HOW NOT TO BECOME A SPY

*A Memoir of Love at the End
of the Cold War*

BY JUSTIN LIFFLANDER

Front Cover: one of several medallions struck by the Votkinsk
Machine Building Factory in honor of the INF Treaty
Back Cover: banned Soviet SS-20 and American Pershing II
missiles on display at the Smithsonian National Air and
Space Museum in Washington, DC.
Photo credit: Cliff1066 / Wikicommons

Front cover concept by Max Lifflander
Additional digital design work by Alex George

ISBN-10: 0692259945
ISBN-13: 9780692259948
Library of Congress Control Number: 2014913053
Gilbo Shed Books
Dobbs Ferry, New York

For Alyona

FOREWORD

The end of the Cold War was a time of leadership. It was a time of open minds and, as my story reveals, open hearts.

Great men like Ronald Reagan and Mikhail Gorbachev took bold steps to make things happen that affected nations and individuals in ways even their wisdom did not foresee. In the pages that follow I give short shrift to their accomplishments in favor of entertainment and a bit of real life drama.

My plan when I wrote this story was to have it serve as an explanation to those at home who might wonder why I'm here, and those here who might wonder who I really am. But my wife likes to remind me of the Woody Allen quote: "If you want to make God laugh, tell him about your plans."

I am sure he was laughing at me when I made my plans to become an intelligence officer, and probably when I planned this memoir.

Leadership is precisely what is needed now. Intolerance, suspicion and sanctimoniousness run rife on both sides of the ocean. The information glut favors superficiality over substance and leaves us susceptible to manipulation and ignorance.

The crisis of misunderstanding has to be addressed. Challenge everything you think you know, take the time to dig deep, to scratch well below the surface. Perhaps my story will help you in that effort. And perhaps one day we can return to a time of open minds and open hearts.

Justin Lifflander
September 2014
Moscow, Russian Federation

This is a true story. It is my recollection of events and I have related them to the best of my knowledge. Some names have been changed for the sake of privacy. Some haven't.

*"Communication is the most important thing, with friends or enemies.
Only through communication with people can you find what you are looking for,
in any depth at all. And the most interesting things are life and what people live by.
The Empire State and Chrysler buildings come afterward."*

—Viktor Nekrasov, Both Sides of the Ocean, 1964

Table of Contents

Prologue: Not Entirely Alone xi

Chapter One: Playing Spy 1

Chapter Two: Rockets, Roads and Reagan 8

Chapter Three: A Reluctant Agent 24

Chapter Four: Mastering the Language, Making a Friend. 33

Chapter Five: Tchaikovsky's Hometown at Ground Zero 51

Map of the town of Votkinsk. 53

Chapter Six: Defending Against Enemies, Real and Imagined 65

Chapter Seven: All Personal Items are Subject to Inspection 75

Chapter Eight: Fish Doughnuts. 83

Map of the Votkinsk Portal Monitoring Facility 92

Chapter Nine: Churches, Hospitals and Hot Tubs Battle Boredom 103

Chapter Ten: Cooking Up Trouble. 127

Chapter Eleven: German Ancestors and a Memorable Dinner 142

Chapter Twelve: Only Blue Push-Pins are Acceptable 167

Chapter Thirteen: Goats, Grass, and Goodbyes 183

Chapter Fourteen: Co-Conspirators and Consumed Mating 205

Chapter Fifteen: "It will be bad for you.". 217

Chapter Sixteen: I Don't Understand. 231

Chapter Seventeen: Trust Your Doctor 246

Epilogue: A Museum Quality Result. 257

Acknowledgments 261

About the author 265

PROLOGUE
NOT ENTIRELY ALONE

I sat on the sill and picked at the frost forming in the gap between my window and its frame. I had been at it for about ten minutes. It seemed like frost picking would be the highlight of my evening. Down on the street Muscovites scurried about in the freezing cold. They were mostly heading to their apartments, which were as dingy as mine.

Because it was a wine night I could still feel my fingertips. They were starting to sting. Had it been a vodka night I could have kept at it much longer. Normally, I would have taped the window frames to protect us from the draft. But there was no us left to protect. I probably should have given up at that point and gone home.

February 1990 was the peak of the last winter of the Soviet empire. No one knew it at the time. Even Henry Kissinger didn't know. He was partially responsible for my predicament. Nearly two decades earlier Kissinger started the disarmament negotiations that brought me to where I was now. And he had seen me off at the airport in Frankfurt three years earlier. I spotted him coming out of the Ambassadors Club lounge. Actually, he didn't even notice me. But I took his mere presence at that moment as a good omen. Someday I was going to be a great diplomat, or spy, or both. Then Henry and I would walk together through those curtained glass doors and sit down to nibble on canapés. We'd discuss Arafat's table manners and the real reason for Gromyko's depression. That was my fantasy. But, things didn't turn out the way I planned.

Instead I wound up drinking alone, far from home, with no idea of how to put my life back together. The capital of the Soviet Union was gray by day and poorly lit at night. Its bleakness only added to my heartache. Several weeks had passed since Sofia left, and I still didn't understand why. They told her they considered me a dangerous element with whom they would eventually reckon. I was sure they had convinced her to break my heart. I wasn't ready to accept any other explanation.

The living room of my rented apartment contained a couch bed and book shelves occupied by the collected works of Pushkin, Lermontov and Tolstoy. Neatly bound, each set had a uniform size and color scheme. A teapot on either end of the upper shelf lent symmetry to the scene. My empty bottles were lined up on the floor along the wall, arranged according to size. A clear one-liter bottle of Moskovskaya vodka, with its green and white label, was followed by two beige bottles of Armenian cognac. Next came three 0.75 liter bottles of Stolichnaya, six dark green bottles of Chianti and three bottles of Miller beer — donated to my cause by friends with precious access to the U.S. Embassy commissary. Not a bad collection for a month's work.

Despite the order, it had become just an apartment again — no longer a home. It was empty, and so was I, no matter how much I tried to fill myself with the contents of those bottles. My personal items were all in their proper places. The pens were on the left side of my writing table. The forks, knives and spoons each lay in their appropriate section in the kitchen drawer. But controlling your loved ones? That's different. They resist. Cutlery never resists. My world had crumbled.

The thick glass screen of the huge Soviet television bulged from its wood-paneled cabinet. It glared at me like a goitered eyeball. I tried to plug it in. After two attempts I got the prongs into the socket. All smart citizens left their television unplugged when not in use. It might spontaneously combust if left plugged in during a power surge.

No wonder my landlord took my first month's rent to the hard currency store and bought himself a sleek new Japanese TV. We had no contract— just trust, based on a handshake. It was as Asian as the Persian carpets that hung on the walls. The apartment looked like a Bedouin tavern, if Bedouins even have taverns.

I planned to watch the weather report after the news, to see if there was Hope — the name of the weather lady. Russian women's names often have meaning, like Glory, Love or Faith.

The TV screen took time to warm up. I caught my reflection in the grey glass. A pale bespectacled figure stared back. Was it really me? The wine? The curvature of the tube? The ringing doorbell interrupted my self-observation.

I opened the door and the usual bouquet of odors wafted in from the landing: stale cigarette smoke, urine and highly organic refuse fermenting in the garbage chute.

"You are the foreigner renting this apartment," said the pensioner standing before me in a frayed winter coat. The ear flaps of his rabbit-fur hat dangled on either side of his head. He held a stack of ration coupons firmly in his wrinkled hand, like a magician holds a deck of trick cards. I recognized him as Kuzmich, a volunteer with the building's communal services department. He recognized me as Justin, the misplaced foreigner.

"I like vodka, Kuzmich," I said, struggling with the simultaneous tasks of not slurring my speech and not screwing the grammar. His appeared dejected as he handed me my allotment.

"...but, sometimes it doesn't like me..." I added.

Kuzmich glanced past my shoulder at the empty bottles on the floor and said with dismay, "What are you doing here?"

It was a reasonable question. His interest could have been tactical...Am I mixing wine and vodka? Why am I drinking alone? Or maybe he was trying to comprehend my strategy...what was I doing here at all, in this country? At this time? Shouldn't I be somewhere else?

I had been having the same thoughts since Sofia left.

There was sympathy in Kuzmich's query. But he was also baffled, as most of my Russian friends were. They knew they were mostly living in poverty — without deodorant or sanitary napkins, or sometimes even soap; in buildings like those the West uses to house its poor. And they assumed the place I came from was better, more comfortable. At the Hewlett-Packard Moscow office where I worked my colleagues would sometimes ask, "Do you really want to be here?" "You came voluntarily?" "Why do you like living in Moscow?"

A diplomat I had known, when asked that question, said, "Well, I don't wear a watch, and you have these large street clocks everywhere. Very convenient. The local mustard is also good."

Those were all the pleasantries of life in Moscow in the mid-1980's that he could think of. There were plenty of intangibles, like the kindness Kuzmich was showing me. But it took time to develop sensitivity to them. I had managed to do that, and felt fortunate. I made friends I knew would be with me for the rest of my life. And I'd learned an appreciation for comfort and convenience that someone who has not lived outside the West will never have. Along the way I had even grown accustomed to the musk of humanity in Moscow's cramped metro. But the illogic of the digital clocks above the tunnel that count how long it's been since the last train left still irritated me.

"Justin, it's not good to mix...but sometimes it happens," Kuzmich said. "Make sure you are having something to eat, too. I recommend pickles or mushrooms if you're drinking vodka, and dried fish if you're drinking beer."

He looked again over my shoulder, grinned, and continued. "We don't get any coupons for wine. I guess that's for the best, since cheese is hard to find, too. But I'll bring you some pickles from my dacha, when I come by next month."

The Russian sense of compassion was almost never out of reach. Scratch the surface and it came right out. Seventy years of being dumped on from above had left them with too much tolerance and too little patience. It facilitated no collective defense, but at the individual level it made for very true friends. Right then I needed the scrap of sympathy embodied in Kuzmich's advice. I guess my situation — a tipsy foreigner alone on a cold evening — was enough of a scratch for him.

I returned his kindness by signing for the coupons and handing them back to him.

"You take my vodka coupons this month, Kuzmich, and the ones for cigarettes. Give them to someone who needs them."

Everyone around me was in need. I could see by his ruddy cheeks Kuzmich had recently addressed his needs by using my coupons from last month. He placed his right hand over his heart and bowed in thanks. Then he turned and headed for the next apartment, earflaps bouncing as he went.

I closed the door and went back to the now glowing screen. My reflection had disappeared, replaced by someone telling me it was going to get colder.

Kuzmich didn't realize that he was part of the answer to his question. But there was more to it than that. I decided that when he came by next month I'd invite him in and tell him the whole story. It was the least I could do in exchange for his caring.

Chapter One
Playing Spy

Kuzmich would have had more sympathy for my parents than I did. Children are inherently ungrateful. If you raise them in comfort they are oblivious to pain and so more easily create it. I saw the preparations for my departure to Moscow in September of 1987 as a logistical challenge, not an emotional one. For my parents it was different.

We collected six camp trunks in the living room of our suburban New York home. I was trying to decide what to include for the two-year tour of duty. My mother, Barbara, had already labeled the trunks as per the instructions of my new employer: *Justin Lifflander / PAE, Motor Pool, U.S. Embassy, Moscow, U.S.S.R.* Now she was supposed to be retrieving my clothes from the laundry room. Instead, I again found her sobbing at the kitchen table.

"What's wrong?" I asked.

"You're going to be arrested there," she blubbered.

"Mom, I'll have diplomatic status…all I'll be doing is driving and fixing cars."

She continued to sob. "Nobody will like you."

"Well, gee," I said, "thanks for the vote of confidence."

My efforts to soothe her had no effect. Her friends' kids were moving to Manhattan or New Jersey after graduating from college. Some might go as far as the West Coast. I was moving to the other side of the Iron Curtain. Barbara was able to manufacture a slew of excuses as to why this was a bad idea for her baby.

She continued to whimper as we filled the trunks. They were a reminder of childhood. My older brother and I had used them to bring home arts and crafts from summer camp, rock samples and the occasional dried amphibian. But that was another time. Now I was loading them with heavy-duty winter clothing, a set of tools and an abridged collection of electronic espionage equipment.

"What is that?" Barbara asked as I placed the night-vision goggles gently in the bottom.

"Something to help me make new friends," I answered with a grin.

I couldn't leave my tradecraft behind. I needed to maintain technical superiority. I saw the embassy job as a training mission — perhaps the last phase of my pre-spy education.

By the time I received my degree I had learned basic Russian and completed internships as a junior intelligence analyst at the State Department and at the Federal Bureau of Investigation. I had even been to Langley. But I was a typical liberal arts graduate: ready for nearly anything, qualified for almost nothing. I had successfully passed the State Department tests to become a real diplomat, but decided to delay further processing. Instead, I signed a contract to work for two years as a driver-mechanic at the embassy. I would make contacts, hone my skills and learn about life on the front of the Cold War. Then I would decide in which organization to make a career. I was sure this approach would help finalize my plan, not destroy it.

My father, Matthew, also had reservations about the move.

"It's a sad place. Why would you want to live there? No cars; lines for everything, dreary," he said.

Matt, as my brother and I called him behind his back, had been to Moscow during the last thaw, in the late 1960s, negotiating a partnership between Hertz and Intourist. His den at home where he'd spend his nights reading briefs and chain-smoking cigars was a shrine to his international adventures. A photo of him on Red Square hung on the wall. The snapshots and memorabilia from his travels were framed by shelves on both sides bearing his collection of military hats from around the globe. And he wondered what sparked my desire to explore the world?

"They are hostile," Matt continued. "It's been clear since the Berlin airlift of 1948. I'll never forget the images of our planes delivering food, coal — even candy bars. The Russians would have used Sputnik to control the world if Kennedy hadn't challenged them. Khrushchev kept saying over and over again that he will bury us! Where did it get either side? We've spent the last 40 years living in fear of each other. The only reason my father didn't build a bomb shelter in our back yard was because

2

he was saving to buy a new Chevy Bel Air. Even now, the paranoia continues. Look how they shot down that Korean Airliner a few years ago."

My own ideology was weak and my historical baggage nonexistent. For now I was driven by curiosity.

I should have thanked my father for inspiring me to want to become a spy. It wasn't just the artifacts on his shelves from far off lands and his globetrotting war stories. He gave me my first bugging assignment. When I was eight Matt had me crawl under a table in the living room and plug in a wireless intercom with the TALK button locked on, so he could monitor Barbara's consciousness-raising group meeting. I had no ethical dilemma about betraying my mother. I was enthralled by the conspiracy and oblivious to the violation of privacy.

Above all, it was the sense of technical superiority that turned me on. Everything became "Mission Impossible" for me. My hero was not Mr. Phelps, the leader of the group of secret agents, but Barney Collier, the tech guru who could bug, blow up, or electronically baffle his way out of any tight spot. With the active support of my parents, my equipment and experience expanded. When I was 12, instead of taking payment for installing telephone jacks in every room of the house, I got Matt to buy me a subscription to the mercenary trade journal, Soldier of Fortune. When I was 14 my mother typed my application letter to the CIA. The agency responded, saying it did not have any programs that accepted secondary school students, but I should study hard, learn a foreign language and get good grades in college. They enclosed a recruiting brochure that described their organization, facilities and career paths. I promptly cut out parts of the brochure and used them to make a fake employee identity card.

By the time I entered high school I was spying on the girl who lived next door. She was my version of the little redheaded girl and I was a mutated form of Charlie Brown — passing half the day with my head in my hands thinking about her and the other half assembling my Heathkit $79 infra–red telescope. The thought of just going up to her at school and talking to her was too terrifying to contemplate. Sitting in a shrub trying to peer through her window was much easier and potentially more rewarding.

I reached my acme of technological skill when I tapped into the school's public address system and remotely played prerecorded programs made by me and my friends of teacher imitations, blaring rock music and belching contests.

But I made the mistake of bragging about our accomplishment to a group of fellow students. I basked in their respect and the feeling of power. "All too often, a man is the hero of his own stories," answered the famous Scotland Yard detective, when asked about the secret to his success at uncovering criminals. Or, as Matt would say, "Loose lips sink ships."

The high school office found out, but they couldn't fathom how it was being done. Word came down that if the programs ceased there would be no repercussions. The perpetrators would be allowed to continue their academic careers and possibly graduate. The show was over and I learned a valuable lesson. Spies need humility. They must be able to live without adulation or glory in order to succeed. It was a way of life that involved denying oneself what the ego naturally desired. Like taking vows and joining a holy order. Would I ever have that kind of self-discipline?

I was dangerous when bored. My parents wouldn't let me go to Manhattan. Nobody's parents did. Most of them grew up in that city, with exaggerated memories of perilous childhoods to back up their paranoid restrictions. They didn't move to the suburbs so their offspring could get mugged in Central Park. We were allowed to take the public bus by ourselves and go as far as the White Plains Mall, 15 kilometers from our house. We were allowed to take the bus back from the mall. It didn't get any more exciting than that. Desperation mounted on all fronts as we muddled through puberty. A fear of boredom became ingrained in my psyche. It was a key factor that sent me down the path I chose.

My love for Kipling and the far away land of stoic tribesman he wrote about ignited my first anti-communist sentiments. I was greatly disturbed by the Soviet invasion of Afghanistan in December of 1979. Reports came monthly in the mercenary rag about heroic resistance leaders, insurgency operations and Soviet atrocities. The Afghanis were fighting for their freedom, aided by the occasional foreign volunteer.

I told my best friend Richie that if a plane landed on my street to take me to join the mujahedeen rebels fighting the *Shuravi* — what the Afghans called the Soviet invaders — I wouldn't hesitate to get on board. He was a talented artist and made a poster to inspire me. It portrayed a viscous looking Russian commando with a red circle around him and line through the middle. The words "Commie Busters" were embossed on the bottom.

I combined my fear of boredom, my passion for surveillance and a faint sense of duty to battle communism into a new college major: pre-cold warrior.

The first semester of junior year I worked at the State Department as an intern-analyst in the Intelligence and Research Bureau of the Soviet and East European Section. All information from, by, and about the Soviet Union, generated or gathered by State and other agencies found its way to our office. It was digested for the secretary of state, who then regurgitated it to the president.

The grey building at Foggy Bottom was enormous and unwelcoming. But inside, our office was a cozy warren. Its stark furnishings and crusty analysts dated from the late 1960's. Donald was the department manager. He looked more like a librarian than a spymaster.

"Margery," he would say to the intercom on his desk, which was connected to the secretary sitting a few feet from his door, "please locate the foreign broadcast translation report for the first week of October and bring it here."

Margery would dig through piles of material stacked in every corner until she found what was requested and toss it on his desk with a slap. None of the documents ever came back out.

"This," Donald said, as he stood in the doorway of my office and waved a manila folder, "is the daily intel file. It contains the interagency communications, classified articles, and relevant embassy cables and reports that we use as a basis for our analyses. We also read all the key Soviet newspapers, transcripts of radio and TV broadcasts, and other open source material, to create a view of people, situations and trends."

It sounded very much like basic research I had supposedly been doing at college. I began to devour the folder's contents. A CIA report on the Soviet space shuttle (the thing looked exactly like ours); an FBI summary of Soviet diplomatic activities at the UN Mission in New York (like students, they favored cheap sandwich shops); Moscow embassy reports covering a broad range of subjects, from consular issues concerning *refusniks* and separated families, to the latest lecture at the Knowledge Society.

The embassy cables always mentioned a Mr. Emboff. He sure got around. He'd meet with dissidents, attend receptions and respond to demarches. How could one person accomplish so much? And with his Russian ancestry, wasn't he a potential security risk? I kept reading. Even if he was a double agent, he was doing a good reporting job.

My adrenaline pumped as I read the folder's contents every day. We were dealing with matters of global importance. This was the real thing. No more muffled gurgling noises from poorly positioned bugs in the bathrooms of girl's dormitories. No more blackmailing my fraternity brothers with transcripts of their compromising phone calls. The facts contained in the daily file helped us make connections, see patterns and draw conclusions. We provided insights that allowed policy makers to gain an advantage over our enemies. The sense of power was strong. But I remained calm and refrained from discussing the folder's contents with anyone outside the office. The analyst work hooked me. I wanted to learn more.

When I informed Matt and Barbara of my plan to become a driver at the embassy they were not surprised. Matt made peace with the idea of me moving to Moscow. I think he was excited about living vicariously. He had always dreamed of being named the U.S. Ambassador to the Court of St. James. Instead, he got a son who had been hired to drive around Red Square. It would have to do. Matt quickly surmised possible fringe benefits of embassy life. "Can you send me Cuban cigars through the diplomatic mail?" he asked.

On my last night before departing for Moscow I headed to the local bar. My friends were throwing a going away party. They had all been observers, participants or victims of my various operations. Over the years several of them, and even their parents, had been interviewed by investigators conducting background checks for the top-secret security clearance I had for the internships in Washington.

Richie gave me a drawing as a going away present. It was a cartoon of me standing in front of the embassy. I had dark sunglasses and looked suave next to the ambassador's limo. In the background, a girl leaned saucily against a lamppost with the letters K G B embossed on her generous breasts. A trench-coated man eyed me through binoculars from a window across the street.

Even the little redheaded girl was at the party. She smiled at me with a kind of knowing smile. Had she spotted me in the bushes outside her window at some point? She and the rest of my crew admired Richie's drawing. They joked that my life as a spy might not be that easy. I realized none of them believed I was really going to be working as a driver-mechanic.

The little redheaded girl gave me a greeting card that said "Congratulations on Entering the Service." And she gave me a goodbye kiss.

The erotic sensation I experienced at that moment was followed by a sense of pride. I knew living in the Soviet capital would be difficult. But I felt I should face the enemy head on. After two years of living in his midst, I'd know what he was really made of. But I had no specific mental image of what he looked like or how I'd interact with him. And it did not occur to me that I would also figure out what I was made of.

Chapter Two

Rockets, Roads and Reagan

In my mind the Soviet enemy was a variation of the menacing creature in Richie's commie-buster drawing. He was bound to be a demon with Slavic features, dressed in an ill-fitting suit. I could imagine him in some poorly lit room, plotting the manipulation of the Cubans, organizing the slaughter of Afghanis and planning further steps to foist his poisonous doctrine on Eastern Europe. In reality, I would not have recognized him.

Vladimir Gennadevich Sadovnikov, the Soviet Union's most decorated nuclear missile maker, was packing for a trip to Moscow at about the same time I was. He would be there for just a few days, and was traveling 1,200 kilometers westward, from a small town in the Ural Mountains called Votkinsk. I was fortunate to befriend his wife, Elena, many years later and she shared their story with me.

Sadovnikov's kindly appearance, neat grooming and cardigan sweater made him look more like the host of a children's television program than a builder of weapons of mass destruction. The 58-year-old engineer had served as general director of the Votkinsk Factory Production Association for more than two decades. The most important products his factory made were rockets. In English, we have "rockets," which take men to the moon and put satellites in space, and we have "missiles," which rain bombs on your front lawn. In Russian, it's the same word, *raketa*.

"Why are they summoning you, Volodya?" Elena asked as she closed the clasps on his bag.

"I'm not sure," Sadovnikov said. "We already had our initial planning meeting in May…the final session is not scheduled until late October."

"Maybe Mikhail Sergeevich wants to promote you," she said.

"I doubt it. I don't fit the profile of Comrade Gorbachev's new young cadres."

Over the years, Sadovnikov rejected several promotions that would have forced him to move to Moscow.

"Besides," he continued, "they need me here. Production is in full swing, and we have planned for a major increase next year in the new long-range rocket."

"Why aren't you wearing your medals?" she asked.

Vladimir Gennadevich had twice been presented with the Hero of Socialist Labor — the highest civilian award in the Soviet Union – for his work in strengthening the defense of the fatherland.

Now he looked out the window of their apartment, across the lake to the birch forest on the other side. The onslaught of winter was already tangible. By the end of the month the yellow leaves would make their final shift to red and brown. Burning brightly for a week or two, they would then succumb to the first frost and blanket the shoreline.

"I don't know," he finally responded. "I just don't feel like it."

"Akh!" she exclaimed, trying to cheer him up, "you want to leave room in case they decide to give you more."

"Perhaps. But somehow I doubt that's what's going to happen on this trip."

In its 200-year history Sadovnikov's factory had run the full gamut of heavy manufacturing: anchors, ships, and locomotives in the last century; artillery early this century. Stalin's war-time evacuation of key military production facilities to the Urals injected Votkinsk and other industrial towns with a new generation of engineers and designers. When Sadovnikov moved there in 1965, his friend Mikhail Timofeevich Kalashnikov — who designed the AK-47 assault rifle following World War II, giving birth to the world's most popular weapon — was already a leading engineer in nearby Izhevsk, the capital of the Udmurt republic. As the Cold War intensified, rockets became an integral part of the Soviet defense doctrine. Votkinsk was selected as the site for manufacturing intermediate and long-range ballistic missiles.

Sadovnikov saw his work as a key element in his country's defense. The SS-20 was deployed in Eastern Europe as the bulwark of nuclear deterrence against NATO, and on the country's southeastern flank to defend against the Chinese. SCUD short-range rockets had been delivered to the Soviet armed forces and those of its close allies. The RSD-12 was the factory's latest masterpiece. Called the SS-25 by NATO, it was a three stage solid propellant intercontinental ballistic missile transported and launched from the back of a giant truck.

Vladimir Gennadevich walked from his Moscow hotel, past the Olympic Stadium, to the Ministry of Defense Industry's headquarters on Ulitsa Shchepkina. Usually the meetings at headquarters entailed approving budgets and agreeing to production targets. As Sadovnikov walked, he wondered if the Party had decided to bolster the country's defense strategy and now production would be increased. He believed in the Party and he believed in Gorbachev. Eighteen months earlier, returning to Votkinsk from the 27th Party Congress where the young General Secretary began to lay out his vision for the future of the U.S.S.R., Sadovnikov was so impressed he told his deputies, "We have a second Lenin!"

But Sadovnikov also had doubts. There were points of the program not yet clear and those that would be difficult to accept. Another crackdown on corruption; rapid personnel changes at all levels; limits on alcohol; and something entirely new: this *glasnost* idea of exposing the nation's ills for public discussion.

Meanwhile, the country seemed to have run out of socks. He could no longer find them at the store in Votkinsk. It seemed that the centralized economic planning apparatus had faltered. Sadovnikov didn't dwell on the idea of a nation without socks. He was still getting the aluminum, cellulose and other materials he needed to make his rockets. Besides, Elena was good at knitting.

Of all the elements of Gorbachev's vision, the one that concerned Sadovnikov most was the General Secretary's cryptic comment during the Party congress that the military might of the future Soviet Union would be based strictly on "reasonable sufficiency."

Vladimir Gennadevich sensed something different as he passed through the second door into the office of the minister of Defense Industry. The beechwood paneling was the same, as was the pungent odor of the minister's filterless Belomor cigarettes. The usual group of factory chiefs, military officers and ministry functionaries were present. But there were also several unfamiliar faces.

"Greetings, Volodya," said the commander of the Strategic Rocket Forces, Sadovnikov's main customer. "How is life in the birthplace of Tchaikovsky?"

"Greetings, Yury Petrovich," answered Sadovnikov as he shook the general's hand. "We hear music every time a rocket exits the factory gate. Of course, it gets louder when you make your payment on time."

"From each according to his ability...," the general retorted.

At that moment, Defense Industry Minister Boris Belousov approached. He was Sadovnikov's close friend and a native of Udmurtia.

"Vladimir Gennadevich," said Belousov, "allow me to introduce you to the Deputy Minister of Foreign Affairs."

'That's odd,' Sadovnikov thought as he shook hands. 'Our entire republic is closed to foreigners. Maybe we are going to discuss a special foreign trade deal.'

The Foreign Ministry man started the meeting.

"Comrades, we are here today to inform you about expected changes that will affect all of us. As we speak, our negotiators in Geneva are discussing a new treaty banning intermediate-range nuclear rockets. If it goes through, it will be the first time in history that the two superpowers have agreed not just to limit their weapons of mass destruction, but to actually eliminate an entire class of them."

The Foreign Ministry man paused to glance at the pensive faces of the group and then continued. "This will affect us all and require enormous work: technical; diplomatic; security; and, of course, work at the factories making these weapons. The General Secretary plans to go to America in early December to sign this treaty."

Sadovnikov was baffled. 'Destroy hundreds of rockets we've worked so hard to make...that the state spent so much money and intellect to create?' he asked himself. It seemed unreal. The two concepts were hardly reconcilable. Build to defend and then destroy to defend? He had heard rumors a few years back that Brezhnev had proposed to eliminate all the rockets of both camps in Europe. NATO rejected the offer, claiming that nuclear missiles were the only feasible defense against the overwhelming number of Warsaw Pact troops. This was the same general secretary who had inspired Sadovnikov with the maxim, "Everything the people have built must be reliably defended."

Minister Belousov took the floor.

"Concerning our work, of course this means a revision of production plans. We can't be making rockets and launchers that are forbidden by the treaty. We recently received a directive to review our consumer goods output and propose new norms. By our next planning meeting I expect to have your proposals for increased conversion of manufacturing lines."

Sadovnikov thought about conversion. It was one thing if the Party decided this was the best way to defend the country. Defense was his life's mission and he would carry it out until his last breath. But was the Party sure he could feed the 100,000 people of his town on the income from baby carriages, washing machines and food processors? Vladimir Gennadevich felt the weight of responsibility pressing down on him. His dedication was unwavering, but the uncertainty of the future was disturbing.

Others who were distraught by the decay of the late Soviet period were trying to escape. A mass of Armenian emigrant applicants surrounded the entrance to the U.S. Embassy in Moscow. It was my first day of work. I needed to weave my way through the crowd to get to the front door.

I showed my passport to the Soviet guard and made it inside. The consular section was closed for lunch. The only people in the lobby were two men with mops. They were deep in discussion.

"He was completely insensitive, Lyle," said the shorter one, who was dressed in a brown puffy insulated jumpsuit, had a red beard and wore a bandana around his neck. He looked like a plump pirate.

"You don't understand. It was an act of self-preservation, Danny," Lyle answered. He was tall, balding, with thick glasses and a scraggly beard.

"Self-preservation my foot. He wanted to get away from his wife since he was getting some on the side. He wouldn't even talk to her in his last days."

"His muse is irrelevant. He had agreed with Sofia Andreyevna that they would communicate through their diaries," Lyle said, waving his mop handle threateningly at Danny.

"So why did he have to leave her?" Danny asked, pushing the garbage cart out of my way so I could pass.

"Tolstoy was suffocating, don't you see?" Lyle answered.

I had never met such literate janitors.

"Sorry to interrupt," I said, "but I am supposed to report to the motor pool. Could you tell me where it is?"

"Ah, the new driver," Lyle said as he extended his hand. "I'm Doctor Benning, PhD in Russian Studies from Brown. This is Assistant Professor Stevens, Master's in Russian Lit, University of Wisconsin. Welcome to Moscow." Danny and I shook hands, too.

"Justin Lifflander, BA in Soviet Government, Cornell." I responded, eager to show I had the credentials to comprehend their discourse.

"Through the glass doors, into the yard. Then take the door in the middle on the right," Danny said as he pointed.

He turned back to Lyle. "You may be right, but that doesn't change the fact that it's your turn to clean the consular section and one of the visa applicants who succumbed to a stress attack at the thought of not getting his shot at the American dream puked all over the floor."

As I headed through the yard I realized that there was nothing surprising about the professor and his mop. There were others like me who wanted to put a practical edge on their formal education and decided that manual labor at the U.S. Embassy in Moscow was just what they needed.

I first heard of this opportunity in the spring of my final semester of college. I walked past a bulletin board in our language hall. A cartoon caught my eye. They were usually easy to read and didn't result in homework, so I took a closer look. A man in a tuxedo was splayed underneath a limousine, tools by his side. A sign on the wall read "Moscow Embassy Garage." Nearby a well-dressed matronly lady held a tray of food. "Would Mr. Ambassador like some hors d'oeuvres?" she asked. "Mrs. Ambassador made them herself." The advertisement next to the cartoon said that the Pacific Architects & Engineers Company was offering contractor jobs at the embassy.

The United States used locals to fill support positions at its embassies around the world in order to save diplomatic slots and maintain a link to the local society. The Soviets always staffed their missions — including cooks, drivers and other support personnel — exclusively with their own citizens. This made for more effective control of the embassy environment, particularly from the counter-espionage perspective.

I had Ronald Reagan to thank for creating this job opportunity. In 1986 he accused 80 Soviet diplomats stationed in the United States of spying and expelled them.

The normal response would have been for the Soviets to do the same to the U.S. Embassy staff in Moscow, but Gorbachev took a clever tack. One day the Agency for

Supporting the Diplomatic Corps, which went by the acronym UPDK and was essentially a subsidiary of the KGB, ordered all of its employees at the Moscow embassy to quit.

The Americans were crippled. They didn't know how to get plane tickets, find supplies, clear goods from customs or even drive. The State Department reduced the number of U.S. diplomats in Moscow and made room for 90 American contract workers to replace the 200 Soviet support staff.

As I entered the motor pool office, a look of relief came over the face of the young Foreign Service officer sitting behind a desk.

"Let me see your driver's license," my new boss, whose name was Brad, asked.

I handed him my New York State license and the international license I had just picked up from AAA in Manhattan.

"So you're the new embassy school bus driver," he said with a smile.

"Bus driver? I just got the international license because I thought I might need it in Europe sometime. They stamped the "Vehicle with 8 Passengers or More" at my request, since I knew I'd be driving a van here."

"Right," said Brad, "and my bus has more than eight seats. Seventy-two, to be exact. My lone bus driver is completely burned out and he's also the only one with a truck driver's license. Congratulations. I am sure the kids will adore you."

"But what if I get stopped by the police?" I asked.

"Don't worry. I'll give the Sovs your international license and they'll issue you a local one. They use the same format."

Somewhere back in America, in a rocking chair on the front porch of the Bus Driver's Retirement Home sat an elderly man. In between facial spasms, he cackled with glee as he pictured "Justin the Terrible" finally getting his just deserts.

"I am to be a bus driver," I told Lyle, when I met him several days after getting the assignment. "It's not what I expected."

"Ah," said the professor, who had taught a graduate course in planned economies, "you must learn to expect the unexpected in Mother Russia. You know the Soviets say, 'The future is bright,' but privately they admit they are one of the few nations with an 'unpredictable past' — history is rewritten regularly. Flexibility and spontaneity are the keys to survival. For example, if you are walking down the street and you see a line, what do you, as a clever Soviet citizen, do?"

"I guess I find out what is being sold."

"Wrong! First you get on line, *then* you ask what is being sold. It saves time. Do you have an *avoska?*"

"A what?

"It's a 'maybe bag,' made of mesh, easily folded up and kept in your pocket. Everyone has one. It's a fundamental symbol of the Russian spirit. Maybe you find something, maybe not. Whether it's something you need is irrelevant. If you don't need it, someone else will. So you wait and buy what you can anyway. Basic communist economics."

"I think the supply situation is getting worse," I said. "Before I got behind the wheel of the bus, Brad said I needed some road experience. He had me drive two visiting diplomats yesterday — to the Foreign Ministry, and then to the British and German embassies. I overheard their conversation. One said he had just come from Geneva where they had been conducting arms reduction talks with the Sovs — apparently some new treaty is in the works. They were discussing eliminating nuclear weapons and the Americans were taken by surprise by the Soviet acquiescence about on-site inspections. Now the two sides will allow each other to visit their missile bases and factories to verify treaty compliance. Then I heard him talk about a strange personal request from his Soviet counterpart."

"The Sov was probably seeking medicine, good cheese, or perhaps an English language book," Lyle guessed.

"Socks," I replied. "He wanted to know where to buy inexpensive socks. The Soviet Union is running out of socks. They have nuclear weapons galore, but not enough socks."

The Moscow embassy school bus was a full-size manual-shift model painted robin's egg blue. Benjamin, the senior bus driver, didn't look like other Mormons I had known. They got security clearances easily, due to clean living and a healthy sense of patriotism. Most of the ones I met at the Bureau and Foggy Bottom were thin, pale and clean-shaven. Benjamin was short and pudgy, with a thick sandy beard that clashed with his otherwise youthful appearance.

Our task was to drive diplomatic offspring between the embassy compound and the Anglo-American School on the south end of town.

My passengers.

"Actually, they are a nice bunch of kids," Benjamin said. "You'll get used to the screaming." I was behind the wheel. Ben sat behind me on the empty bus, coaching me on my first practice run. We were stopped at a traffic light near the zoo, not far from the embassy. It was a warm day so we left the door open. Before the light changed an elderly man approached.

"Is this the American Embassy Bus?" he asked in Russian.

"Yes it is," I answered officiously. I guessed he hadn't noticed the unique red and white license plates the Sovs issued to all diplomatic vehicles. But now he would understand we represented private transportation. It was not possible to confuse us with the over-crowded public version. Instead, the man mounted the steps. He headed for a seat in the rear.

"Gosh dang it!" Ben muttered. His religious beliefs limited him to using curse words that one might hear on a 1950's television show. It was an endearing habit, but I suspect he'd have preferred stronger language in this particular case.

Ben got up, crossed his arms and blocked the man's path. "Listen," he said, "you may not ride this bus. It is U.S. government property."

"But I have these bags, and you are going towards the embassy aren't you? I live nearby." The old man was ejected, bags and all.

"I understand the guy's confusion," Ben said. "When the Sovs were working in the motor pool they were operating their own private transportation company, ripping us off blind. Not everyone in Moscow is aware of the staff changes. Some people expect to be able to hail any U.S. diplomatic vehicle."

He was outraged by the fraud. I had never met such an excitable Mormon.

Despite Ben's lessons, the cumbersome bus took getting used to. On one of my first school runs I overshot the access road. I checked the mirrors, shifted into reverse and began to slowly back up. A gentle crunching noise caused me to hit the brakes. At first I thought I hit a go-kart. But it turned out that a Zaparozhets had made the error of parking behind me. One of the smallest Soviet cars, it came from the Ukraine and was often given by the state to invalids and war veterans — some kind of cruel joke. It had the model number "960M" on the front grill, which locals said was the number of meters it would travel before breaking down.

I shifted into neutral, applied the parking brake and stepped out to greet the driver. A middle aged man was calmly surveying his bent hood and broken headlight.

"I am sorry," I said, "I did not see you." My emaciated vocabulary cheated me of sincerity.

"But I saw you, and you kept coming," the driver said.

His license plate started with a lower case letter, so I could tell it was not a state-owned vehicle. A small group of interested citizens observed the spectacle from the curb. I had given the bus some flair by painting the hubcaps red and the lug nuts white. I wanted it to be a patriotic advertisement. But from my victim's perspective it was a rolling American flag of destruction, and it wasn't even scratched. Not that there was any doubt as to the country of origin. No other such vehicle existed on the roads of the Soviet Union.

The senior and junior mechanics and the rolling American
flag of destruction next to the embassy wash bay.

The situation disturbed me. I took the role of citizen-ambassador quite seriously. In all likelihood I was the first American this unlucky fellow had ever encountered, not to mention been smashed by. I had no reason to think of this guy as the enemy, but at this moment he probably wouldn't believe it.

There were other pressures to deal with as well. Soon a group of high-strung Foreign Service children would be waiting a block away with their lunch boxes, artwork and jeers. According to embassy policy I was obligated to file an official report with the traffic police. But to save time and face I decided to abrogate it.

I surveyed the damage to his car once more and said, "A little hammering here, some paint, a new headlight. Maybe 30 rubles." The citizen grimaced. I added, "... and a pack of Marlboros."

"Well," the citizen said after a pause, "I am not an expert in such things, and don't know what it'll really cost to repair." He leaned back against the fender, waiting for another offer.

"What do we do?" I asked aloud in English. "Wait for an expert to walk up and offer an estimate?" The citizen shrugged his shoulders and lit a cigarette.

Why can't you have sex on Red Square? Because there will be too many people around giving advice. There is always someone around to give advice in Russia. The Russian word "*soviet*" means both "council" and "advice." My professional and diplomatic reputations were at stake. I motioned to a competent-looking spectator to join us.

"Excuse me," I said, switching back to Russian. "Please give us your opinion on how much money it will take to solve this problem."

The spectator played his role perfectly. He surveyed the damage and fingered the wounds. He could have easily passed for an insurance adjuster or used car buyer. Then the cajoling began. The two men spoke quickly. I could only catch snippets of the conversation. It appeared the spectator was telling the victim to be polite to the foreigner and accept the offer. The victim was unmoved. The spectator waved his hand in disgust and wandered off.

I checked my watch. In 45 minutes the children would be standing in front of the school, colorful insults and nasty songs rehearsed, ready to go home. I urgently needed a traffic cop.

Called GAI ("*guy-ee*"), the abbreviation for the State Automobile Inspectorate, the traffic police were one of the staples of an embassy driver's conversational diet. They were there to make sure pedestrians and motorists observed all the legal nuances of socialist transportation culture. They tended to be fat. The layer of blubber was necessary to endure low temperatures. A mustache was also common.

There was only a slight chance I could locate a GAI, get him to the scene, complete the necessary paper work and still get to school on time.

I jogged to the main road, but no GAI were in sight.

A bit further south, on Leninsky Prospekt, I found one standing in the center of the street. He was twirling his black and white striped baton, alternately stopping vehicles and pedestrians at the crosswalk. Embassy drivers called the baton a "*pozhal-sta*" or "please" stick. It could be lit-up for nighttime use by a squeeze of the palm. Minor variations of angle and direction of the *pozhalsta* stick meant the difference between a request to "please pass" and one to "please pull over." The GAI's other key tool was his whistle, which he would blow loudly at anyone who ignored his stick.

I prepared the vocabulary in my head and began.

"Excuse me but I have had a small road transportation incident."

"So what?" the GAI responded, without even looking at me.

"I would like you to come and fill out the documents." The GAI continued his crossing duties, wholly uninterested in my dilemma.

"Listen, I am an American diplomat and my bus has struck a Soviet vehicle. Could you please help?"

"You are an American?" the GAI said with a sudden burst of enthusiasm. "I thought you were a Finn." He picked up his white gloves and ticket book and hailed a passing car. We got in. As we passed the U-turn necessary to get to the scene, I pointed. "The accident is there."

"Yes, yes," the GAI responded, "but we must go meet my commander at the next intersection. How do you like my badge?" He jiggled the oversized brass plate on his breast like an infant with a crib toy. "You don't have them like this in the USA."

I realized it was going to be one of those situations that flows at its own pace, impervious to external influence.

"Yes," I smiled back at the GAI, "your badges are bigger."

The shanghaied driver was soon freed. The inspector and I marched across three lanes of sparse traffic, his *pozhalsta* stick our only protection. The commander was nesting in an aluminum enclosure mounted on top of a three-meter pole.

"Comrade Captain," the GAI said with a salute, holding the ladder with his other hand, "I have an American here who has had a small accident." Comrade Captain began his descent.

"An American?" he said with even more interest than the first GAI. A provincial approach, but many Moscow GAI were imported from the provinces. We all shook hands.

"Was it a state-owned car or a private one?" Comrade Captain asked.

I answered. Clearly Comrade Captain had different priorities. "Oh, don't worry then," he said with a wave of his hand.

"How long have you been here?" he queried. "How do you like it?" "What do you do in your free time?" "Do you like your new embassy building? I used to be posted nearby, on Prospekt Kalinina."

"Well," I answered, "we cannot move into the new building yet, because it has many microphones."

"It was a strange decision by your government to allow us to build it for you," Comrade Captain said.

"I agree," I said. "I guess once our workers remove the microphones, then we can move into the building and the Soviet diplomats can move into their new building in Washington."

"Did Americans build microphones into the structure there?" he asked.

"No, I think the Soviet side was smarter and did the construction themselves."

"I was on leave in Odessa last month," the first cop chimed-in, "and saw a movie with Dooglas."

"Fairbanks?" I asked, not wanting to seem uninterested.

"No, it was with Romans. Keerk Dooglas. It was called 'Spartak.' He is very manly. And there was a woman." He made the appropriate outline with his hands.

"Yes, a very beautiful woman," said Comrade Captain. "I have read Jack London, as well," he added. At this point he dismissed the first GAI and changed the subject.

"You must realize this very important fact." His gray eyes stared at me intently. "Things are different now. Our two countries can coexist together. That is what everyone wants...here... there."

I was touched by his sincerity. I decided I'd write Barbara that evening and let her know I couldn't get the police to arrest me even when I fled the scene of an accident.

Comrade Captain wished me all the best and returned to his perch. Another step towards world peace, I thought, as I jogged back to the accident scene. I had made no progress in solving the immediate problem, but everything had fallen into perspective. It was the first time I realized my mission might be greater than I originally thought. I had quickly found commonality with a Soviet law enforcement official. All I did was to try to speak his language and express interest in what he had to say.

There was no common language to be found with the driver of the Zaporozhets. By the time I got back to the scene of my crime, he had given up on me, the 30 rubles and the pack of Marlboros, and driven off. I made it to school on time.

February 10 1988

   Dear Mom and Dad

   I apologize for not writing sooner. I enclose a roll of film I finished at the end of the year. Please mail me back the prints. You will see I have made some friends. Please also send me a typewriter ribbon and some socks, too.

   Dad, I decided to try my blending-in skills and buy you a hat at the central military department store. I think they are only supposed to sell things to officers. I took a border guard's hat from the shelf, put on my sternest face, and got on line to pay for it. I made it to the cash register when the woman behind me said aloud, "He's not one of us." The cashier took the hat and sent me on my way. I will think of another tactic and try again later.

   Despite the dreariness of Moscow and the deficit of supplies, foreigners live well and know how to have fun. I joined a strange club called the Hash House Harriers. We go jogging through a park every Sunday for about an hour. The locals stare in awe. They think we have stolen something and are running away from the police. Then we go to one of the embassy bars to drink beer for about four hours. The Americans are the best at running and the New Zealanders the best at drinking.

   A few restaurants have sprung up. They are part of new rules allowing cooperatives —— basically, family-run businesses. We frequent one called the Taganka Bar —— it has decent food, a fountain with albino frogs in the middle, a rooster that wanders around and an owl that lives up in a corner of the ceiling. They have entertainment, including a belly dancer, a jazz ensemble and a fiddler who plays havanagila. There is a male contortionist who places himself into a box measuring a half a meter on each side.

   Life on the streets is interesting. Embassies and foreign businesses are the only ones to have imported vehicles. The locals are quite enamored of automobiles. I did see one privately owned Mercedes and was told it belongs to a famous actor. Whenever I park somewhere, not near the embassy, small crowds gather to inspect my car and interview me about its characteristics. My language skills are very primitive still, but when I let one young man sit in the driver's seat of a van, I think what he said, as he stroked the dashboard and fondled the steering wheel was, "She is like a beautiful woman, but she would be obedient...."

   That is about the extent of my interaction with Russians.

   You'll see my pictures from the celebration of the 70th anniversary of the communist revolution in November. Lots of military personnel (with nice hats, of course) and vehicles on display. You'd love it. In the evening we saw a son-et-lumiere presentation at the giant Lenin statue on

October Square. It was as if he had come to life. Colored lights flashed behind him. A booming voice told of the glory of the revolution and how we were building the socialist future.

There was a peace protest outside the embassy last week. I counted about 20 young people. They gathered to voice their concern about America's nuclear ambitions. They had posters decrying U.S. imperialism, 'revanchism' and several other 'isms' I had never heard of. The foreign media showed up to film the scene and lauded it as a sign of free speech. They didn't notice the truck on the side street where the protesters picked up and returned their pre-printed placards. One young lady told me she had been given a half day off from work to "express her peaceful feelings."

Even the circus is a platform for propaganda. We went to the show the other day. The talent was amazing: a strong man shaped like a cylinder who could lift three times his weight; an elephant that could pick up a ballerina on the tip of his trunk; a troop of cats that shimmied up poles, rode dogs, jumped through hoops and even drove little bicycles. I never believed a cat could have talent! But at the end of the show there was a pantomime routine in which the chief clown, who just wants to pick flowers and play with children, gets pursued by a giant bomb decorated with $$$ signs that descends from the ceiling and eventually crushes him. They don't do the happy-ending thing here.

Speaking of bombs, I heard that that the U.S. and U.S.S.R signed a new peace treaty in December, but I don't have any details. My International Herald Tribunes come weeks late. Please see if you can find some articles on the subject and mail them to me. There could be some interesting job opportunities related to the treaty.

Love,

Justin

Chapter Three
A Reluctant Agent

In the spring of 1988 both sides were ramping up staffing and logistics operations in order to fulfill the obligations of the treaty to eliminate intermediate-range nuclear missiles that Reagan and Gorbachev signed at the end of the previous year.

Two graduates from the Lenin Language Institute exited the Moscow metro on the way to an interview at the Ministry of Defense Industry. The government had provided them with free education. Now they were categorized as "young specialists" and required to accept a three-year work assignment from the state.

"How bad could it be?" asked Sofia. Her long chestnut hair was blown back by a gust of wind as she exited to the street. She had blue eyes that changed their hue depending on the clothes she wore. An indigo scarf encircled her neck and accented her round Slavic face.

"Better the devil you know, Sofia" responded Maria, who was an Abkhazian from Soviet Georgia. Her hair was jet black and her eyes nearly as dark, but her complexion was as fair as any Russian aristocrat. She had the kind of face you'd expect to see if the veil of a princess in an Arabian fairytale suddenly fell away. "The only other choice they gave me was a teaching job in Kyzyl," she added. "It took me ten minutes to find it on a map."

"You're lucky to get an opportunity so far away," Sofia said. "They offered me a kindergarten in Ivanovo."

"Why do you want something far away?" asked Maria. "You have a five-year-old son you'll bring along, don't you?"

"That's the point. I'm trying to get away from his father. As far away as possible."

"Well, perhaps the ministry can grant you your wish," said Maria as they entered the building, "the job they're offering sounds pretty remote."

The two women were eventually summoned to a meeting room at the personnel department.

"So, girls, are you ready to serve your country?" the Defense Industry man asked as he leafed through their files.

Sofia and Maria looked at each other. They were unable to comprehend the patriotic summons. Sofia remembered what one of her teachers had said: "If you get involved with the defense or security apparatus, you'll never be able to get out. They won't leave you alone." Then she thought about the last time her ex-husband came to Moscow from their hometown in the Ukraine. He wouldn't leave her alone, either. Only a threat to summon her father convinced him to retreat. Sofia was 24. Her education had been delayed by the unexpected pregnancy. After two rejections, she was finally accepted into the Moscow institute, whose quota for provincial students filled quickly. She was less concerned about a long-term connection to the defense industry than a short-term escape from her ex-husband. Sofia was ready to sign.

Maria was not. The daughter of a high-level Party functionary, she learned gumption early. Having been raised by a bureaucrat, she knew how to handle one. She pumped the ministry man for details.

"The work concerns the new treaty on elimination of medium range rockets," he said. "It requires we escort American inspectors when they are on our territory. Right now we are looking for two types of escorts with good English skills to work at the Votkinsk factory. There will be technical escorts who work with the Americans on the inspection activities, and there will be escorts who travel with them from Izhevsk to Votkinsk and accompany them on social activities during their stay."

"How long will the project last?" Maria asked.

"The treaty runs for 13 years. The Americans will work in shifts of a few months each," he said.

"Will there be special benefits?" she pressed.

"Yes, yes, there will be significant benefits to those who join this important mission," the bureaucrat said. He took the cue to relate another selling point. "Escorts will receive apartments and special allotments of food and clothing."

"How many hours per week are the shifts? And what kind of bonuses will be paid?"

The ministry man stood up from his desk and said with a shrug, "Look, I don't know anything more. No one knows. It's all completely new. The only other

information I can tell you is that the general director of the factory is famous for taking good care of his employees."

The girls walked out of the building and parted company. Maria was in a hurry.
She had errands to run, people to visit. She was just that kind of person — fated by
character and circumstance to be successful and get the most out of every opportunity.

Sofia was never in a hurry. She decided to stroll along the city's ancient boundary,
the boulevard ring. She loved Moscow in May. The air was fresh and people were in a
better mood with the arrival of spring after six months of winter.

'What did he mean when he asked if we were ready to serve our country? What
kind of service?' The questions gnawed at her. The ministry man did not specify, but
the implication was clear.

Vitaly Ivanovich, her English tutor and mentor, taught her to despise the KGB.
He had planted a fear and hatred of the organization whose acronym he avoided
pronouncing, just as the old religions avoided saying the almighty's name. When
he would tell stories about how he and his friends were harassed by them, Vitaly
Ivanovich would refer to the Committee for State Security using superlatives like *the
all-pervading, the omnipresent, the all-seeing, the all-hearing, the all-knowing.*

She pondered the adjectives. They were the same terms her grandmother used
to refer to God. Vitaly Ivanovich used to say that if the Soviet economy functioned
the way the KGB did, then the USSR would rule the world. She sensed a sacred awe
as he lowered his voice when talking about them. It was this sublime power that she
now found herself momentarily attracted to. The apostasy would be perverse, but
the feeling of security was soothing. She would be protected from the stalking of her
ex-husband. All she had to do was cooperate and she too would become untouchable.

But the revulsion had become ingrained. Another common term for the committee was "organ" as in organ of power. She associated the word with an organ of the
body — a bloody, pulsating thing not meant to be exposed.

Sofia remembered the disgust she felt the previous year when she underwent a
debriefing after returning from a two-week long student exchange in England. She
lay awake the night before trying to figure out why she had been summoned.

Vitaly Ivanovich once introduced her to his neighbor, Nana. She was an old
Jewish lady who had lived through the Stalin era. One day she revealed the reason
why she was alone at the age of 90, although there were pictures of her family on the

cupboard — everyone she loved had been arrested and sent away. Sofia could still see the sorrowful figure sitting in that apartment telling her sad story.

Sofia recalled approaching the inconspicuous building in the center of Moscow. No one would ever guess that it was one of their offices. She was terrified. None of the other girls received such an invitation, or so they said. She was convinced that the officer planted in their student exchange group had reported on her and the other two girls.

That co-traveler was the first KGB official she ever met. Or at least the first one she knew was from the KGB. She would never have suspected that the short, plump, spectacled older student was one of them. He did not fit the stereotype of "Iron Felix," the founder of the state security apparatus. Few of Vitaly Ivanovich's adjectives could be used to describe him, except perhaps for *all-watching* and *all-eavesdropping*.

The girls knew when they stole away that evening to have dinner at the home of one of their English host students that it was an infraction. But it was too tempting. They had met Martin in Moscow the previous year when he was on an exchange. His mother was very insistent on returning the girls' hospitality during their visit by preparing a six-course dinner. The students were happy to oblige. And they were hungry. They had been saving their 30 pound per diem to buy jeans and other clothes to bring home. Canned food brought from Moscow was their main sustenance for the week.

Sofia was relieved when the debriefing officer only expressed interest in getting information about another English host-student from Guilford University named Andy. The officer said they suspected Andy of having been trained by MI 6. He never mentioned the dinner at Martin's home. "Maybe they are not so *all-seeing* after all," she thought.

The KGB wanted to know about Andy's behavior, habits and lifestyle. Sofia lied and told the officer her English skills were not good enough to understand such nuances. The officer seemed disappointed but scribbled his phone number on a piece of paper and handed it to her, in case she remembered anything and wanted to contact him.

'But Stalin was dead and families no longer disappeared, at least not in their entirety,' Sofia thought as she exited the building. She threw the piece of paper in the gutter and made a conscious effort to erase the image of the KGB man and the location of his building from her mind. Sofia preferred to spend time reviewing pleasant memories. This was not going to be one of them. By the time she made it back to her dormitory, the officer's face and the appearance of the building were just a blur.

Now, after parting with Maria, as Sofia continued her walk and turned off the Boulevard Ring onto a side street, she recalled the miracle that had allowed her to travel abroad.

It was all thanks to her faculty advisor. Salmas Shamilyevna was a mousy woman of Tatar origin with a long nose on which her thick glasses rested. She was generally disliked by the students. She lacked a sense of humor, occasionally espoused Communist or patriotic slogans and had no tolerance for breaches of discipline. Though she seemed to favor Sofia, the girl was surprised when Salmas suggested she apply to participate in the exchange to England.

The idea of travelling to a foreign country was beyond the ken of nearly all Soviet citizens. It just didn't happen. Going abroad remained at the level of fantasy. It was something to daydream about or experience only through literature or movies — especially for a poor girl from the provinces.

The competition for the trip was fierce and the criteria stringent. Only 10 out of the 150 students in her class would be selected. Sofia looked at the list of qualifications necessary to make the cut. She was not optimistic.

Grades: A student had to excel. She barely got enough above the average to qualify for the 30 ruble monthly stipend.

Attendance: Sofia regularly missed classes because she worked nightshifts at the kindergarten in order to secure a place for her son Max and earn some extra money.

Active participation in the social life of the institute, through clubs, societies, etc: Another weak spot. Sofia tried to shun society, not join it.

Perfect discipline record: She was almost expelled the previous summer for getting caught drinking with fellow students during their "Summer Practice." Why the institute considered potato-picking a good practical experience for those learning English was a mystery to her and the other students compelled to take to the fields.

It was also a mystery to her as to why Salmas had decided to coach her through the exchange trip application process. First, approval from the all-seeing, omnipresent ones was required. But somehow Sofia got that. She was amazed. Salmas said it helped that Sofia came from a workers' family and not one of intellectuals.

The last and most difficult blessing to obtain was that of a special committee of Communist Party Members. They were the gate keepers charged with measuring the political and moral health of the candidates. It was up to them to judge the students' dedication to the ideals held sacred by the Party, its mission and the proper presentation of its face to the outside world. This was done by rigorous examination of the results of the other committees' work. In a final interview they would test candidates' knowledge of the Komsomol — the Party's youth league. Being well versed in Party history was also obligatory. Finally, they evaluated the student's personal life.

Sofia was excited to have made it this far. But when Salmas described this last step, she understood she was doomed. Sofia had never been able to force herself to care enough to master the highlights of even one of the Party Congresses. All she knew was they happened every four years —or was it five? Even more damaging was her personal situation. She was divorced. This was a cardinal sin for hard-core Party activists. They regarded the family unit as the foundation of Communist society that decent citizens, and especially party members, were obligated to construct and preserve.

"All you need to do is convince them you did everything in your power to keep your family together," Salmas told Sofia as they sat in the advisor's office preparing for the review. "I want you to rehearse your speech. And you need to wear a long black skirt and bright white shirt, like a proper Komsomolka — nothing short or flashy."

"I only have a blue skirt," Sofia said.

Salmas passed her beady eyes, enlarged by the thick lenses, over the student.

"All right, let it be blue," she said.

The tribulations of Sofia's personal life required no rehearsal. Her husband, Yury, had tried to kill her in a drunken rage while she was pregnant. He threw an axe which missed her head by a few millimeters. But she found it in her heart to forgive him for the sake of letting her son have a father. She also pitied Yury. He had come from a broken home. Sofia held out hope that maybe her love could somehow bring him back. But it was the common self-deception of an alcoholic's victim. The last straw came when, in another fit, he shoved her into a bookshelf. A radio fell from the top. Sofia caught it just before it would have slammed into her terrified infant's head.

Still, she was sickened by the idea of having to expose this private ugliness to a group of strangers. She promised Salmas she would do it, as it was the only chance to soften their hearts. Secretly, Sofia hoped the review committee would never even get to the inquisition about her personal life. She knew she'd crumble early on, during the scrutiny of her Party knowledge.

Sofia entered the room and sat down before the committee. Her skirt covered her knees, which began to tremble as soon as she saw what she was up against. It was like an aged hydra, sitting behind a long table at the far side of the dimly lit room. It was almost motionless except for the odd cocking of a head from one side to another to look at a neighboring head. Hercules was nearly destroyed by such a creature, she thought. I have no chance.

She tried to focus on the wrinkled faces of the Party members, but they seemed identical, genderless. They had penetrating stares and thin, dry lips. They wielded enormous power —enough to fulfill or destroy her dream — just as their organization did over the fate of every citizen. Their tentacles shuffled some papers on the table. Then the first question came.

"Why were you divorced?" asked one of the heads in a sharp but monotonous voice, which might have been female.

Sofia panicked. She realized she needed to urgently adjust her strategy. If she started telling the truth, she knew she'd quickly break into tears. The explanation had to be short. She suddenly remembered what her mother-in-law had told her about why her own husband had run away when their son Yury was born. Whenever Sofia tried to get consolation or understanding from the woman, she'd hear the same story.

"Imagine what he answered when I asked him, 'Why are you leaving me?' " her embittered mother-in-law would say. After a dramatic pause to make sure she had Sofia's full attention she would articulate each word slowly.

"My husband said, 'With the birth of this child, evil has entered our home!'"

The phrase sounded hideously dramatic, like so many of the phrases the Party spewed about the glory of Lenin or enemies of the state. And since it wasn't her husband who actually uttered the phrase, it was easier to transfer the blame to him than it was to reveal her equally as pathetic story.

As she repeated her mother-in-law's statement Sofia went pale. She knew it was a lie. She believed Yury had loved her and Max in his own way. He could never have repeated what he knew his father had said. She sat there trembling and ashamed.

Something happened to the torpid Party creature. Its stares no longer pierced her. The heads became animated and began to discuss something amongst themselves, like bystanders who just witnessed a bloody road accident.

"What kind of bastard says a thing like that about his own child?"

"How can our society produce such a citizen?"

"We have to consider the effect..."

The snippets reached her at the far side of the room. Then the monotone returned. Sofia heard the phrase she had wanted so badly to hear.

"You are free to go."

Her advisor was surprised to see her emerge from the room so quickly. Sofia started sobbing. The whole process was embarrassing and grotesque. She was angry at herself and at the committee. Why do those people get to decide if she goes or not? Who are they to question her personal life? Who gave them the right?

Salmas led her to the end of the hallway where no one could see them and held Sofia while she wept. There was sincere compassion on Salmas's face. Maybe she understood the real reason for the girl's tears. Sofia sensed that there was a big and generous heart in that little body. Despite the usually stern expression on her advisor's face, Salmas's smile confirmed to Sofia that the woman was truly a kind person.

"I've never seen you smile before," Sofia said, after she had calmed down.

"All your girlfriends have influential parents and contacts," Salmas said. "You have no one in this world that will help you. Your life won't be easy. I know you've been through a lot already, and you will have to fight for your happiness alone."

"Why are you so interested in my fate?" Sofia asked.

"My family was decimated by those bastards. Those that didn't die in the camps returned with the life drained out of them. And I am barred from ever travelling abroad," Salmas said. "You'll just have to do it for me, and then come back and tell me all about it."

Sofia embraced her and felt her strength.

A year later Salmas insisted Sofia go to the interview at the Ministry of Defense Industry.

"The world is changing," she said. "I think for the better. You should be part of that change. It won't be easy, but this will be a big chance to improve your life and perhaps find real happiness."

As Sofia remembered this admonition, she looked up and found herself next to Pioneer Pond. Muscovites still called it by its prerevolutionary name, Patriarch's Pond. It reminded her of her favorite book, "Master and Margarita," in which Satan

31

comes to Moscow along with some of his henchman and moves into an apartment not far from the pond.

'Perhaps if I reread it,' she thought, 'it would help me to understand this strange feeling of excitement and fear. Do I need to go to the devil himself for salvation? Can I play their game? What will Vitaly Ivanovich say when he finds out I've become an agent of the organ?'

Chapter Four
Mastering the Language,
Making a Friend

Lyle and Danny joined me and Benjamin for lunch at the cafeteria on the new embassy compound. It was a good chance to catch up and trade stories. Danny's tray was piled high with enough food for two. He had worked up an appetite by unloading a cargo shipment with a forklift, changing the snowplow's oil and preparing the riding mower for winter storage. He was one of those multitalented Midwesterners that could operate any kind of machine. Lyle was just an East Coast vegetarian.

After a few months of embassy life I was beginning to figure things out, but I still had many questions. I knew I could learn a lot from the experience of these two veterans and Benjamin's piquant observations.

I noticed a kernel of popcorn taped to the back of Lyle's badge, which was hanging around his neck and now hovering over his salad plate.

"What is that for?" I asked.

Lyle nodded toward the front of the compound.

"I'm protecting myself from the church across the street — Our Holy Mother of Constant Observation. A friend in the embassy engineering department told me yesterday that they detected elevated levels of microwaves coming from the steeple. When my kernel pops I'll know it's time to get inside."

Across the street from the new compound entrance was an abandoned church. From time to time men could be seen moving around in the bell tower. It was rumored to be used by the KGB to monitor the comings and goings of embassy staff and visitors.

I learned about counter-intelligence the summer I worked for the Federal Bureau of Investigation. As far as I know they weren't using any churches as lookout posts. Judge Webster decided to stimulate the intellectual level at the bureau by hiring college students as interns. The summer after my junior year I reported for duty to the J. Edgar Hoover building. I stepped out of the elevator in search of Division Five — the department tasked with identifying and tracking foreign spies. It immediately became clear this was a peculiar place.

A sign across from the elevator bank read: "If you do not have direct business with Division Five, you do not belong on this floor." I reassured myself by looking again at the assignment letter in my hand. Yes, I have direct business. It says so right here.

There weren't any other signs or instructions visible. I wandered the dim corridor in search of my unit. I heard the sound of a mail cart coming towards me. I figured I'd ask the clerk for directions. The sound got louder and louder until I thought it was on top of me, but there was no mail cart visible. It was on top of me. I ducked and observed a laundry-basket-like cart on a miniature railway suspended from the ceiling tooling along, carrying documents to an unseen destination. Just before it should have slammed into the wall at the end of the hallway it made a sharp turn into a hole in the wall and vanished. I continued my search, too intimidated to knock on any door.

Again, I heard the sound of wheels coming my way. This time I could feel the floor vibrate. I turned the corner. A rolling brown and gray box about the size of a refrigerator, with a flashing yellow light on top, was heading my way. Again, no visible human driver. It stopped next to a door and began to gong. Shortly, the door opened and a young man stepped out, opened the refrigerator door and retrieved some papers. The organization seemed to be interconnected by an automated flow of paperwork. But at least a human had appeared in the process.

"Excuse me, sir," I blurted out, my assignment letter in hand in case he proofed me. "Where is the database unit?"

"The corridor opposite this one, third door down on the left," he answered.

I found the right door and went inside. The unit chief, Mr. Ohlson, got up from his desk and shook my hand.

"Nice to have you aboard." Indeed, coming in from the dark corridor to the well-lit office filled with busy people felt like entering a submarine.

He led me around, introducing me as the college kid they had been awarded for the summer. "This is Alan. He's in counter-terrorism. Walter handles the Freedom of Information Act inquiries. John here manages the diplomatic database."

John turned from his desk. "Shall I give a demo, chief?"

"Sure," Ohlson said.

"Where do you live in DC?" John asked me.

"23rd and Ellicott," I answered. After a few keystrokes, a month's worth of statistics on which diplomatic vehicles of hostile countries had been sighted in my neighborhood appeared on the screen.

"Which are Soviet?" I asked.

John smiled. "All the ones with "FC" on the plates. Used to be 'SX,' like 'SEX' — easily recognized from a distance. That got leaked to the Washington Post and the Sovs complained. The head of the Bureau's Washington Field Office changed it to "FC"… for "Fucking Communists.""

The atmosphere at the bureau was very different from Foggy Bottom — younger, more relaxed, less intellectual. More acronyms: Bu-cars; Bu-bats (the older secretaries); Bu-babes (the younger ones); and even Bu-burgers in the cafeteria. The camaraderie and sense of mission were high. The agents and analysts in my unit were helpful. That summer I wrote a briefing document for agents who interview émigrés.

I lived alone in a three-room apartment in the south of Moscow. If it had been a normal Soviet apartment, there would have been between six and 10 people living in the amount of space I had. But the building was owned and operated by UPDK and was occupied exclusively by foreigners. About half the residents were Americans working at the embassy. The rules for contractors stated that I was not allowed to own a car for the first year of my tour so I usually used the bus and subway to get to work.

As I exited the front door of my building one morning, I saw a political officer getting into his car. He offered me a ride. His name was Jack Downing and he was the CIA chief-of-station in Moscow. I wasn't sure of this at the time — it was only confirmed 10 years later in an article in the Washington Post entitled "Legend Returns to the CIA," which told the story of how Jack had come out of retirement at the request of the Director of Central Intelligence to once again head the Operations Directorate.

I had only met one other person from the CIA. One day, during my summer at the FBI, Olson offered me the opportunity to talk with a real agency officer.

As I stood at the door to the garage entrance I probably looked like an excited puppy waiting for its master to come home. I assumed the CIA man would pull up in a Lotus or Jaguar, and be wearing a tuxedo. I kept looking in both directions to see if I could spot him. The top of the hour came, and went. No sign of him. One heavyset rumpled man waddled towards me. It was clear from the sweat stains on his shirt and his wheezing that he was suffering from the heat of the DC summer. He looked me over for a moment and introduced himself as "Peter." This CIA officer looked more like Jerry Garcia than James Bond, his scruffy mustache and open collar adding to his disheveled appearance.

We sat in a conference room and he played a tape recording of a forlorn Bu-agent conversing on the phone with his émigré girlfriend, who was a Soviet swallow.

"When can I see you?" the agent asked.

"Perhaps you come up this weekend?" she answered.

"I really miss you," the agent said.

"I love you," the swallow answered. "Did you get the manual?"

"Yes, I made a copy."

'What a fool,' I thought, 'falling in love with a Russian!'

Peter stopped the tape.

"Someone in the office spotted him making copies of a manual from Quantico and tipped us off. She had told him her cousin was interested in joining the bureau and wanted to get some information on the training program," he said. "This was one bad guy who was easy to catch."

For counter-intelligence officers there are good guys and there are bad guys — nothing in-between.

Peter fingered an unlit cigar. "You see, Justin, recruitment is everything. The ultimate high. For the bad guys...for us," he said. I admired his smugness and the order to his world. "To be able to influence someone to do what you want them to," Peter continued, "and have them want to do it, even if it means betraying their country...It just doesn't get any better than that. I remember a time in Nairobi..."

HOW NOT TO BECOME A SPY

I didn't know if Peter was a typical intelligence officer or not. My only other interaction with the CIA prior to meeting him was a visit to Langley. It lasted 10 minutes.

One day during my State Department internship, my boss Donald stopped by and handed me an envelope. "Would you mind taking these unclassified summaries over to the agency? I promised them by five and the regular courier has already gone."

The Agency. The Central Intelligence Agency. A warm flush came over me. I saw myself pulling out of the Foggy Bottom garage in a Corvette, part of a special pool of cars reserved for such missions. I'd speed across Theodore Roosevelt Bridge and out toward Virginia, the documents on the seat next to me and a standard issue Walther PPK in the glove box.

"The interagency bus leaves from the D Street entrance every 15 minutes," Donald said, somehow reading my mind. "It's an old tub, but it will get you there. Just show your ID when you get on."

We rolled along the tree-lined parkway and turned off at a sign for the Federal Highway Administration. I was sure I was surrounded by case officers, valued assets and minor revolutionaries. The crowd looked suspiciously like a bunch of secretaries and bureaucrats, but I assumed it was just good cover work. The bus turned left. After a brief check at the gate, it stopped under an awning.

Most of the passengers got out and walked into a tunnel that served as an underground entrance for agency employees. The covered bus stop allowed them to get inside without being photographed by enemy satellites. As a mere delivery boy, I had to use the front door, exposing my cranium, just beginning to fill with secret information, to the hostile heavens. I paused along the sidewalk to take in the sights. I had memorized the features of the facility described in the recruiting brochure — the round theater, the research center in the distance, the statue of Nathan Hale, America's first spy, a noose fixed around his neck.

Walking into the lobby, I savored each step. There it was: the mosaic in the floor with the agency seal. Just beyond it, a freestanding sign listed the rules: "No Photography," "No unauthorized electronic devices," and oddly, "No Gambling." To the right was the wall of honor. There was a star etched in the marble for each employee lost in the line of duty. His or her name was inscribed in a classified book sealed in a case standing nearby. The reality of a premature but honorable death did not register with my youthful sense of immortality.

I left the documents at the reception desk. As I dreamily walked back to the bus stop, I envisioned my future office on an upper floor: the cute secretary with a black-belt in Tai-Kwan-Do, my desk drawer filled with an assortment of advanced electronic trade craft and loaded pistol clips.

Jack Downing operated in the real world. There were no outward signs of his mission. He epitomized the humility necessary to be a great intelligence officer. He was the equivalent of a decorated hero waging the Cold War from the trenches. Yet he drove a four-cylinder Zhiguli model No. 7 with manual choke. At least he didn't have to take the bus.

I knew all was not as it appeared to be. It wasn't just because Jack very much resembled "Mission Impossible's" Mr. Phelps, with his neatly trimmed gray hair and dispassionate demeanor. The 46-year-old career diplomat had the suspiciously low rank of second secretary — the same as me, the 23-year-old driver-mechanic.

There were other clues to his real occupation. Some of the Foreign Service officers I met during my internship at Foggy Bottom were now at the embassy. They asked me to help them with a research project. I was given an upgraded security clearance and permission to work in the "core"— the cramped and dusty secure section of the old embassy building where classified work took place. Access to the core was via the small elevator to the top floor. Past the Marine guard post, steps led to the various section offices below: Political, Economic, Agriculture and so forth. My work had me in the political section, but the number of desks didn't match with the number of listed diplomats, and Jack was never there. From the top of the stairwell I would occasionally see him moving about on a lower floor, coming and going through a door with a cipher lock.

Jack had a degree from Harvard. He served two tours in Vietnam as a Marine officer before joining the CIA, where he'd been for the past twenty years. There was an ironic twist to his career: before coming to Moscow on this tour, he had designed a graduate course for the agency's best spies. It taught the art of disguise and stealth activity to help officers and agents learn to move undetected in hostile environments. One of the graduates was Edward Lee Howard — a KGB mole. He and Aldrich Ames, another Soviet spy, had been handing over the names of Soviets working for the CIA. When Howard was finally uncovered, he used the skills he learned in Jack's course to evade capture and flee to the Soviet Union. By 1986 the majority of the

CIA's agents in Moscow had been caught and executed. Jack was now supposed to rebuild the network.

This seemed to be an impossible task. In an age before high quality wigs, plastic rocks and blue tooth communications, how did a spymaster identify, meet, vet, recruit and run agents in the tightly controlled environment of a police state? Did disgruntled or greedy citizens just walk up and offer their services? I was curious about the challenge, but never asked any questions.

One point was made perfectly clear to each arriving embassy employee during the initial security briefing: "Do not openly hypothesize about the activities of any of the embassy staff and what their true responsibilities might be." Jack and I didn't converse much on those rides to the embassy. Usually he'd put on his favorite tape — the Smithsonian Collection of American Popular Song — and we'd hum along.

One spring morning on our way in to the embassy we got pulled over at the GAI post where I had met comrade captain several months earlier. A different officer was on duty. He politely requested Jack's diplomatic ID and car documents. Jack chatted with him in flawless Russian, and we were sent on our way.

"Your Russian is great," I said.

"Sometimes I feel like answering them in Mandarin, just to confuse them," he said with a grin.

"You speak Chinese, too?" I asked.

"Yeah. I learned it in college. Got to use it in Vietnam."

That was the trick. Study a language, and then use it. At least I was on track. I had been persistent and stayed with Russian for all four years in college. It was torturous. The alien alphabet was intimidating. One Cyrillic letter could equal up to four Latin consonants. The grammar, syntax and phonetics frightened away all but the most masochistic students.

There were times when I wanted to give up. During one of my internships in Washington, a friend who was member of the old boy's network introduced me to a fossil of a man named Ernie Cuneo. Ernie had been President Roosevelt's advisor on intelligence matters and one of the architects of the precursor to the CIA. He inspired me not to quit by paraphrasing a quotation by Charlemagne. "Another language is another heart," Ernie told me.

College Russian teachers could be divided into two groups. Some were Slavic émigrés from Eastern Europe, the Baltic States and Ukraine. An undertone of resentment that you were not studying their native tongue was added to frustration at your slowness in grasping the imperial language. The atmosphere in class was always tense. The other teachers were Soviet émigré intellectuals primarily from Leningrad and Moscow. They were more relaxed, but had a sadness about them. It was as if they were not whole. In certain looks and phrases, particularly when we talked about life in Russia, you could detect their melancholy.

They educated us about Soviet life through humorous dialogs:

"Where is the General?"

"He has disappeared."

"This happens."

At the time I had no idea under what circumstances I might get to use such a phrase.

The Marine guard sergeant at the embassy had a simplified course for members of his detachment who might be called on to welcome Russians into the building or usher them out.

"Gentlemen," the Gunny said, "repeat after me: 'Does your ass fit ya?!'"

The soldiers repeated it.

"Excellent. Now if you practice saying it quickly a couple dozen times, you will arrive at the Russian word for 'hello,' which is *zdrast-vui-tye*. Next, when a Soviet citizen is departing our premises, you may say to them, 'Just leave us.' This phrase, once you have also practiced saying it quickly with no pauses between the words, will sound like '*shas-lee-va,*' which is a very friendly way to say 'goodbye.'"

The two-phrased Marines were probably more comfortable in their conversation skills than I was at that point. I frequently had trouble making myself understood on the rare occasions I got to speak to ordinary citizens. My latest blunder had me demanding that a cafeteria server give me her tits instead of her hotdogs. Unoffended, she gently corrected me as she placed the wieners on my tray, but I was mortified.

"I'm still struggling with my vocabulary," I told Jack as we approached the giant statue of Lenin on October Square. "A guy came up to me on the street the other day in front of the embassy when I was changing a brake light on a van. He was curious about the engine and other parts but I could barely find the words to describe eight cylinders and power steering."

"How long have you been here?" Jack asked.

"Almost nine months," I said.

"You got your language test, albeit a bit late into your tour."

"What do you mean?" I asked.

"Think about it. Average citizens are not allowed anywhere near our building. Had that happened on a side street somewhere, it might have been legitimate. But sane Soviets do not engage embassy staff in conversation in plain view of the police guards. Such behavior would lead to an interview around the corner in the shack."

He was referring to what we called the "little rubber house." Observation revealed that up to 50 milimen, as we called the local policemen (from the Russian word *militsionaire*) could enter the nine square-meter wooden structure at one time. The little rubber house still stands there today. How many more floors exist below the street remains a mystery.

"If the less-than-sane citizen offers any resistance," Jack continued, "he'll receive a complimentary 'wood-shampoo,' administered by the miliman and his club. I'm pretty sure the inquiry about American automotive achievements was really just a language test by the KGB. They do that from time to time to gauge how much of a threat you are. Don't worry about it. It's standard operating procedure. You should still try to get out as much as you can and talk to the locals, to improve your skills."

The sound of boots marching into the embassy cafeteria announced that part of the Marine guard detachment had come in for lunch. They were bunched together in a small group. They only broke formation to get on the food line.

"Those guys aren't allowed outside anymore, except to move the 300 yards between the two compounds — and they have to do it four at a time," Ben said as he ate breakfast one morning with me, Danny and Lyle.

"Their contact rules are even tougher than ours?" I asked.

I wanted to practice my language skills with the natives as Jack recommended, but embassy policy inhibited interaction. If I were ever going to learn the art of recruiting agents, I needed to spend time talking to Russians in order to figure out how they think.

"Well, it was discovered last year, before the contractors started arriving, that two Marines had been fornicating with Soviet nannies working at the embassy," Ben said. From the sharp inflection he put on the word fornicating, it was clear he did not get to use it as often as he might like.

"One night these ladies convinced the Marines to allow the KGB to enter the secure offices and communications center, which the guards were supposed to be protecting, and compromise all the diplomatic communications equipment," Ben continued. "The new detachment is even more limited in its freedoms than we are."

In addition to microwave bombardment, the sense of isolation was an element of the siege mentality I felt from the day I arrived. All newcomers received a security briefing:

"Embassy staffers are forbidden from personal interaction with Soviet citizens, except within the framework of a strict contact policy. Any pre-meditated interaction with locals requires the presence of at least two Americans. Following such contact, a report must be submitted to the Regional Security Officer (RSO)."

"But if they hadn't betrayed the country and the corps, there might still be Soviets working here, instead of us!" Danny said.

I was not the only one who was frustrated by the contact policy limitations.

"I took this job in order to learn something about the country and meet the people," Lyle groaned. "I'm not having a lot of luck fulfilling that goal emptying garbage cans and scrubbing the consular toilet bowl. I'm thinking of asking for a transfer to the labor crew."

This was a group of contractors that roamed the city in two Grumman step vans. Their primary tasks included retrieving food shipments from the train arriving from Helsinki and moving appliances, furniture and personal shipments to and from embassy apartments. They were also responsible for picking up the increased load of diplomatic mail from the airport — the embassy communications systems were still considered unsecure. The laborers went around town most of the day, talking to the proletarians, meeting strange people and having fun. They even filmed a music video of their adventures that was circulating in the contractor underground. Their collective had attained a cult status within the PAE-Moscow Embassy hierarchy.

I had come to the conclusion that my father was right. Moscow was a sadder and drearier city than the one he had seen in 1969. Its buildings were now decaying and the majority of its citizens were engaged in a daily struggle for survival. A few were beginning to admit privately that their system was failing. But the labor crew somehow managed to find humor and even beauty in their interactions. They represented the other aspect of embassy life: it was as if we were on a mission of interplanetary exploration, seeking out any opportunity to meet aliens and understand their customs and behavior.

The embassy's political officers were there to figure out what the Politburo was up to, but it was the citizen ambassadors of the labor crew who knew the answer to the far more pressing question of where cheese was being sold that day.

"I heard the laborers had another successful *lyudi* handoff yesterday," Ben said.

"A what?" I asked.

"That's when they are driving around and spot a truck with soldiers or laborers sitting on benches in the back, under a canvas cover. The tailgate is usually marked 'lyudi,' to make it clear the vehicle carries 'people.' The laborers pull up behind and make eye contact with the occupants, one of whom usually makes a hand signal indicating he needs a smoke. Then it's like a tanker plane performing a mid-air refueling — they match speed and get parallel, pulling in just close enough to pass a pack of cigarettes to the hopeful Sov. In return they get a smile and thumbs up, before disengaging."

Well, I thought, at least it's some form of contact. More intimate than the one I had recently enjoyed.

"I think I found a place to buy light bulbs yesterday," I said.

"A seriously deficit item," Danny said with interest.

"I was heading home on the trolleybus on Leninsky when a young woman got on at the stop in front of the Moskva department store. She was carrying a small bag containing light bulbs."

"She probably nearly missed the bus while they were testing each one at the counter. Soviet bulb quality sucks, though they are a lot cheaper than the Hungarian ones, when you can find them," Danny said.

I continued to savor the memory. Though the light bulbs first caught my eye, it was her hands, delicate and pale as they held the railing inside the bus, which made me want to talk to her. She had long blond hair and a gray fur coat. Her hands seemed to glow with warmth in the muddy gloom of the crowded bus. But by the time I finally summoned my courage she had disembarked. I had no intention of violating the contact policy or betraying my country for light bulbs. But I was surprised and a little bit alarmed at my near-act-of-courage. Even more worrisome, it wasn't an intelligence gathering exercise for me. I was attracted to a Russian woman, or at least her hands and her household goods. I could have written a report to the RSO explaining the need for light in my apartment as an excuse for unsanctioned contact, and not mentioned my attraction to her flesh.

One day while standing at a bus stop I discovered an empty BIC lighter in my pocket and tossed it into the garbage can. A thin young man with a bushy beard and wearing an army issue windbreaker saw me do this, scowled in my direction and pounced on the lighter. At first I thought I might be about to get another language exam. I decided not to cooperate. "It's empty," I said in English.

"Now, empty," he responded in his own version of English. "But when I finished…" He produced another lighter from his pocket, fitted with a tiny valve. "No more empty," he said and flicked the flint wheel. "Do you know where more can be obtained?" he asked. In Soviet Russian, the verb "to obtain" is more important than the verb "to buy."

This was very suspicious. Was I being set up for a black market deal in dead lighters that would eventually be used as an excuse to declare me persona non grata?

Perhaps the plot was even more sinister: the tiny valves doubled as microphones. They thought I'd give one of these nefarious examples of recycling as a present to Jack? No, it was too absurd. I was disappointed with myself for being paranoid.

Then I considered the possibility that this would be a safe way to practice my recruiting skills, though I had no inkling of what this muppet-like fellow might be able to reveal that would contribute to our national security. I let my guard down and decided to get acquainted. I was less likely to have issues with the RSO if I made a male friend, though homosexuality had been successfully used in the past to blackmail agents.

What my first Russian friendship lacked in romance it made up for in eccentricity. Refilling lighters was just one of Valery's business ventures. He also designed and manufactured titanium gynecological instruments — he had a friend who could obtain the metal and another with access to the machine tools necessary to produce them. "One friend is worth more than 100 rubles," according to the maxim. I enjoyed Valery's ingenuity and entrepreneurial spirit. He was a fringe element. With nothing to lose, he had no fear of the authorities. Our socializing was limited to public events and the occasional dinner at his home or mine. Not very strategic reading for the RSO reports. In the end, it was he who recruited me with his warmth and humor.

Valery was very patient in explaining the subtleties of socialist reality to me and enthusiastic about expanding my understanding of Russian traditions.

"You see label?" he asked, after we successfully purchased a bottle of Stolichnaya ("Capital") vodka, following an hour of standing in line.

We were going to drink it in something called the *banya* — a communal sauna facility.

I had offered to buy the vodka in a Beryozka, or "little birch tree" store. This was a chain of about a dozen shops located throughout the city. Their non-descript storefronts belied the fact that inside a whole array of goods was freely sold — as long as you had hard currency or the right official coupons, and permission to shop there. But Valery insisted we obtain our vodka, "like the common people do."

"Yes, I see the label," I said. "It's a picture of the Hotel Moskva."

"No just that," said Valery, waving a finger. Though still confused by article usage, his English was getting better from hanging out with me and the other contractors I introduced him to. "Look closer," he said. I did. But all I could see on the red, white and black label was the hotel.

45

"It is also lesson in history, paranoia and what you capitalists call marketing… First, look at the façade of Moskva Hotel," he said as he pointed to the small drawing.

"You see left half is a small bit different in design than right half?"

It was. The left side of the façade had larger windows and was more ornate than the right.

"This is showing the fear that Mr. Steel — you do know Stalin name means 'steel,' yes? — the fear he put in people. Architect makes drawing with two possible façade designs. Great leader puts check mark on drawing, not noticing difference. No one has courage to tell him he make mistake…that he was supposed to pick one or the other design. They construct building with two different facades.

"Moskva hotel was built by same people who built your embassy. It was stuffed with microphones. This because hotel was used by regional Party and government officials who come to city for meetings. Stalin wanted to watch and listen for disagreements, dissensions. But small problem: little bits of freedom — provincial leaders would stay at apartments of friends or relatives when they came to town.

Stalin wanted just to order them to stay at the Moskva, but his head of security, Lavrenty Beria, says 'Let's have more subtle approach.' Beria ordered Stolichnaya brand to be created, and put the picture of the hotel on label. It was sold and poured freely only at the hotel. Beria convinced Stalin that visitors would associate good times they had with the hotel, and be more likely to stay there."

"It's the first instance of Soviet subliminal advertising!" I said. "Is there any evidence the strategy worked?"

"No," said Valery. "All results kept secret. We have other advanced inventions. Our telephone system is build so that you can see who is calling you…I mean from what number. Now cooperatives are selling the phones that can do this; but before it was only for big officials and Chekisti." He used the nickname for KGB officers that comes from the abbreviation of one of its predecessor organizations, the Cheka.

"It's also brilliant," I said. "Your geniuses can make things out of nothing…"

"We have very strange geniuses in this country. Sometimes when they get identified as geniuses, the KGB puts them in special prison for geniuses — where they work in laboratories making even more genius things for the state. Our genius of rockets — Mr. Korolev — he put Gagarin in orbit on a rocket he first designed in laboratory prison. The telephone system for seeing caller number — also designed in prison. Solzhenitsyn writes about it in his book…which, of course, can only be read in underground edition."

"It seems scary, if you happen to be a genius," I said.

"This correct. So we all pretend to be fools," said Valery. "Though some don't have to pretend. When KGB invites me to Lubyanka to ask what I talk about with Americans from embassy, I tell them everything, which is really nothing."

"Aren't you afraid?"

"Maybe, just a little. But while I am talking to them I keep left hand in my pocket and hold the Solzhenitsyn book about gulag you gave me. From this I get courage…"

In between adventures beyond the embassy walls, we had work to do. My sense of purpose grew. As the spring of 1988 approached, high level delegations began arriving from Washington to finalize details of the new arms treaty. Reagan and Gorbachev were scheduled to exchange ratification documents at a summit in Moscow in June. I was given the task of dispatching a fleet of 20 black Volga cars for the advance team. The cars and their drivers had been assigned to us by the Central Committee of the Communist Party to shuttle the herd of visiting diplomats around the city. I stood at the embassy gate and practiced my language skills.

I instructed the first driver: "You take this lady to the Ministry of Foreign Affairs, then go to Spaso house where the ambassador lives to retrieve the man waiting there, then return here." Verbs of motion are the hardest to master.

"I take the lady to the ministry, then I go have a quick bite to eat, then I come back here," said the Volga driver.

The verb of lunching had several variations, but fortunately I caught it.

"No. You drive the lady to the ministry, then drive to the ambassador's house, and then you come back here. Lunch will happen later."

"Ok. Lunch later."

I was finally putting my education to good use.

The fleet waiting for instructions.

We drove the bigger groups in embassy vans. I delivered five people to the Ministry of Foreign Affairs meeting house on Spiridonyevsky Pereulok. It used to belong to businessman and art patron Savva Morozov, but the Communists appropriated it when they came to power. It was a beautiful building in Russian-Modérn style, a derivation of art nouveau – a grand entrance hall, wood paneling and stained glass windows. I followed the diplomats inside to see if anyone needed a lift back to the embassy. There was no one around. As I headed out, I saw a Soviet general's cap on the rack among the tweed coats, fur hats and wooly scarves. I identified it by the scrambled eggs on the brim. Matt taught me that is what the raised gold laurels were called. I remembered the term, since it was also the only dish he ever cooked. I picked the hat off the peg and fondled it. My pulse quickened. Then a revised dialog from my Russian language course began in my head:

"Where is the general's hat?"

"It was here."

"Maybe the American driver stole it?"

48

"This happens."

I decided not to. I'd get other chances of scandalizing their treaty and adding to my father's hat collection.

A stamp commemorating the 1988
Reagan-Gorbachev Moscow Summit.

Ella Fitzgerald sang to us from Jack's tape deck that she was an old-fashioned girl, but his mind was elsewhere.

"They're not having a lot of fun in there," he said with a nod as we drove past the North Korean embassy.

"What do you mean?" I asked.

"If they want to watch a soccer game they have to go to the nearby barber shop. They're not allowed to have televisions. At home in Pyongyang they can't even put curtains on their apartment windows…citizens are obligated to watch each other all the time."

It was as if he had x-ray vision and could look at a place or, I imagined, a person, and give insights that were invisible to the naked eye. This was powerful. But there was a subtle sadness to Jack. It seemed a lonely existence, abnormally humble and anonymous for the fame-conscious American way of life.

"I read that Gorbachev signed the intermediate-range missile treaty with Reagan when he was in Washington," I said.

"It is a big deal," Jack said, "eliminating all missiles with a range of 500 to 5,500 kilometers. I hope the Chinese and the Europeans will at least say thank you."

"And a lot of work, too," I said. "Do you think it will all be done by only military personnel, or there could be some contractor jobs too?"

"For sure, there will be contractor work. There aren't enough language specialists at DOD or the Ministry of Defense to make it work. They'll need people for the elimination process and to work on the continuous monitoring aspect," Jack said. "I'm sure there'll be many opportunities for both sides to learn a lot about each other."

Chapter Five
Tchaikovsky's Hometown
at Ground Zero

"Why are there no other airplanes here, Mama?" Max asked, as they crossed the empty tarmac after landing in Izhevsk. 'Because we've arrived in the middle of nowhere,' Sofia thought, but instead responded, "I don't know."

No one from the factory met them at the airport. Maria negotiated a taxi ride to Votkinsk. She agreed on four packs of Marlboros, though the driver wanted five. Along with the sock crisis, the country's cigarette manufacturing infrastructure was breaking down. To avoid social unrest Gorbachev was forced to spend precious hard currency on imported cigarettes. But few of them made it beyond Moscow.

"Are you going to work on the treaty?" the taxi driver asked, puffing on his fare as he pulled out of the parking lot.

"Yes," answered Maria. "Have there been a lot of people coming in?"

"Not so many. I think a few people from Izhevsk are working there. You know we had no idea what the Votkinsk factory was making until the treaty was signed."

The slopes intimated the beginning of the Ural mountain range. The decaying road had buckled for a stretch of 20 kilometers due to severe temperature swings. The driver swerved regularly to avoid large chunks of shattered asphalt.

An hour later they were rolling down the hill into Votkinsk. The GAI post at the edge of town was abandoned. On either side of the road were small wooden houses, called *izbas*, which made up half the dwellings of the town. Brightly painted window frames and shutters contrasted with dingy brown logs. The roofs were trimmed in carved filigree. Max's face was plastered to the car window as he sat on Sofia's lap. He stared at the goats and chickens wandering the yards. Each house had a garden plot attesting to self-sufficiency. Every few hundred meters a common well provided fresh water. An *izba* had no indoor plumbing, but TV antennae on every chimney confirmed the presence of electricity.

Reaching the bottom of the hill, the taxi driver slowed at the corner of the lake. A massive iron anchor lodged in concrete served as a monument to the factory's expertise in metal working of the previous century.

"Over there, on the other side of the pond is Tchaikovsky's estate, where he was born. His father was a manager at the factory," the driver said with pride. "Most people think the composer came from Klin, but he spent his early years here."

They drove over the dam on the southern edge, to the main square. The ubiquitous Lenin stood proudly, his left hand clutching his cap. His right arm pointed towards the factory headquarters building. Along the upper cornice of the red brick structure were two giant medals in the shape of Lenin's head — awards received for excellence in production. The plant spread out for several square kilometers like an appendix hanging off the narrow end of the lake. A tall concrete panel fence attempted to obscure the gray-brown scene within — workshops, smokestacks and exposed piping.

The town center consisted of stucco and brick buildings. The two-story structures were from the turn of the century. Three-story buildings along the embankment had been constructed by German prisoners of war after the war. Other buildings of standard Soviet design from the 1950s and 1960s dotted the hillside above the lake. The most recent construction was the factory's Palace of Culture, built by Sadovnikov a decade earlier. Its six Doric columns looked out over the promenade along the lake's edge.

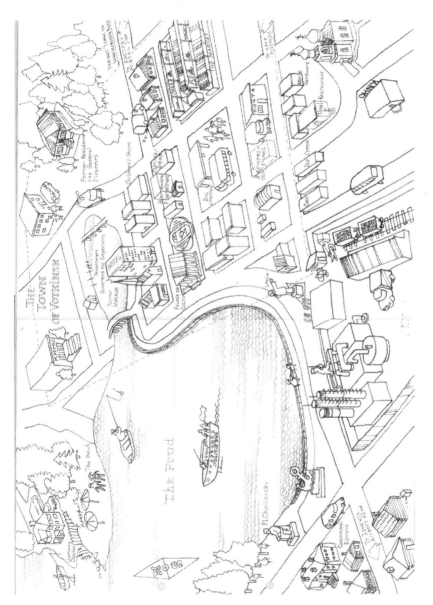

Map by Mikhail Kononov

The streets were as poorly maintained as the facades. The decay surprised Maria. "I thought defense-industry towns lived a lot better," she told Sofia.

After stopping for directions, the taxi driver found the *barak*. It was a two-story building in a workers' neighborhood next to the factory. On each floor, six rooms along a common corridor were home to as many families. They shared a 12-square meter kitchen and one bathroom. Sofia and Maria were assigned the two empty rooms next to the toilet.

Maria rapped on the door of one of the neighbors to inquire whether beds or mattresses were available.

From behind the door a woman slurred, "Why don't you ask Department 162?" With a bitter laugh, she added, "We hear they have lots of privileges for the Americans' escorts."

Sofia didn't own luggage. She was transporting her belongings in a sturdy cardboard banana box she had found at one of the Moscow markets. They made a bed for Max out of Maria's suitcases, and he promptly fell asleep.

"I'll bring up the furniture issue with the department tomorrow," Maria said. "I am sure this is just temporary until our apartments are ready. Let's go for a walk."

As they strolled along the central street, Sofia was surprised to see a Soviet rendition of Audrey Hepburn staring at her from a poster on the wall next to the only cinema in town.

"I waited in line for hours at the Illyuzion to see 'My Fair Lady,' " she told Maria, "and here it is playing in this backwater."

"I'm sure it's a sign. We are meant to be here and our work with the foreigners will blossom into something magnificent," Maria said.

Strolling along the embankment, they admired the beauty of the pink June sky. It faded to gray as the sunlight finally disappeared behind the trees above the composer's house on the opposite shore. 'This seems like a good place to hide,' Sofia thought.

By the summer of 1988 preparations to implement the treaty were also in full swing on the American side. The sounds of destruction emanating from a basement storage room in the old embassy served as proof. The tinkling of glass and crunching of metal echoed down the hallway, as if a car crash had just occurred within the building. I peered inside. Danny was attacking a large copying machine with a sledgehammer.

"Ok, three strikes. Now it's my turn," said Lyle, with the determined glee of a child waiting for his turn on a roller coaster ride.

"What are you up to?" I asked Danny as he passed the sledgehammer to Lyle.

"Well, there is a new office going in here and we were told by the General Services Administrator to dispose of this old copier. The embassy Security Officer won't allow it to be donated to the Sovs. They might decrypt its dust or something… It's easier to take out in pieces…"

"In small pieces," Lyle shouted, as the hammer sliced through the machine and it split in two.

"Who are they going to put in here?" I asked. "I mean, after you've cleaned up?"

"The Arms Control Implementation Unit. That's the group which will be handling implementation of the new missile treaty," Danny said. "I hear there is going to be a staffing contract. Six figure salaries. Three months of vacation. All for just watching missiles in the middle of nowhere. I found this welcome-pack in their mailbox and made a copy. It even has a hand drawn map of the town. Have a look…"

"Vot, Votkinsk! (Here's Votkinsk)

Welcome to Votkinsk and the Udmurt Autonomous Soviet Socialist Republic — the birthplace of Tchaikovsky and now the location of the United States Portal Monitoring Facility. Take advantage of some of the social activities, buy some shashlik (shiskebab) from an Armenian vendor in the city marketplace, or simply join the locals in a stroll along the lake next to the city center. You will acquire a unique perspective of the Soviet Union. Not only will your work be history making as you help implement the INF treaty, but also your chance to observe ordinary life in the heartland of the Soviet Union will be a memorable experience. We hope your witnessing and being a part of a new era in Soviet-American relations will be professionally productive and personally rewarding. Vsevo Khoroshevo — All the best!"

I remembered a book that Jack had lent me. It was the 1985 edition of a glossy public relations piece published by the U.S. Department of Defense called "Soviet Military Power." One excerpt read:

"We must not be overawed by Soviet Military capabilities, though they are formidable. Rather we must strengthen our resolve to preserve our freedoms and our national security, and

fashion an enduring program for our collective security. Only in this way can we, our allies and friends secure the blessings of liberty and freedom for ourselves and our posterity in the years ahead."

The Defense Secretary who penned those words had not foreseen eating *shashlik* in the heartland of the enemy as one of the ways of securing liberty for the years ahead. Even Henry Kissinger couldn't have foreseen it.

As the copier demolition continued, I thought about the future. My first year in Moscow was nearly over. But something was missing. I had front row seats to observe diplomats, counter intelligence officers and spy masters. The nature of diplomatic work was now clear: a journalist whose beat was the country of posting and whose audience was a limited universe of readers back in Washington. I had passed the State Department exams. The Foreign Service gave me a deferral, which allowed me time to decide if that was the path for me.

I also understood the vigilant grind of foreign counter intelligence, or FCI. I remembered an FBI agent at the Washington Field Office. His nickname was "Mad Max," though I don't know why. He had a neatly trimmed handlebar mustache and was responsible for surveillance. I met him in the coffee room one morning.

"How was your shift, Max?" I asked, expecting to be regaled by a story of chasing traitors down dark alleys.

"It was great, Justin," he said sleepily, "I spent the whole night watching a doorway."

As for spymaster Jack, I couldn't comprehend how he, in his anonymous humility, could function in such a hostile environment. I wasn't even able to change a brake light without being manipulated by the KGB while he was supposed to recruit sympathizers in the enemy's midst and get them to willingly provide secret information. It seemed an impossible task.

But I was sure that any pasture would be greener than the mud-filled wash bay in the embassy garage. The welcome pack was evidence of an entirely new kind of opportunity: a chance to live in a rural Russian town and be part of an historic agreement between the two countries. There were undertones of adventure and glory. There was no glory in that wash bay.

Benjamin had just returned to the embassy from home-leave in Utah. His beard had grown bushier. I could see under his shirt he had already donned long underwear.

"Seems a bit early for the long-johns," I said. "I normally don't put mine on until October."

"Criminy, Justin!" he snapped. "They're not long johns. I took the holy endowment when I was at home. These are my temple garments."

I continued to look baffled. He realized I wasn't mocking him.

"It's not something we talk about with outsiders, but the short version is we take what you might call 'communion' and then we are allowed to wear the garment. It shows respect to God and protects us from harm. Clear?"

I nodded politely. He was beginning to remind me more and more of some kind of old-testament warrior — ready to sack Babylon or Jerusalem, depending on which side he was on. The frustrations of life in Moscow were famous for giving people short fuses. I decided to change the subject.

"Have you heard about the new arms treaty?" I asked.

"We've heard of it," he said, "and at first we were apprehensive."

"We? Who is we?" I asked.

"The Utah Mormon community," Benjamin said. "It turns out that the Sovs picked the Hercules missile plant near Salt Lake City as the site that they want to do continuous monitoring at. This means that 30 godless commies will live at the entrance of the factory and have the right to check all of the production coming out. The church leadership thought it was a disaster."

"Why? It's a chance to be part of history, to build world peace and so forth. Don't you guys believe in that?"

"Sure, but we're not much on welcoming outsiders, particularly heathens. We were also afraid that letting the Sovs live at the factory would mean we'd be less likely to win sensitive government contracts in the future. The State Department reassured our elders that would not be the case. And they said this would be a good chance to show the Soviet inspectors the glory of our way of life, so now the elders have decided to welcome them and treat them as honored guests."

Votkinsk factory director Vladimir Sadovnikov was one of the first of those guests. As both sides worked on finalizing the detailed protocols that would allow the treaty to be implemented, they also organized initial exchanges of key personnel to tour factories and bases and facilitate mutual understanding. In the spring of 1988 Sadovnikov joined a delegation that visited the missile factory in Utah. What he saw there changed his life forever.

"The defense minister didn't like it when I told him that we live like aborigines compared to the Americans," Sadovnikov told his wife, shortly after returning home.

"Are you out of your mind, Volodya?" Elena said. "Aren't you taking *glasnost* a bit too far?"

"The defense minister has never been to America. But I saw it with my own eyes."

It had been his first trip abroad. Directors of secret factories are not usually allowed to travel to foreign countries. He thought he was properly prepared. The propaganda about how poorly the Americans live amidst the detritus of capitalism, about the misery of the exploited workers — it was all well known. In reality, the information available to someone even of his level was very controlled. But the rocket maker was a man of insatiable curiosity. While in Washington, Salt Lake City and New York he took every opportunity to ask questions of everyone he met.

"I felt as if a long closed door had been opened, Lena. There had always been unanswered questions, but now, as we read in our own papers here, we are supposed to ask questions. We don't have to fear. I understood that they have never felt fear there. So I joined in. No subject was forbidden. At first I didn't quite believe what I saw and heard, but I quickly realized that they don't see themselves as being in competition with us. So, there was no reason to lie. The Americans shared their problems — if you could call them that — just as freely as they did their triumphs."

"Last week," he continued, "I told the local Party chiefs that the U.S. has achieved the goals of socialism, while we are still struggling. The people there are happy... smiling...content. They have cozy homes and well-stocked stores — it was no illusion, Lena. There is a sense of both personal and communal achievement."

Sadovnikov was looking out the window at the lake. His hair was grayer and his body thinner thanks to long hours at work and the progress of Parkinson's disease.

"One of my managers asked me if it was true that America is covered in litter. I had to disillusion him. When I landed in Washington I was met by a nice young man from our embassy. We drove toward the city. I looked out the window for the first ten minutes in shock. Finally, I could stand it no more. I asked him 'Where is the garbage?' He smiled and said that the situation was not as bad as we had believed."

"Volodya, this talk is dangerous," Elena said, pouring him a cup of tea made from herbs that supposedly had curative properties. She was worried. She had seen others brought down for speaking their mind. Sadovnikov's hands trembled as he brought the cup to his lips.

American military personnel were now passing through the embassy with greater frequency as they ramped up missile inspection activities. I wanted to learn about how the treaty was being implemented. I had no idea what it might be like to work with military people, though I knew they had nice hats. The U.S. Army colonel running the Votkinsk site was scheduled to visit Moscow in a couple of days. I arranged to be his driver.

Colonel Francell was more than six feet tall. He approached the car with a gentle ursine lumber. The colonel's enormous boots occupied the entire floor space. His short black hair, trimmed with gray, gave him an air of wisdom. Treaty inspectors wore civilian clothing when on an official visit to the inspected country. No military hats. His plaid shirt made him look more like a lumberjack than a commanding officer. I was intimidated and intrigued, never having met a colonel before.

A young lady crossed in front of us at a traffic light. Her short skirt fluttered in the fall breeze, revealing shapely legs. I sighed.

"Yeah, there are a lot like her in Votkinsk," the colonel said, reverently removing the toothpick wedged between his teeth.

"Sir, would you mind if I asked a few questions about your work?"

He slowly looked me over from head to toe then said, "Not at all; go right ahead."

"What is the routine in Votkinsk like?"

"I've done two tours here as a defense attaché at the embassy, but this program is something completely new. We're working hard now to finish the main inspection facilities at the factory. It's located about 12 clicks outside of town. We monitor everything that comes out. If it's a treaty-limited item, we measure and inspect it."

"Have you actually seen any missiles?" I asked.

"Oh yes. They still make intercontinental ballistic missiles, so we're checking to be sure they don't hide a banned medium-range missile inside a bigger one. Of course, that would be a silly thing to do. But as President Reagan said, our mission is to trust but verify."

"Is it dangerous?"

"There are no warheads there. In Votkinsk they only do final assembly of the solid rocket motor and send it on its way."

"How are the living conditions?"

"Not too bad. We're housed in a basic Soviet apartment building in the middle of town. They call it a hotel. We'll be there for a few more months until a new facility out at the missile factory is finished...I mean *next* to the factory. We're not allowed inside the production facility. For now we're taking our meals at a local café. It's edible and it's a heck of a lot better than what the natives get. When we move out to the site, we'll have our own kitchen and food supply."

"What is it like working with the Russians? Here, at best, I get to talk to traffic cops and if it goes beyond an exchange of smokes I have to report it to the RSO."

The colonel smiled. "We work together 10 hours a day, setting up the site. That's in addition to inspection work where each side has four people on a shift. The factory department is very professional and hospitable. There is a social program during free time. Both sides have a two-man rule. We also need their permission to go anywhere off site. In the end, it works.

"We live by the rules of the treaty, which gives us the right to travel within a 50-kilometer radius around the factory. That gets us to a few nearby towns, some recreation areas, meetings at schools and farms. We're sort of local celebrities...Maybe 'oddities' is a better word, since the place has been closed to foreigners since the end of World War II. We're allowed to wander around downtown Votkinsk without escorts in a limited zone. Sometimes they take us to Izhevsk, the local capital, even though it is 58 kilometers from the site. We've met Kalashnikov there and gone to the ballet a couple of times."

I got a good feeling from this man. A combination of calm and curiosity. The colonel agreed to pass my resume to Hughes Aircraft — the company which had won the contract to staff the site. They needed to ramp up quickly. I had Russian language skills, a security clearance, and was already in country with a diplomatic passport and visa.

By early fall Hughes had contacted me and made an offer. It was twice my current salary. They would take me onboard following more processing stateside. I was going home for Christmas anyway. I signed the contract and mailed it back. I wasn't going to miss Pacific Architects & Engineers, and I didn't think they were going to miss me.

A security debriefing was standard procedure for departing embassy staff. It took place in the "cone-of-silence" on the seventh floor in the RSO's area. This was a box-like room within a room, perhaps 10 square meters, sound-proof and immune to all forms of radio frequency interference. Two departing State Department employees and I were present.

"Hostile intelligence services," the RSO said, "will sometimes attempt to make contact with embassy personnel who are finishing their tour of duty. Whether this happens or not depends on a number of factors, including the diplomat's rank, background, next posting and behavior while in country."

"What do you mean by 'behavior'?" I asked.

"Well," he said, "in the case of a contractor, I don't think you have much to worry about. But the military attaches sometimes have problems, particularly if they've gotten some good photographs during their time here."

"What kind of problems might they have?" asked one of the diplomats. "What is the nature of this contact?"

"It takes different forms," the RSO said. "It could be a conversation on the street in an effort to get a better file photograph. It could be a half-hearted attempt to compromise or recruit the individual. Maybe they take a crap in your apartment toilet while you are out. For the very- poorly-behaved it could be more severe punishment — tires slashed, food poisoning. A few years back a military attaché was thrown down a flight of steps. The police said the perpetrators were a group of 'unidentified hooligans.'"

"Are there any steps we should take to protect ourselves?" I asked.

"Not really. Just behave as you always have and report any suspicious encounters to me."

I had seen a "hostile" intelligence officer once before. While I was at college a delegation of Soviet students came to visit. There were about ten young men and women, and one slightly older "student." He should have had "Hello, my name is KGB control officer" written on the sticker he wore at the welcome reception. It was spring and already warm in Ithaca, but he insisted on keeping his long black trench coat and sunglasses on everywhere, even indoors and at night. He so resembled the cartoon stereotype of a Soviet spy that I expected him to start asking if anyone had seen the moose and squirrel.

My suspicions were confirmed at a question and answer session. The lounge was packed with curious students. I could only get a seat behind the table where the Soviets were sitting.

A student from the Hillel society approached the microphone and asked one of the young ladies, "How come you don't let Jews study Hebrew in the Soviet Union?" The interpreter translated the question.

"This is not correct," said the Soviet student. "They freely study Yiddish. We even have a few books published in that language."

The young man in the yarmulke repeated the question and emphasized he was talking about Hebrew, not Yiddish. The bewildered Soviet girl leaned back on her chair and turned to trench-coated Boris.

"What is Hebrew?" she asked him in Russian.

"The Jews have two languages, Irina," a flustered Boris whispered to her.

Though clearly baffled by the newfound knowledge, she maintained her composure.

"Well," she said, turning back to the student, "everyone in the Soviet Union speaks Russian, and this common language is enough for all our nationalities to communicate with each other. Next question..."

Two weeks before the end of my job at the embassy, Jack invited me to celebrate Thanksgiving with his family. I had purchased a car — a Zhiguli 2105 — the previous month, so I hadn't seen much of him lately. I was pleased to have the chance to catch up. A pecan pie purchased at the commissary was on the back seat of my car. I pulled out of the embassy garage to the gate of the compound. My window was open. Konstantin, a miliman with whom I had become acquainted while dispatching cars from the front gate during the Secretary of State Shultz's visit, was on duty.

"Did you give up your big cigars?" he asked, having observed the cigarillo in my mouth. We had never discussed my smoking habits, but his job was to observe all activity at his post. I didn't feel like explaining I was out of the bigger models.

"That's the way it goes!" I said with a shrug and drove off. I observed Konstantin in my rear-view mirror making a call into the radio microphone on his lapel. Perhaps I would meet a cigar peddler at the next traffic light. As long as they weren't from the same box the CIA wanted to present to Castro, I'd probably buy them.

A snowstorm began to blanket the city. 'A few neon lights,' I thought, as I drove through October Square, 'some colorful signs, sand blast the building facades and this place could really be beautiful someday.' I made it to the driveway of my apartment building at Leninsky 83. It had begun to feel like home. Maybe it was just because I knew I was moving on. Or maybe I had grown accustomed to being in Russia.

Bread Store No.72, the bakery on the corner, was doing brisk business prior to closing time. Shoppers came and went. Fluorescent light from the store window feebly illuminated the yard and part of the driveway. I drove slowly along the side road. In the headlights I could see large snowflakes moving horizontally in the wind. A pale round face under a fur hat appeared in the middle of the road ahead of me. I stopped the car. I assumed he had dropped his loaf of bread in the road.

Instead of bending down to pick it up, the man walked quickly to my side of the car. He indicated with a nod that he wanted to talk to me. I rolled down the window. He leaned his head toward me, the bristles of his beaver-fur *ushanka* nearly touching the car. His hand shot up and passed an envelope through the window. I took it without thinking.

"Take thees to yer seekoority peeple," the round face said in poor English. At first the words did not register. The phrase was out of context. I expected to hear a sentence in Russian like, "Please don't run over my bread." The man ambled off into the darkness. I rolled up the window as the meaning sank in. Contact had been made.

I drove slowly to the parking lot of my building. I tried to analyze the situation and suppress panic. The miliman stood indifferently in front of his booth. He was staring up at the falling snow. He then went to his booth to presumably make his usual note of an arriving vehicle's license plate number as I parked.

My pulse raced as I turned off the engine. The previous year an American journalist in Moscow had found himself in a similar situation and was arrested as a spy — the documents he received having turned out to be "classified" information. The black passport in my pocket protected me from permanent incarceration but that did little to ease my nerves.

Fear of arrest was only one part of my reaction. What really irritated me was the feeling of being manipulated. The situation was orchestrated and not under my control. I imagined the pale-faced man before my arrival, sitting in a car nearby with his colleagues, plotting our interaction.

Now what? Would they pop up from behind the lone shrub next to our entryway and arrest me as soon as I got out of my car? No one was visible in the shrub. I opened the unsealed envelope. Inside was a standard Soviet post-card. On one side was a photograph of a Moscow park. On the other, carefully printed in the same English handwriting that all Soviets have, was the following message:

"I have to write to you again. Ready to cooperate. Still no way to go abroad. Need connection for Moscow. Address: Main Post Office, on my name.

Juan Pablo"

Juan Pablo looked much more like Ivan Ivanovich. If he really was "one of ours," I thought with a dilettante's disdain, he was a complete fool for trying to facilitate communication in such fashion. His handler should be fired for not teaching better tradecraft. I decided to put the envelope under the seat of the car and pass it to the RSO the next day. I walked past the miliman, into the building. I was overcome by a feeling of disappointment. 'Is that the best they could do?' I thought. 'I deserve more attention than that!'

I must have still had a wild look on my face as Jack opened the door.

"Is everything alright?" he asked.

"Just fine," I said, handing him the pie. "I'm moving to Votkinsk to monitor missiles."

"Outstanding!" said the former Marine. "You're in for a unique adventure."

CHAPTER SIX
DEFENDING AGAINST ENEMIES,
REAL AND IMAGINED

The Sadovnikovs had driven to the outskirts of Votkinsk to finish harvesting their garden plot. With the onset of winter they would pickle and can most of what the 600 square meter space yielded. In the past, tending vegetables was not a hobby that Vladimir Gennadevich relished. Elena would tease him, reminding him that his last name meant "gardener." Lately, however, as Parkinson's disease began to take its toll on him, he found the activity therapeutic. Today, it gave him the chance to have an important conversation with his wife of 30 years.

"It's incredible, Elena," Vladimir Gennadevich said as he stooped to pull the onions from the cold ground. "They have destroyed 72 of my rockets by static ignition. Three years of production. And do you know what?" He didn't wait for her to answer. "Not one single failure!"

His voice was energized with pride. In his mind's eye he was watching the technical triumph take place and savoring the result of all those years of careful engineering and manufacturing.

"Each one worked perfectly, from ignition to final burn," he said, making an arc with his hand as if he was following a rocket's path across the sky. "The American military observers complimented us on the quality of our production."

"You should be very pleased, Volodya. I am proud of you," Elena said.

She had seen the man she loved grow from a respected engineer to the leader of an entire factory and its town. Vladimir Gennadevich's hand trembled as it stretched toward the onion sprout. He was concentrating very hard to make his fingers move in the right direction. She wanted to reach out, to help him steady it. But it was his balance of self-confidence and humility she loved most of all. She restrained herself.

"I am proud, Lena. Which is why I didn't put up a fight when they told me yesterday that I must retire. I realized they were going to get me one way or another. My best products are no longer needed. Perhaps I was a little too free in my speech lately; though the Party officials say the reason for my retirement is to leave me time to take care of my health. They went on and on about my years of service, how I deserve my pension…"

Elena felt relief. No more 12-hour workdays. No more complaint letters from workers who didn't get the apartment they wanted, or petty accusations that the general director was seen using his official car for private purposes. 'We're done with that kind of ingratitude,' she thought, as she rubbed the soil from her hands and embraced her husband. A cool wind came up from the lake.

Elena was a strong and creative woman. But, as the wife of a man in such a powerful position, her life was her husband. She shared his joys and concerns, managed his schedule, fed him and raised their sons. Her entire existence was an extension of his dedication. He was her only friend.

"You are not giving up, are you?" she asked, kissing his cheek. Vladimir Gennadevich looked perplexed. "What does this mean? Give up? Don't know the phrase. You've seen me running 10 kilometers every day, doing an hour of yoga? I'll double it!"

"But no more fasting, dear. Please."

"We may all be fasting soon. They are going to put Palyanov in my place. I said when I shook his hand to congratulate him, 'Alexander Ivanovich, don't forget: the people can't eat rockets!'"

Vladimir Gennadevich seemed to have made peace with the situation. But Elena, though relieved by the news, had trouble imagining her husband without his work. It had been as much a fundamental part of his existence as his family was. His lifelong goal had been to be useful. Retirement seemed like a death sentence.

The worst nightmare for the head of the Votkinsk branch of the Committee for State Security had come true. Every three weeks a plane landed in Izhevsk filled with

American spies. They would make their way to his town, where they would be given intimate access to the most sensitive product made by the factory, which he had been protecting for the last 12 years.

Before the treaty, Gennady Petrovich Shuvalov, who had steel gray eyes and short-cropped mustard colored hair, managed three engineers. They were responsible for the security of the Votkinsk Factory Production Association, whose main facility was located downtown. It had a branch, innocuously called Workshop No. 95, located 12 kilometers outside of the city. It was there that missiles were assembled. Solid rocket fuel was dangerous to work with and best not handled in the middle of a population center.

Shuvalov's task was to minimize the factory's visual, thermal and electronic emissions. They could be analyzed by foreign satellites and other technical reconnaissance. So far he was successful. The entire Udmurt republic had been closed to foreigners since shortly after World War II. This was necessary due to the nature of the work of the factory and dozens of other military enterprises located throughout the republic. Udmurtia was also home to storage facilities of enough chemical weapons to kill a trillion people. That stockpile would eventually be reduced beginning in the late 1990s through a joint project with the Americans.

But as far as Shuvalov was concerned, the world he was dealing with in 1987 was already fraught with enough change. His office on Ulitsa Lenina, across from the downtown factory headquarters, was getting significant support from Moscow. Workshop No. 95 outside of town had even been renamed "The Votkinsk Machine Building Factory."

'It's ironic,' Shuvalov thought. 'Thanks to an arms reduction treaty, everyone got a promotion. A workshop became a factory; factory workers became participants in an international treaty; and my own team doubled in size and was given new responsibilities.'

'Now, instead of hiding the factory from the enemy, we have invited their intelligence officers to live at its front gate. Is this what the Party means by a 'Bright Future?"

It was hard for him to accept, but respect for authority involves an element of faith. Shuvalov's faith in the Party and the Committee was unshakable.

The work life of Shuvalov's unit had become more interesting. Their mission expanded to include cooperation with Department 162, the group created at the rocket factory to escort and manage the Americans spies. He would now get to study the foreigners firsthand and gather information about them that would allow him to better protect the facility. Gennady Petrovich had never seen an American before. He had started his career 12 years earlier as a junior engineer in the KGB, but now he was interested in the human intelligence aspect. In "humint," recruitment was everything. KGB headquarters in Moscow had declared active recruiting of the Americans off-limits due to the significance and visibility of the treaty. He could live with that, for now. There was enough counter intelligence work to keep him busy. Several of his officers were working in Department 162, and he was in the process of training some of its staff to be agents.

Gennady Petrovich viewed the new paradigm as an opportunity to gain an advantage over factory Department No. 1, which had formal responsibility for the physical security of the plant as well as personnel vetting and access control. This included liaising with Department 162 and the escorts. The rivalry between the two security organizations intensified as preparations relating to the treaty got underway. The KGB was interested in the escorts because they could help identify any immediate threats — it was clear the Americans would use the opportunity of being close to the factory to try to gather information and possibly compromise workers or the facility itself.

"The Americans are our enemies. They come here to spy," Shuvalov told Sofia and the other escorts in Department 162 during their initial security briefing.

It was a logical conclusion. Why would the state spend so many resources building weapons to defend against the United States if they were not enemies? History was full of examples of America's aggressive attitude to the U.S.S.R.: General Patton's well known plan to attack the Soviet Union after the end of the Great War; Kennedy's blockade against Soviet ships trying to support Comrade Castro; Eisenhower's deception of Khrushchev with the U2 over-flights; the provocation of the Korean Airliner. As a guardian of the state, Shuvalov could not believe otherwise.

He did his best to teach the escorts techniques that would help his effort. "Those of you who know a third language should keep it to yourselves. It is possible that the Americans could decide to exchange secret information amongst themselves in that language; you could learn something valuable." That tactic had worked for Stalin and his secret police chief, Beria, who was also a Georgian. They frequently spoke their mother tongue together when they didn't want their Russian underlings to understand what they were saying. Shuvalov, however, was clearly unaware of the poor status of foreign language study in the American school system.

The task of defending the fatherland added an element of righteousness to the work carried out by Shuvalov and his team. But, as in police detective work, the criminal had predictable goals and known methods. The mission was to foresee risks and eliminate weak points while making the enemy's efforts as difficult and transparent as possible. If you could turn a defensive play into an offensive one, that was the acme of skill.

"What should we do if we learn something that seems interesting?" Maria asked Shuvalov at the meeting.

"Send me a *spravka* (a brief report about an event or incident) with the details," Shuvalov answered.

"This would be in addition to the *spravki* we already write for Department No. 1?" Sofia asked.

Shuvalov was surprised. He thought he was the only one demanding *spravki*.

"You mean they have you writing reports, too?"

"Well...yes," she responded. "They told us it was part of our job and that our monthly bonuses and our chances to improve our housing would depend on how diligent we were."

"In that case, yes. Please send me a duplicate of any report of interesting statements or behavior by the inspectors."

Sofia didn't care. If a little more paperwork would help her and Max get away from the cockroaches of the *barak* and obtain a decent apartment, she was willing to put in the extra effort.

I was eager to make it to Votkinsk. But before I could be cleared to start working on the treaty I had to go to the On Site Inspection Agency's headquarters in Washington, DC for additional processing.

I realized I got off at the wrong stop as soon as the bus doors closed behind me. There was no sign of a federal building. But I could see how the area came to be called Buzzard Point. Faces peered from the yards of the few inhabited dwellings, interspersed between burned out buildings and rusting automobile carcasses. I easily imagined scavenger birds circling overhead.

After a 10-minute walk, I came to Fort McNair, situated at the bottom tip of the diamond that makes up the District of Columbia. My expectation of how a military facility should look —walls decorated with maps and citations, weapons secured in neat racks and other signs of organized aggression — was incorrect. Boxes and papers were piled in corners. Furniture was stacked along the corridor. A layer of dust attested to the last occupant's long forgotten retreat. The On Site Inspection Agency, or OSIA, had been created by the Defense Department only a few months earlier. It was juggling its ramp-up with ongoing treaty implementation activities.

There was one manifestation of aggression present. It was not displayed on the wall or secured in a gun rack. It was sitting behind a desk. And it was breathing. The badge on the breast of its uniform and insignia on its collar indicated it was called Captain William Knight, USMC. It did not smile at me as I entered the room. It simultaneously created a reassuring feeling of security for the nation and a subtle threat to the safety of my person. Perhaps the hostile vibrations emanating from the Marine were of a general nature and not directed specifically at me. I decided not to yield to my instinct to run away. I couldn't. I needed help to find my way out of Southwest.

The captain's shape made me uneasy. He was defined entirely by straight lines. A large young officer, he had a generous complement of requisite muscles, especially pectorals. Arms and shoulders met at right angles that paralleled his linear cranium. Rectangular glasses sat on a square nose. As he looked through them at me even his eyes seemed angular. He was clearly made of interchangeable parts. If damaged in battle, they could be easily exchanged with new ones.

Knight acknowledged he was familiar with the purpose of my visit and handed me some forms to fill in. Then he began to ask questions.

"So, you work in Moscow now?"

"I'm a driver and mechanic at the embassy," I answered.

"You work for the State Department, then?" There was a clear inflection of disgust as he asked this question.

"I'm a contractor."

"Did you come to Washington especially for this interview?"

"Actually, I had to be here anyway to process some forms for the Foreign Service."

"So you want to become a diplomat?" His tone was definitely colder now.

"Maybe. I'm not really sure. It's an opportunity I'd like to explorer further."

As the words left my lips I realized my error. There are two reasons why Marines have an inherent antipathy for the State Department. First, Marines are charged with defending U.S. embassies abroad, which can be a thankless task. I remembered how at Foggy Bottom the Marines would come through the building at night on training exercises. This meant all security measures had to be triple-checked — papers away, doors locked, typewriter ribbons secured. Second, the two organizations are diametrically opposed in their approach to foreign countries — State prefers airports with red carpets and canapés, while Marines prefer beaches, landing craft and cover fire.

Realizing I had already lost Knight's heart and mind, I struggled to continue the conversation. Knight had been to Votkinsk, so I asked for details about the site and the treaty work.

"Everyone pulls inspection duty," Knight explained. "A shift team includes one OSIA officer and three contractors, one of which is a translator. The Sovs sit shift just like us, across the hall. Our interaction with them is limited to treaty work. We observe all vehicles coming out of the factory. Those of a certain length or more, we inspect."

"What length?" I asked.

"That's classified. You'll find out after we finish your clearance. Once per shift we do a perimeter patrol of the factory. It's about five kilometers. Usually the Soviet guards patrol the other side of the wall, along with their attack dogs."

"Attack dogs?"

"It's not a problem, except where there are holes in the fence. In the winter the patrol is done on skis. But in the summer it's a swamp. We do it in waders and special anti-tick suits."

"Anti-tick suits?"

"There is an epidemic of tick-borne encephalitis in the area. The suits don't always work. So we strip down after each shift and inspect each other head to toe."

I imagined inspecting all the places where the naked captain's lines intersected. I hid my revulsion.

"Sounds like pretty basic work," I said.

Knight appeared disappointed at his inability to dissuade me.

"Lieutenant Taylor can give you more details," he said, pointing to the pudgy army officer with round spectacles, auburn hair and mustache who had recently entered the room. "I've got to report to the operations center," Knight said, and went out.

"Don't worry about Will," Taylor said. "His mission is to make sure nobody gets in trouble over there."

Will was clearly a man with a mission. In the future he would take on the nickname "Captain Ahab." His white whale would be Saddam Hussein, who personally called Will a "Hyena" thanks to the captain's relentless efforts to uncover weapons of mass destruction in Iraq. Will would also have the courage to tell General Norman Shwarzkopf that the general was mistaken in his claims to have destroyed Scuds. They were just fuel trunks. The general, unaccustomed to making mistakes, had Will reassigned to the front. In Russian, Will would be called a *Borets za Pravdu* (Fighter for Truth) — a fanatic idealist. To his credit and detriment, he would let nothing get in the way of completing his mission.

"Bug spray takes care of the ticks most of the time," Lieutenant Taylor said. "Besides, we're inoculated by the site nurse."

"Have you ever seen Knight naked, lieutenant?" I asked.

"Not that I can remember. And please call me Jake. I've just been recalled from reserve duty. I'm happy to limit the formalities."

"Thanks," I said. "So it's not that tense?"

Jake smiled. "No, not really. Actually, perimeter patrol is a relaxing break in the monotony. We do it with the Soviet escorts. It's a chance to get acquainted. In the winter the drifts get so high you can even see over the wall sometimes. The summer is short but stunning. The escorts tell us about the flora and fauna. There is a field of brilliant yellow sunflowers on the east side that blooms for a few weeks. You can even see the occasional moose posing at the edge of the woods. I find it quite pleasant."

After the chilling interlude with Knight I began to feel warm again.

"Are you ready for the polygraph?" Jake asked. I had been so distracted by the two opposing impressions that I forgot that there would be a polygraph.

"Yes, I'm ready."

"Then I'll take you upstairs to meet Brock," Jake said.

Compared to Brock, Knight was scrawny. My hand was lost in his massive palm as he greeted me. Brock was a polygrapher.

It was supposed to be a counter intelligence exam only. This involves a series of questions that clarify whether you are, have ever been, or are planning to become an agent of a hostile foreign power. The more dreadful type of polygraph is called a "Lifestyle Exam." It lasts several hours, and addresses everything from political persuasion to sexual deviation and substance abuse. It is given to those who enter the intelligence world in a deep way: high ranking military officers, National Security Agency employees and CIA officers.

The effectiveness of a polygraph exam depends on the skills of the polygrapher. The Naval Intelligence Service, for which Brock worked, was reputed to be the most professional of government polygraph administrators.

Free of perversions and believing it would be the first of the two types of polygraph exams, I was initially unafraid. The principle behind the polygraph is simple. It simultaneously measures heart rate, blood pressure, respiration and galvanic skin resistance — essentially, your sweat level.

The assumption is that if you are not telling the truth your body gives you away. In order to have a scientific approach to this not entirely scientific process you are connected to the machine and given a baseline set of irrelevant questions. You are alternately instructed to give true or false answers. This allows the polygrapher to obtain a profile of you when you lie. Finally, you are asked the exam questions.

"Is your name..."

"Do you live at...."

"Have you ever been in contact with agents of a hostile foreign government?"

"Are you now in contact with any agents of a hostile foreign government?"

"Would you like to be in contact with agents of a hostile foreign government?"

The exam takes place in a special room with no distracting superfluous decorations. You sit with your back to the whirring needles of the machine and the piercing glances of the polygrapher.

It is possible to skew the results. One option is to keep a thumbtack in your shoe, jamming it into your toe when telling the truth on a baseline question. This increases pulse rate and blood pressure artificially. A similar effect occurs if you suddenly contract your anus at the right moment. In a hostile polygraph exam you sit in a special chair that inhibits such movements. Polygraphy is ineffective on a pathological liar who believes what he is saying, since no biometric anomalies are revealed. So, pathological liars have a good chance of being hired.

I was completely confident that I was not an enemy agent. But the last question on the exam disturbed me.

"Have you ever put false information on any official government document?"

The question is designed to root-out income tax cheaters who can potentially be blackmailed. This is grounds for denial of a security clearance. At that instant, I recalled the fake ID business I ran during high school. One stroke of a straight razor and a firm pencil applied to a New York State driver's license was all it took to change the ᑲ5 to ᑲᗱ, making my friends and I instant 18 year olds. I could feel the microscopic sweat surfacing on my fingertips. There was nothing I could do. With feigned confidence, I answered, "No."

The machine stopped whirring. Brock tore off my chart.

"Just sit and relax," he said. "I'll analyze this and be right back."

Ten minutes later he returned. "Everything checks out just fine," he said, "except you seemed a bit unsure of your last answer."

He paused and looked down at me intensely. I stared back trying to appear as innocent as possible. "I am not too worried about it," Brock continued. "Congratulations and good luck in your new work."

My hand again disappeared into Brock's as I thanked him. Exiting the office, I half believed there were several New York State Troopers waiting in the corridor to arrest me for forgery and underage beer consumption. And I half believed I was on my way to Votkinsk.

Chapter Seven

All Personal Items are

Subject to Inspection

The taxi driver grumbled in German the entire seven-minute ride from Frankfurt airport to the Rhein-Main airbase. He pulled over, removed my bag from the trunk, took my 10 Deutsche marks, and sped off. How was I supposed to know it was a short trip?

The On Site Inspection Agency's European field office was at Rhein-Main. The base was a symbol of the ups and downs of U.S.-Soviet relations. It had been the staging area 42 years earlier for the Berlin airlift that had left such an impression on my father. By 1992 it was time to help the defeated enemy. The chaos that followed the end of the U.S.S.R saw a shortage of not only socks and cigarettes but also food and medicine. Rhein-Main was the hub for the humanitarian effort called Operation Provide Hope. For two weeks in February of that year the United States and NATO used C5 and C141 transport planes to deliver several hundred tons of emergency food and medical supplies to hospitals, orphanages and other needy recipients in cities throughout the 12 newly independent former Soviet republics, including Russia.

When I arrived at the base that day in March 1989 it was the logistics center for the INF treaty. From its airfield U.S. inspectors flew to dozens of locations across the Soviet Union and Eastern Europe to observe the destruction of missiles, verify their absence from launch sites and monitor former production facilities.

The sign above the gate read: "Rhein-Main Air Base: Home of the 435th Tactical Air Wing."

'I bet there are a lot of nice hats to be had in here,' I thought.

The guard looked at my diplomatic passport and one-page order. Then he pointed me in the direction of the hotel.

I lugged my bag towards the building. I left most of my useful belongings in two trunks at the OSIA Moscow office for forwarding directly to Votkinsk. The jet lag left me weary and the gray morning sky offered no inspiration or energy. The lobby of the hotel was decorated in late 1960s split-level-American-living-room motif. The brick walls were complimented by vinyl furniture and aluminum lampshades. I stood at the end of a line of burly soldiers waiting to check in. As I handed the lady soldier behind the desk my order, I half expected she would turn me away because I looked younger than my 23 years. She checked a list and passed me a key.

"You'll be rooming with Mr. Seward. The elevator is behind you, to the left."

The room was decorated in the same fashion as the lobby. Seward was asleep on one of the beds. He was dressed in jeans and a leather vest. A cigarette burned in the ashtray on the side table next to his head, which was covered in a gray tousle of hair. He looked like an old version of James Dean. Seward was a manager at Hughes Technical Services, the contracting company I was now working for. He was in charge of our inspection team.

As I put down my bag, he sat up and offered his hand.

"I'm Jim, but you can call me Uncle Lou."

The expression on my face made it clear to him I couldn't see the link between the two names.

"The nurse on site said we have too many 'Jims,'" Lou continued, "and that I remind her of her uncle, so the name stuck.

"I guess you're the long lost inspector!" he said out of the corner of his mouth, still not accustomed to his recently acquired dentures.

"I can hardly believe it myself," I said as I sat down on the bed across from him. "They had me at the Albuquerque training site for five weeks. I really wanted to get back here...I mean to Russia, as fast as I could."

"Well," said Seward with a skewed laugh, as he put his Popeye-muscled forearms behind his head and stretched back on the pillow, "sounds like the pencil pushers tried to screw you pretty thoroughly."

The Pacific Architects & Engineers contract manager at the embassy and his State Department counterpart made a fuss when I left. They accused Hughes of poaching contractors. State refused to issue me a new passport. It took an army of lawyers from the Defense Department to convince them they risked a lawsuit if they tried to keep me from taking the inspector job.

"How are things at the site?" I asked.

"Well, we're almost eight months into treaty implementation. The basic inspection equipment is set up. But there's plenty left to be done — trench-digging, cable pulling, wiring and so forth. It's chaotic, but we're getting along with the Sovs and things are progressing."

"How many people are working there now?"

"The treaty allows for up to 30 inspectors at any given time. Usually it's the site commander from OSIA, three or four of his deputies, and 25 of us contractors. I understand you're our handyman. You can help connect the appliances and get the supplies in order."

My job title was "Custodial Maintenance Engineer." Mr. Bellman, the Hughes site manager for Votkinsk, assured me it didn't mean I would spend all my time cleaning toilets.

"So what do we do now, Lou?" I asked.

"I like to get some shut-eye before the team goes for dinner," he replied. "We usually wind up at a beer house nearby and guzzle as much as we can before going in-country. There's no drinking on site, and the o-five hundred reveille is so god awful early, you're better off half in the bag anyway."

At about the time we were gathering in Frankfurt, the Nuclear Risk Reduction Center, the Soviet counterpart to OSIA, sent a list of incoming inspectors to Department 162. Alexander Vladimirovich Losev, the head of Department 162, reviewed the list before handing it to Sofia, who had just started working part-time as his assistant.

Losev worked as a technical manager for the final stage of solid rocket motor assembly at Workshop 95 before the treaty was signed. He had a reputation for patience and meticulousness —two characteristics that factory and ministry officials agreed would be essential to successfully implement the treaty and deal with the Americans. He had thick glasses and was nearly bald. The slide rule he used to carry in his breast pocket was now replaced by a pen. But he was an engineer at heart.

"Sofia, tell Nikolai I want him to lead the trip to the airport for the inspector rotation. You and the girls decide which of you will go along. I've got a meeting with the new factory director."

"Yes, Alexander Vladimirovich," Sofia answered.

"Oh, one more thing," Losev said. "Find the file that has the customs reports. Department No. 1 wants to see the list of what's in the trunks of that inspector that never showed up. I think his last name is Lifflander. The trunks were cleared three months ago and he's on the list to arrive tomorrow. And have one of the drivers deliver the trunks to the hotel."

Sofia went to the file cabinet and retrieved the memo with the notes from the customs inspector. She read it before putting it on Losev's desk:

22 December 1989; Moscow, VIP Terminal of Sheremetyevo Airport. Customs Officer Captain Ivanov, Oleg Ivanovich: report of contents observed during standard rotation inspection of personal luggage of incoming inspectors. Attending U.S. Embassy officer delivered two trunks, which the officer stated belong to an inspector that would be going to Votkinsk on next rotation.

Description: Two trunks, standard size, black, labeled "Justin Lifflander / PAE Motor pool, U.S. Embassy, Moscow, U.S.S.R."

Contents:

<u>Clothing</u>: *Fur hat, several pairs of synthetic gloves, one blue winter jumpsuit with embassy label, winter underwear — white, with holes. Several pairs of thick wool socks. One pair of work boots.*

<u>Documents</u>: *Approximately 15 books; authors noted include Bukowski, Dostoyevsky; Manchester; Approximately 8-10 Magazines, including National Geographic, Soldier of Fortune, National Lampoon. No pornography detected.*

<u>Personal Items</u>: *Audio cassette tapes: approximately 100, several with Jewish names written on them (Cohen, Simon), others with Anglo-Saxon names visible (Marley, Prince, Byrne); 1 Electric typewriter, 1 ream of paper, packages of spare ribbons for the typewriter; 2 Flashlights; 3 Cigar boxes; 6 decks of playing cards; a small selection of tools, including electrical tester, screwdrivers, wire cutter. At least 12 rolls of black electrical tape — more possibly hidden in the socks.*

No further details possible due to limited time and close supervision by American inspector.

An interesting collection of items, she thought. Why would he need to bring all that tape? Hughes has plenty of its own equipment in the warehouse. She didn't recognize the musician's names, but was glad to see that at least one of the Americans was interested in Russian literature. No videos — that was different. Usually they brought lots of video tapes.

She looked at the other names on the incoming inspector list. She wasn't good at remembering people's names, and wanted to get them right this time.

Mr. Seward — she remembered him well. He always had candy. Looked something like a cowboy.

Darlene, the translator — big glasses, worked hard. Accent not so bad.

Lieutenant Jake Taylor — one of the more friendly military officers; cute red mustache; passable Russian.

She looked at the rest of the names of inspectors on the list, some of whom she had met several times. But try as she did, she couldn't remember their faces.

At the airbase it was still dark outside. We exited the bus next to the C141 military transport plane that would take us to Moscow. I glanced over at the civilian side of the airport. There was no activity. On our side of the tarmac a massive C5 Galaxy transport plane was parked in a hangar behind us. Technicians swarmed over it like ants. Above the hangar doors the phrase "Mission Success" was written in large letters, illuminated by flood lights. My mission remained unchanged. Two years living in a provincial town as a missile inspector would hone my language skills and give me unrivaled insight into Soviet life. Jack's parting comment about the uniqueness of the opportunity echoed in my ear. Being blessed by him was like kissing the pope's ring before starting a crusade.

I entered the hatch of the plane and took a seat. I felt like I was inside a green whale. Its ribs were visible and a partially digested lunch lay in a heap at the back. The heap was actually a pile of inspection equipment and luggage that had been strapped to the rear deck. There were only two small windows midways along the belly. Nine passengers sat facing the back of the plane.

Lieutenant Jake sat down next to me. It was the first familiar face I had seen in several days.

"You finally made it! Welcome!" he said.

"A victory over the bureaucracy," I replied.

"We fought hard for you back in Washington. The general finally laid it on the line and the State geeks conceded."

"Sorry about the trouble. It was supposed to be easy."

"Don't sweat it. Ambassador Matlock signed off on the last cable where they confirmed it was nothing personal against you."

The engines started and we had to shout.

"How did you wind up here?" I asked.

"I'm the world's oldest lieutenant. I was called up from reserve duty because I speak some Russian." His knees wiggled as he talked. His constant fidgeting made him seem younger than his 38 years.

Our voices were soon drowned out by the engine noise. A crew member came down the aisle and handed out foam ear plugs. The plane began to taxi.

After we were airborne most of the team fell asleep. A few occasionally awoke to return the rented German beer to the port-o-potty bolted to the floor near the front of the cabin.

Four hours later we touched down at Sheremetyevo airport. The bay doors behind the equipment pile opened. It was like looking at a movie screen. I saw all the familiar features of the airfield. The Pan Am flight from New York was parked at one of the jetways of the new terminal. We taxied to the other side of the field near the old terminal, which was used for domestic flights and diplomatic delegations.

The hatch opened. Two border guards with green epaulets and caps stood at the bottom of the tiny ladder. Several officious middle-aged men in civilian clothes stood behind them. Jake handed them a stack of passports belonging to the inspectors and the air crew.

"The Nerk reps will now compare our names to the master list of approved inspectors and the official notification OSIA sent about this rotation, to make sure it all jibes," Jake said as we walked across the tarmac.

"What's a Nerk?" I asked.

"Nuclear Risk Reduction Center. They manage the escort process and also the logistics of getting inspectors to where they need to go inside the country. The funny thing is that they approved our first master list of inspectors two weeks ahead of the treaty deadline, while the FBI wanted to reject several of the inspectors on the Sov list because they had them listed as Soviet military intelligence officers. Our general had to remind the bureau that both sides were using such experts, since they are the ones who know foreign languages and the enemy's hardware."

We went through a side entrance at the end of the small terminal and entered a lounge.

"Now we go through customs," Jake continued. "Only our documents are diplomatically inviolable. Since we live and work so close to a strategic site, everything else — personal items and inspection equipment — is strictly controlled. On the last rotation they tried to take dental floss away from one guy. They thought it was fiber optic cable."

We were ushered into a lounge where two customs officers were x-raying luggage. I was glad I left behind my night vision goggles and wireless microphone collection. While the bags were scanned, we milled around the bar drinking bitter instant coffee from India – a delicacy in Russia. There was one woman on our team. From the conversation the previous night I gathered she was a former Army sergeant now working as a translator.

Darlene was short, about 30 years old, with long blond hair and large eyeglasses. She was standing alone. The other team members seemed wary of her. I tried to strike up a conversation.

"Must not be easy being one of the few females on this program," I said. From her facial expression I could see I hit a nerve.

"Listen, kid," she barked, "everyone here is a professional and you're better off acting the same if you know what's good for you."

"I wasn't implying…" I stammered, taking a step back in anticipation of a possible blow. Before she could resume her tirade, Uncle Lou summoned her to the x-ray machine.

He had a sheepish grin on his face. "Assuming this is your bag, I'll let you explain to them what's in there."

The screen showed the outline of an elongated cylindrical object with batteries inside, like a flashlight but with a tapered end. I'd never actually seen a dildo. I had no idea it could be so large.

Muffled howls of laughter came from some of the team members. "Is that diesel powered?" someone asked from a safe distance. Darlene's face turned red and a seething sound emanated from her pursed lips.

The customs man motioned her to remove it from the bag for closer examination. Darlene contemplated resisting, but sensing surrender would provide a more rapid close to the incident, she opened the bag and handed the vibrator to him.

"What is it?" he asked via the Nerk translator.

"It's a personal relaxation device," she responded through gritted teeth.

"It's a Thunder Dong" said Lou, reading the label on the bottom.

More laughter from the other side of the room. But the customs man was genuinely perplexed. He understood it was a personal item, so no treaty violation was suspected. But it didn't fit into his understanding of human sexuality. Here was a group of nearly 30 men and just a few women. Why would there be any need for the women to find artificial satisfaction?

The Nerk translator tried to explain to the customs man. He translated the word "Thunder" literally — *grom*. Darlene squirmed.

"And 'dong'? What is 'dong'?" asked the translator.

"Uhm..." Lou thought for a moment. "...Well, it's kind of a slang for, uh... member," Lou answered, and pointed to his own crotch.

"Ah, *chlyen*," said the translator, turning to the customs man.

"Yes, *chlyen*," said Darlene, and snapped in Russian, "*mi konchili?*" Which is close to, "are we finished?" but actually means, "did we climax yet?"

"*Gromni chlyen*," said the translator to the customs man.

"*Ogromni gromni chlyen*," said the customs man, "*i mi zakonchili...*" as he gently placed Thunder Dong back in Darlene's bag.

"Huge thunderous member," said the translator to Seward, without a trace of emotion, "and we *are* finished."

A half hour later we boarded a chartered Aeroflot plane to Izhevsk. I sat down and got out the welcome pack. I scanned the cartoon-like map drawing made by the OSIA advance team. In some ways Votkinsk resembled the village I had grown up in. Although not quite a single-factory town due to its proximity to New York City, Hastings-on-Hudson's economic life had been dominated for nearly half a century by the Anaconda Wire & Cable Company. In Votkinsk, the factory was the town. It sat at the foot of the lake, while the streets wended their way up the hill, dotted with shops and apartment buildings. I imagined myself wandering around, mixing freely with the locals, using my Russian. After nearly six years of struggling with the language, I was finally beginning to make myself understood and to understand. I knew that this empowerment would be critical to my happiness.

Chapter Eight
Fish Doughnuts

The Izhevsk Airport was a sad little building. The absence of other aircraft and lack of activity on the tarmac reinforced the sense that we had reached the end of the line. Birds fluttered around inside the aluminum and brick structure. The outgoing inspection team met us in the second floor waiting room. Everyone shook hands. Seward introduced me and then went to huddle with his counterpart. A stocky older man with a white beard and a sack on his back approached me. He was clearly the guy who wore the Santa suit at the Christmas party. Even without the red outfit, the resemblance was striking.

"…And these are yours," Santa said, as if he was now including me in an ongoing conversation. He extended his free hand which held a small set of keys. "I lugged in your trunks two months ago. Hope you've got some whiskey in there."

"Well, if I do, I wouldn't admit it," I said.

"I'm Thom Moore," he said. "I'm a translator here."

I looked curiously at his sack.

"It's the outgoing mail," he explained. "I'm dropping it at the embassy on my way out. I've got a couple of gigs in Dublin next week. I'm sure looking forward to my rotation…"

"Gigs? What do you play?"

"The guitar," he said, clearly crestfallen that I didn't recognize him. "Ever heard of the group Midnight Well?" I shook my head. "What about Pumpkinhead?" I shook my head again.

"You're just too young, lad. Must've led a sheltered life. We'll fix that when I'm back. See you in three weeks!" He patted my back and headed off with his sack.

The Nerk men from Moscow said goodbye and we boarded a bus for Votkinsk. The police escort with its flashing blue light seemed extravagant, though I noticed we took a route via the outskirts of the city that prohibited a close look at any of Izhevsk's factories.

It was nightfall by the time we rolled down the hill into Votkinsk. We went through the center of town to the opposite side of the lake. The driver maneuvered among the homogeneous buildings via the poorly lit streets. I observed the dark scene through the bus window. A sense of ambivalence overwhelmed me. On the one hand I was pleased with myself that I had followed through and come this far. But at the same time I had an intense feeling of loneliness. I had come to the end of the earth to work as a janitor among strangers and enemies.

The "hotel" was a typical Soviet apartment building. A matronly woman with thick forearms and purple hair sat behind a desk too small to hide her bulk. On the desktop she had a clipboard, stack of papers, teapot and a house plant. Jake greeted her.

"Nelli Petrovna, *kak dela?*"

"Vsyo OK, Mister Taylor," she said with a broad gold-toothed smile, and gave him a thumbs up. She began to distribute room keys to the incoming inspectors.

"Velkom in Votkinsk, Meester Lifflyander," she said as she handed me a key.

The first room of my temporary quarters served as entryway and living area. For a space-starved Soviet family it would also be bedroom. Maybe 20 square meters total, it was called a *prokhodnaya*, meaning "pass through," since people living in the inner bedroom had to pass through to get to the rest of the apartment. The layout saved the state the expense of a few square meters of additional corridor construction.

My trunks were in the middle of the floor. The walls were papered in a floral print, though three of them had one kind of paper and the fourth another. The furnishings were an odd mixture of synthetic and natural materials. A polyester couch with wooden arm rests. The floor lamp had a glass dome and gold-plated plastic tendrils. If you filled the room with people it might take on a warm glow. Empty, it resembled a poorly crafted movie set ready to be dismantled.

The toilet bowl was in its own room the size of two telephone booths. The sink and bathtub were in an adjacent room about three times as large. Keeping the sanitary facilities separate maximized their accessibility.

The layout of the space seemed familiar. I realized the apartment was the same configuration and size as the home of my friend, Valery, and began to recall the good times I had spent there.

Valery lived with his wife, their twins and his mother-in-law. They were fortunate. His late father had reached the rank of colonel in the tank corps and received the apartment after only twelve years — faster than average wait. There was no private ownership of real estate, but it was their home. And anything was better than the dormitory they had lived in before.

Valery's twins and mother-in-law slept in the main room on a fold-out bed. The kitchen was the center of domestic life. I could remember getting haircuts from Valery's wife, Lena, while sitting on a stool in that kitchen. I'd stare at the Beatles calendar on the wall and occasionally steal a glance at her luscious smile as she'd rattle on. She was a great cook, too. While Valery and I distracted the kids in the main room, Lena and her mother would prepare dinner. Since the twins went to bed early, we'd eat in the kitchen. The tabletop would disappear under plates of sliced ham, salami, cheese, fresh brown and white bread, butter, smoked fish, a dish called *kholodets* (minced meat in gelatin) and sardines "in a fur coat"— buried in mayonnaise and sliced beets. Fluted glasses for mineral water and spirits alike, a soda can for an ashtray and aluminum cutlery rounded out the accouterments. On a good day, one bottle of Moskovskaya vodka and one Moldavian White Stork cognac would fill any remaining gaps between the plates. All this on a tabletop slightly larger than a Scrabble board.

We'd spend the evening eating and drinking. Neighbors would drop by unannounced, having let themselves in via the unlocked door. Lena would open the small *fortochka* window in the hope of dissipating the cigarette smoke. Valery would strum his guitar and try to teach me to sing along with his favorites: a group called Akvarium and a cult bard named Vladimir Vysotsky. I could hardly understand the meaning of the songs — the bitterness of the water from the faucet of a railway car; the man who thought he was a submarine and wanted to linger at the bottom of the sea — but the warmth of the people and the hospitality they showed me in that kitchen didn't require any translation. I could forget for a few moments that I was in a strange land. I was just another human, with no inhibitions but my limited language skills, which inevitably improved with each verse and each shot.

The memory of our camaraderie faded as I looked at the identical table in my kitchen in Votkinsk. Its top was as empty as the rest of the apartment. It would hardly be obscured by one bag of microwave popcorn and a Styrofoam bowl of instant soup. But this was my home for the next nine weeks, until I headed out on my first rotation.

Before my eyes could scan the walls for any indications of eavesdropping devices, the doorbell rang. A voice from the corridor asked in English, "Is anybody there?"

"I'm here," I answered, talking to myself as I went to turn the lock. On the other side of the door stood Uncle Lou.

The fact that he had let himself be renamed underscored his easy going nature. "Justin," he said, "you do realize it's Friday night."

I got excited. "Does that mean something special is going on?" I asked.

"No," said Lou, shaking his head. "Actually, every day is almost the same here. The routine hardly changes."

That's what I needed — a routine. I had the uneasy feeling one gets when one finds oneself in completely unfamiliar surroundings. Here everything and everyone was new and different: the coworkers, the town, the job.

"Actually, Fridays are when they hold the pea counting contest at the Kosmos Kafé…that's the local restaurant where we eat our meals now. We never see fresh vegetables but when we get canned peas we compete to see who has more on their plate. I heard Captain Knight won tonight, with 17. Lieutenant Colonel Blackstone came in second with 12."

At that moment a snowball bounced off my windowpane.

"Pretty much on time," Lou said, glancing at his watch. I looked out the window to see a gaggle of children below. They were staring expectantly in our direction from behind the low fence that surrounded our building. "This room was mine last rotation," Lou said. "Those are some of my friends. Let's go take a walk."

As we exited the driveway the kids rushed up, practicing their English greetings. They lived in a place closed to foreigners but still studied a foreign language. And now that effort was yielding a dividend. Lou's Russian was non-existent but the candy he doled out was plentiful, especially for those who said 'please' and 'thank you.' He was a one-man Berlin airlift. But it was personal for him. He addressed several children by name.

"I love the kids here," Lou said. "I love the women, too…Platonically, of course. I even like some of the men. I like all the people here."

We walked toward the lake. Up close, the town looked more real. But the contrasts were stark. There were Soviet apartment buildings constructed in the course of the last 30 years that looked like they might last a few more; there were also the quaint wooden houses built over the course of the last 200 years. They looked like they'd outlast all of us, despite the warped beams and sagging walls. The embankment was lined with solid looking four-story buildings that were neither Soviet nor ancient.

"They seem a bit substantial for pre-revolutionary construction," I said.

"Triple A told me they were built by German POWs right after the war. Their freedom was even more restricted than ours. At least we can walk around downtown in our zone. Triple A told me that 'zone' is also slang for 'prison' in Russian."

"Who is 'Triple A'?" I asked.

"He's one of the escorts. A young guy, but a real Party man. His name is Anatoly Alexeyevich Anisimov, but as far as we are concerned it stands for Anatoly the Amazing Asshole. He can be pretty difficult sometimes. But he means well, and is always happy to explain things…in a condescending way of course."

"I look forward to working with him."

"You won't have a choice," Lou said. "We'll probably move to the permanent housing out at the factory next month. Then you'll need Anatoly to get a haircut, buy bread, or just stroll by the lake. You'll need me too. But you're lucky: I like to go out and do things. Many of the inspectors don't.

"We're divided into two groups. The mercenaries are here for the money. They aren't particularly interested in what's going on. They spend their free time watching videos. They start counting down the days from the moment they rotate in.

Then there is another group, including our translators, a few of the military guys, the nurse — we're here for the adventure and to try to understand Russia better. Even if you don't know the language, you'd be surprised what you can figure out from context.

"Whoa!" Lou suddenly blurted out. "We stop here." We had walked the embankment towards the factory headquarters and were now facing the administration building and the main gate.

"The end of the zone," my guide explained. "Imagine there is an invisible line. It's a nice privilege and we don't want to lose it. I hear the Soviet inspectors in Utah don't have such rights. Let's turn left toward the center of town."

We crossed in front of the triumphant Lenin statue and headed up the main street.

'The bus is arrived,' Sofia scribbled on a piece of paper as she sat at the desk in the hotel lobby. She thought her spoken English had improved after a few months of working with the Americans, but there were still moments when she lacked confidence.

She muttered the phrase to herself to see how it sounded. No, that's not right. 'The bus had come.' No, also something missing. 'The bus is arriving.' No good. Not urgent enough. 'The bus wants to go.' Well, that does imply it's here, but it also implies the bus has a mind of its own. Frustrating. She could read Shakespeare and Vonnegut with complete comprehension, but to say one simple phrase without making an error...that was a challenge.

Nelli overheard her muttering, tapped her arm and stood up. "Don't worry. I'll show you how to do it." She went to the bottom of the steps, cupped her hands to her mouth and shouted at the top of her lungs, "BOOS IST HERE!" Nelli's generation had studied German in school.

The bellowing roused me from my slumber. I had overslept. The crappy feeling of waking up in an unfamiliar place was exacerbated by the embarrassment at being late for the first day of work. I dressed quickly and went down to the lobby. I missed the breakfast run to the Kosmos Kafé. I'd survive. The next van would go directly to the site. A young woman with brown hair was taking roll call, writing down the names of inspectors who were present.

"Sofia, don't forget the new one," Nelli barked.

The brunette came up to me. I recognized her as Sofia. Colonel had described all of the women at the site. He had neglected to mention her blue eyes.

"What is your name, please?" she asked. A slight accent made her English charming.

"Justin," I answered.

She knew everyone else's name but mine. Why did that bother me? I knew her name. It didn't seem fair. She handed the list to Nelli and we piled into the RAFik. It was the Soviet equivalent of a passenger van, named after the Riga Automobile Factory. The curtains on the windows were drawn closed. Was this to hide us from the locals, or the locals from us? I sat behind the driver, pulled aside the curtains, and took in the sights.

After passing through one of the three traffic lights in town we made it to the top of the hill and started down the eastern slope, toward the outskirts. We passed more wooden houses on the way. A pleasant smell of pine came from the lumber mill. It was quickly followed by the rancid odor of carrion from the meat processing plant. My nostrils flared. Sofia noticed my reaction.

"The inspectors call that the 'perfume factory'," she said.

The road headed east towards the Kama River across a broad plain, which was now lightly dusted with snow. We crossed a small bridge from which fishermen were casting their lines. A rusty road sign indicated we were passing through a settlement called Gavrilovka, which consisted of a dozen *izbas*. The paved road was briefly replaced by cobblestone before starting again.

A spy with knowledge of the Soviet defense industry would have noticed several clues to the presence of a hidden factory. Across the plain, high-voltage power lines stretched over metal towers and ran into the woods. Here and there along the road, small brightly-painted signs warned of buried gas pipes. If the spy were to sit on a bench in front of one of the log cabins of Gavrilovka he would note the heavy truck traffic, as well as the convoys of buses going to and from at regular intervals, indicating a shift change. The *lyudi* trucks, each carrying a dozen guard troops and one German shepherd must have a destination other than the riverfront settlement of Stepanovo, to which the road ostensibly led.

As the road reached the top of the hill and the woods began, a lone rail line emerged from between the birches and pines. Finally, the road divided. The right fork went towards the Kama River. At the left fork there should have been a sign saying "Secret Missile Factory" or "Welcome to the Home of Thirty American Spies." But there wasn't. The sign in the form of a simple white circle with the red rectangle inside was anticlimactic. It was called a "brick" in Russian, and it clearly communicated entry was forbidden.

I decided to strike up a conversation with the driver.

"Are you sure we are going in the right direction?" I said, motioning to the sign.

"That's what makes me sure," he said. "You speak Russian well."

"My name is Justin; originally from New York, but I've been living in Moscow for the past year and a half."

He extended his hand backwards and said, "I'm Valentin…always from Votkinsk. Never been to New York. A few times in Moscow. Is that where you learned Russian?"

"I didn't get to practice much there. I was a driver at our embassy. The only Russians I got to talk to were the traffic police. Fortunately, not too often."

"The traffic police here are as much of a problem as everywhere else in Russia," Valentin said confidently. "My father was in Utah once. He said he didn't see any GAI there."

I asked how his father happened to be in Utah.

"He was the general director of the factory," Valentin said. "He visited America at the start of the Treaty."

"What did your father think of Utah?" I asked.

Valentin's expression became serious. In a quiet voice he said, "He liked it very much. The people were kind and seemed to live well."

"Our traffic police are probably paid better," I said, "so that may be why they behave."

We drove the rest of the way in silence. The rail line went into a clearing where a small yard was located. It had a fence around it and a few guards. The tracks came out the other side of the yard and continued parallel to the road.

We rounded the final bend and stopped abruptly at a patch of asphalt next to a newly constructed two-story building. I had arrived at what the Americans called the Votkinsk Portal Monitoring Facility, or VPMF, also known as "the site."

On the left side of the road was an awning on top of a train siding where a railcar could be parked for detailed inspection. This is where the giant x-ray machine was being built to scan the car to be sure a banned smaller missile was not hidden inside a larger one. Next to this was a warehouse. The Americans referred to it by its Russian name, sklad. The inspectors got out of the van and several of them headed toward the building. It was made of the same gray-yellow brick as all the new structures at the site.

The road and rail line led to the factory's main gate. A train was parked on the tracks directly in front of it. To the right of the gate was an administration building with a small square in front. Buses disgorged workers who then entered a building that served as the main entrance to the factory complex.

On the right side of the factory entrance was a three-story building. Valentin said it was the headquarters of the Soviet inspection and technical escort department. Then came the American housing. Four two-story buildings in a row, with 10 apartments in each of the first three. OSIA named them Washington, Jefferson and Lincoln. The fourth building, where we had pulled up in the van, was farthest from the factory gate. It was called Roosevelt and functioned as the American administration and recreation building. Two smaller buildings were next to it, on the edge of the woods.

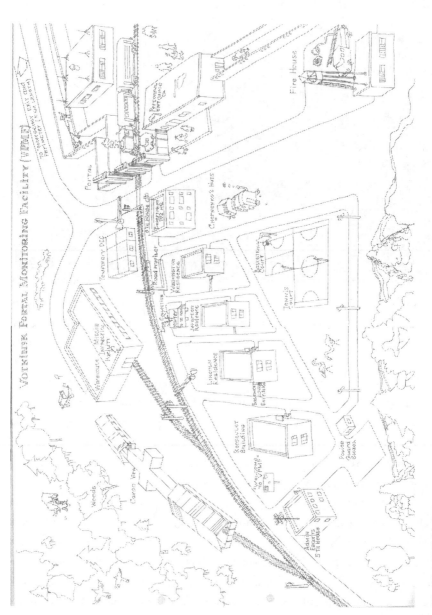

Map by Mikhail Kononov

The tiny one was the police guard shack. The first floor of the larger two-story square building, called "the fifth house" was the office of the administrative escorts who ran our social program. The purpose of the second floor was unknown.

I walked down the road towards the factory gate. Called the "portal" in treaty parlance, it consisted of two gray metal gates each about five meters high and three meters wide. The right gate served road traffic, mostly ZIL and GAZ trucks, which were not big enough to carry a missile. The train track led under the left gate. The tops of the factory buildings were visible beyond it. There were lightning rods every few meters along the roofs. They made the factory look like a castle battlement. Errant electrical charges are unwelcome at a solid rocket motor plant.

The missile factory's main gate.   Courtesy of the Votkinsk Machine Building Factory

The portal sat at a "T" intersection, with the turn to the left heading to the factory's emergency exit located about a kilometer down the road along the northern side of the perimeter. A turn to the right brought you past the bright yellow factory administration building to the end of the road, where the fire station was located.

The Americans had installed semaphore gates, called *shlagbaum* in Russian, in front of both of the factory vehicular exits. After the *shlagbaum* they had set up white metal beams on either side of the rail and road lines. They contained infrared sensors used to profile the size and shape of departing vehicles.

The train now standing outside the portal consisted of a diesel electric locomotive, a midsize buffer car, a long gray metal car and a rundown wooden caboose with a bench on its rear balcony. I saw two young soldiers with machine guns standing on either side of the long metal car. Captain Knight popped out from a small door on its end, followed by one American and two Sovs. The four of them were all wearing blue smocks and big white gloves. They looked like they had just come from Mickey Mouse's art class. As Knight stepped down from the car he made a note on his clipboard. The senior Soviet technical escort looked at him.

"OK, Mr. Knight?"

"Just one question," Knight asked. "This one isn't going to be aimed at Dallas, is it? I have relatives there."

One of the Soviets translated the inquiry to the other technical escort. He gave a stern glance and then cocked his head as if he was reading some invisible marking on the side of the rail car.

"No," the escort responded, "this one will be targeted at Washington." I stared intently at the rail car. All I could see was two terse sentences stenciled in black Cyrillic letters: "Don't bump the car; Don't let it roll down hill."

They all laughed. The soldiers hopped on the caboose and sat down on the rear bench. The traffic light turned green. The engine gave a toot and the train started down the tracks away from the factory.

"Some dark humor to get your morning off to a good start, captain?" I asked the Marine as he removed his gloves while the train disappeared around the bend.

"Well, it's Justin, the long lost inspector. You finally made it." Knight's tone was friendly. Clearly my mere presence at the site had moved me up a notch on his ladder, probably to somewhere just above flower-child.

"Captain, you just let an intercontinental ballistic missile that will be pointed at the United States get away. How did you suppress the urge to throw yourself on the tracks?"

"The treaty dictates all my actions. My emotions are another story," Knight said.

We made small talk for a few minutes in the cold. I had decided back in Washington that I didn't like him. But now I was pleased to see Knight. He represented purpose and security, and something familiar. 'They probably keep his interchangeable parts on a shelf in that warehouse,' I thought.

"Where can I get a cup of coffee here, captain?" I asked.

"Check the new DCC," he said, pointing at a glossy white trailer, situated between the road and the Jefferson building and decorated with Soviet and American flags. The acronym stood for Data Collection Center. It was the nerve center of U.S. treaty inspection activity. Its modern appearance was a bright contrast to the drab Soviet buildings. About 10 meters wide on each side, it sat on pylons, with aluminum stairs leading up on either side. It looked like something you'd live in on the moon.

I walked towards it and mounted the steps. At first I thought the vestibule resembled an airlock on a space ship. But cross country ski equipment was stacked in the corner. Snow shoes lay against the wall, giving the appearance of a sporting goods store. Macintoshes and waders hung on hooks — as if a bunch of New England lobster fishermen had dropped by. Next to this heavy duty footwear was a line of winter parkas with fur-trimmed hoods for some unseen Eskimos. No coffee machine was visible.

I entered the main room. It looked like a cross between the broadcast booth at a radio station and a satellite launch control center. All the cables from the monitoring equipment — cameras, infrared scanners, semaphore gates, traffic lights — culminated in a panel that ran the length of the window facing the road and portal. Uncle Lou was on duty, staring blankly out the window. Lieutenant Jake was at a desk behind Lou, gesticulating with a telephone receiver. Colonel Francell, who I had met at the embassy in Moscow, sat at another desk across the aisle.

"The Sovs did not give permission to fire up the x-ray machine," Jake shouted into the receiver. "What? The x-ray machine…ah…this sucks. What? No sir, I meant the line. The phone line. What?…We think we'll get a test car next week." He continued shouting. "Next week," he repeated slowly, as if non-native English speakers had taken over the OSIA operations room in Washington.

Francell scowled at him.

"We're hoping for the end of March," continued the lieutenant even louder. "March. Maaarch." He half sung and half screamed.

"Have you considered using the phone, lieutenant?" the colonel asked.

This "rank" thing was interesting. One guy could give another guy a hard time based on which small metal decorations he had on his shoulder. Although neither was in uniform they addressed each other as officers. There was no derision in the exchange, but the lieutenant's facial muscles clenched as he attempted to carry on the discussion with some semblance of demeanor, since there was also a colonel on the other end of the line getting the highlights of the weekly report shouted at him from the depths of the Russian hinterland.

Uncle Lou wasn't the least bit tense, even though he was responsible for the communications systems.

"It could be due to snow on the microwave dish," he postulated aloud.

Lou had installed earth stations in the Iranian desert and wired telecom switches in Thailand, but snow on a Russian antenna was not something he had any control over.

"Could also be the land line from Izhevsk to the embassy in Moscow," Lou continued, with an intonation of apathy that added to the officers' frustration.

"It could also be a moose humping the antenna tower, Seward, but that doesn't help us to improve the connection," the colonel snapped.

"Colonel, the antenna tower, along with every other part of the circuit between the DCC and the embassy switch board are completely under the Sov's control. The treaty stipulates that they must provide us with a connection back to our embassy but it doesn't mention anything about the quality of the line."

"Note the continuing line quality issue in the log, Seward," Francell said. "Lieutenant, put it in the daily report."

"Yes sir," Jake said as he hung up.

I sat next to Uncle Lou and he gave me a briefing on how the systems worked.

"It's pretty simple. A non-treaty-limited-item, or "TLI" as we call them, might be a train car or truck less than 14 meters in length. This is about the size of a decent mobile home. When one comes out of the portal it triggers the induction loop. We look at it, and if it's obviously undersized we confirm it's OK, open the *shlagbaum,* give a green light and note it in the log as "ATP" —Allowed to Pass. For anything larger, which would, in reality, only be a missile rail car — empty or full — the Sovs come over with a written declaration in advance."

He thought for a moment, and then continued. "This job used to be a lot more fun when we sat in the temporary DCC with the Sovs in the next room. We drank tea together on breaks and gave them advice on how to play our Monopoly game. They could never understand how a hotel could be more valuable than a private house."

"It sounds cozy," I said. "So when do you get to see them now?"

"They're over in their building and we are here. We only see them when they bring a notice of a TLI coming out. Then we inspect it together. Well, we do interact with them twice a day when we patrol the five-kilometer perimeter of the factory to make sure no one has made a hole in the fence and snuck a 60-ton missile out the back. It's good exercise and good social time too.

"Anyway, when a rail car big enough to carry a missile exits the portal, we meet the technical escorts outside, measure the car, and then they open the door so we can verify that the car is empty. When they announce it has a missile in it, we go inside and measure it, then send it on its way. We have a giant x-ray machine. Eventually we'll use it on any rail car with a missile, to verify they haven't hidden a smaller, banned missile inside a bigger one…but the diplomats are still negotiating the finer points of that procedure. As long as the weather is nice in Geneva, we probably won't be allowed to get that system up and running."

"Thanks for filling me in, Lou," I said. "Can you tell me where I can get a cup of coffee?"

Lou led me out the back door to direct me towards Roosevelt and the coffee machine. Behind the four American buildings was an oval yard surrounded by a fence on the far side. A half dozen surveillance cameras sat atop the fence posts. One more was mounted on the roof of the escort building.

"Are they really watching us all the time?" I asked, somewhat shocked at the idea of being constantly under observation.

Lou didn't answer, but smiled as we walked towards the yard. He stopped next to one of the three pink plastic flamingoes impaled in the ground.

"Observe," he said as he picked one up and walked about 10 meters along the path toward one of the other buildings. The camera on the post in the far corner rotated in our direction.

"Try to look serious," Lou said as he sized up the plot of land, carefully selected a new resting place for the bird and jammed it into the ground. Nodding to himself in approval, he returned to the path. "The colonel likes us to move them every few days. Keeps the Sovs on the upper floor guessing."

He motioned towards the second story of the social escorts' building. "It must be a pretty boring job sitting up there all day watching us move around."

Pointing to an asphalt rectangle inside the yard, Lou said, "That will be the tennis court... someday."

Two small wooden shacks sat outside the far end of the oval, close to the Soviet administration building. "What are those huts?" I asked.

"Ah," Uncle Lou replied with a grin, "That's Colonel Chernenko's office. He's the military construction chief who built the missile factory and our buildings here. We're working closely with him to finish the site. He's really decent. He'll invite you in for tea...or something stronger when no one's looking."

"But it would seem there is always someone looking," I said.

"He's a special case. I guess because he does such an important job, he gets the privilege of dealing with us when and how he pleases."

I entered the Roosevelt building. Other than the *sklad,* it was the only one of the Soviet-built American structures in use. A buzz of activity came from the kitchen and dining room off to the right. But I headed down the left corridor to where the offices of the OSIA site commander, the Hughes site manager and the nurse were located. From that direction I heard the familiar gurgle of a Mr. Coffee machine and promptly followed the sound.

To my delight, in addition to a fresh pot of coffee, there was a plate of jelly doughnuts on the desk. I was beginning to feel at home.

I put 15 kopecks in the empty cup on which "Donations for Doughnuts" was scrawled, and grabbed one. The powdered sugar melted on my fingertips as I put its round body into my mouth. But when my teeth met the upper and lower surfaces of the confectionery delight, my nose picked up a strange scent. It was neither jelly nor doughnut. The deceptive muffin split open along my bite line to reveal ground fish meat. The mixture of coffee, sugar, dough, and fish was enough to trigger my gag reflex. At that moment a woman in a white doctor's coat entered the room.

"Oh," she said with a giggle, "I see you've tried our doughnuts. Actually, they were meant for the officers and managers. Oh, well, there are still enough left for them. My name is Jane. I'm the nurse here." Her accent was Midwestern and her large hoop earrings gave her a funky 1970s look. Her manner had the reassuring warmth one expects from a nurse, and she was attractive. Her short curly blond hair helped her appear younger than her 40 years.

I spit the remains of the fish doughnut into the garbage can near the door and took back my 15 kopecks. "You're a nurse?" I asked. "I thought nurses were supposed to induce health in their patients, not vomiting!"

She laughed again, "Well, I was in town yesterday and found those and just couldn't resist. The powdered sugar was my addition."

Jane's job was to monitor the inspectors' health, distribute Aspirin and cold medicine in the winter and inoculate against encephalitis in the summer. But she clearly worked hard at her practical jokes too. I decided that her attitude was a sign of good mental health.

"Well, I'm glad my nose and teeth saved me…"

Suddenly, she got serious.

"Teeth. Yes. Very important," she said and stepped closer to me. She had pleasant perfume, or maybe it was her soap. She smelled like a young school teacher.

"Open your mouth wide," she said, and whipped out a tongue depressor. I assumed it was some sort of obligatory examination and didn't resist. She wielded the stick like a samurai, flapped my cheeks and lips back and forth for a few seconds and then smiled.

"You have beautiful teeth," she said. "I've already figured out how to make a fortune here. A toothpaste factory. Have you seen these people's teeth? Nothing but gold and rot."

Clearly she could think outside the box, and didn't take the environment too seriously. Her warmth and ingenuity were infectious. I realized that with people like her around I might enjoy myself in this strange place.

I went down the corridor back toward the kitchen and dining area. Outside the dining room, facing the bulletin board that hung on the wall, a man stood with his back to me. He was stocky, with red hair, a red complexion and no neck. He was posting a document, meticulously selecting push-pins from little corrals on the board. First he tried four white ones. Muttering to himself, he gently pulled them out — apparently not satisfied by the lack of contrast with the notice he was posting. He replaced them with blue ones and stepped back to view his work. Pleased by his effort, he patted the notice with his hand and turned around.

There was a feral glint behind his Jiminy Cricket glasses for a split second, as he realized he had been snuck up on. Then he smiled and extended a hand.

"Justin Lifflander, janitor," I said, as I extended mine.

"Lieutenant Colonel Ray Blackstone, deputy site commander. Welcome! I was just posting the notes from our weekly meeting with Department 162."

I remembered how Jake described Ray on the flight in. A deeply religious man, simmering below Ray's smile was a sincere hatred of communism. Jake said that Ray did a good job playing the bad cop in our local negotiations. Then Jake added a cryptic comment that he was glad Ray was on our side in Vietnam.

Now Ray stood before me, smiling. "Have a look," he said. "It's a good way to get acquainted with life at the site." He walked down the corridor toward his office as I began to read:

"Memorandum for the Record

1. On Tuesday, 3 March 1989 a meeting between the U.S. and Soviet side was held on the second floor of the Roosevelt building. The meeting began at 10:00. In attendance were Site Commander Colonel Francell, and Lieutenant Col. Blackstone from the U.S. side; Mr. Losev, and his interpreter, Sofia, from the Soviet side.

2. Lieutenant Colonel Blackstone opened the meeting by providing Mr. Losev with a status report of the leisure activities of the Soviet portal inspectors stationed in Magna Utah. Then Mr. Losev read the plan of approved social activities for the American inspectors in Votkinsk for the coming quarter. It includes:

--An accordion festival at the Votkinsk Palace of Culture

--Possible visit to Izhevsk for Swan Lake Ballet (to be confirmed)

--Visit to the Sharkan farm region

--Standard shopping excursions to locations within the approved zone of downtown Votkinsk

--Weekly skiing activity

--Weekly skating activity

--Sauna on demand

Colonel Francell then brought up current points of contention. The Soviet side had rejected a *zayavka* (written request) to go to midnight Easter service at the church in Votkinsk next month. The colonel pointed out that the inspectors had been allowed to go to the church for Orthodox Christmas; and that there was no midnight service scheduled during the daytime.

Mr. Losev responded that the issue had already been discussed with the local authorities, and that the main concern was about guaranteeing the safety of the inspectors. The police ended their shift at 24:00, with only a single duty officer on after that time, and the authorities had refused Department 162's request to allow the Americans out after midnight. Mr. Losev said he would ask again.

3. The colonel then brought up the issue of the party planned at the Kosmos Kafe this coming Saturday. The U.S. side had asked that it end at 02:00, but the Soviet side insisted it end at 24:00. It was pointed out that the Soviets in Magna have no such curfews. Mr. Losev suggested using the dacha, which is out in the woods, far from hooligans. He indicated it was only a matter of paying additional dollars for its rental. He also suggested the party start earlier.

4. The colonel then said he had two issues which should be escalated.

a) The U.S. side needs a test rail car to run through the x-ray machine. Mr. Losev said it would be provided soon, but could not name a specific date.

b) Control of the basements: The colonel reiterated the American position that the basements were part of the diplomatically inviolable buildings that according to the treaty protocol were to be provided to the Americans. Mr. Losev repeated the Soviet position that basements were considered common property throughout the country and should be left under Soviet control for reasons of technical service and safety. The colonel reconfirmed that the move to the site would not take place until the basement issue was resolved.

5. Lieutenant Colonel Blackstone then summarized the unresolved issues that would be put on the U.S. General's list:

--Control of basements

--The incomplete tennis court

--The poor condition of the factory perimeter

--Absence of places to jog

--Grounds maintenance, specifically snow removal and grass cutting

Mr. Losev said he was awaiting a report from construction manager Mr. Chernenko on the tennis court and work would be done following that. Regarding the perimeter, he said the Soviet side was still investigating the possibility of taking action. If the investigation proved successful, work on the perimeter will start soon thereafter. As far as jogging was concerned, Mr. Losev stated that he saw jogging in the downtown stadium as more advantageous, but would investigate the possibility of some route somewhere outside of town, perhaps in the woods. Regarding grounds maintenance, Mr. Losev said he was still waiting for guidance from Moscow.

The meeting closed at 11:00."

The memo sounded like a report from a retirement community that had been set up in a war zone. The treaty contained no specific references to rights and obligations about jogging, tennis or lawn mowers. But they seemed like reasonable issues to focus on if their resolution helped both sides feel comfortable while they built mutual trust and made the world a little less dangerous. The human interaction would be the most interesting part of implementation.

Chapter Nine

Churches, Hospitals and Hot Tubs
to Battle Boredom

After a few months, the nobility of the mission faded. A routine took shape. I found contentment fulfilling mindless tasks. As I approached the fax machine in the Data Collection Center, I realized it didn't take A3 paper. My tracing of the Czechoslovakian-made toilet seat barely fit on the large page. OSIA was still demanding the Sovs provide new toilet seat bolts to replace the original defective ones, but had also requested the tracing so that Hughes could try to source bolts in America. The urgency was triggered by a corpulent three-week mutant who, along with the free-floating seat, slid off and got wedged between the toilet and the wall in the Roosevelt first floor bathroom.

Three-week mutants were temporary inspectors that came to the site for short periods. They were not Hughes or regular OSIA staff. There was simply not enough language or military hardware experts on either side to fulfill the mission. It was prudent to take personnel from any government organization that could provide bodies. The mutant that got stuck must have made some negative comments in her trip report to whatever agency employed her. This reflected badly on OSIA's ability to properly maintain the site, which led headquarters to chew out the site commander, which in turn compelled him to hammer the Hughes site manager. He naturally turned to his janitor. So I took action. The work gave me a sense of purpose. Not quite as much as if I had snapped a useful forbidden photo, recruited an enemy agent or discovered a treaty violation — but ensuring the functionality of a crapper on the front line of détente was some kind of contribution.

Inspired by the importance of my mission, I finally figured out I could cut the page in two and fax it that way. It took five minutes for the image of the toilet seat to make it 8,000 kilometers to Washington. I'm sure the duplicate rolling off the fax machine at KGB headquarters on Lubyanka was causing some confusion.

There was enough mundane work to go around. Just about everyone was involved in finalizing the set-up of the facility and monitoring equipment — pulling cables through conduit, installing curtains, cleaning video camera lenses (ours), replacing a *shlagbaum* that had fallen victim to a truck driver's impatience. I had already done about a half-dozen inspection shifts. We'd sit in the DCC for 12 hours at a time hoping a missile would come out, logging vehicle license plates and rail car numbers of exiting traffic. Everyone sat shift except nurse Jane and Chuck Biasotti, the new chef. He arrived six weeks after me. For now he was working out the food import logistics, seeing what we could source locally besides bread, and advising on kitchen construction.

Chuck was ideal for the position, having spent many years as a tuna boat cook. He was content making institutional food 12 hours a day, watching video tapes the rest of the time. Even though we weren't ready to prepare food yet, he'd come to work in his whites, and move between the kitchen and the warehouse with a cigarette permanently dangling from his lip, which was topped by a small grey moustache. Chuck was easy to get along with and had a positive attitude, so we hit it off.

I was working on the kitchen wiring, which was more satisfying that fixing leaky toilets and squeaky doors.

"Have you heard if they found a second chef yet?" he asked.

He was very concerned about this, as he would have to rely on this person to help him feed 30 inspectors three times a day.

"Nope. Maybe Uncle Lou knows."

"Why don't you be my deputy?" Chuck said. "Women love men who cook. Later on you can get a job anywhere in the world. You'll never go hungry!" His dangling cigarette jiggled as he spoke.

"Don't you think the inspectors will eventually tire of getting nothing but scrambled eggs and chocolate chip cookies from me?"

"I'll teach you everything I know. All my best recipes." He said this with a sincere belief in their inherent value. "Give it some thought," Chuck added, and went down the hall.

I thought about it as I sat on the tile floor connecting the wiring of the giant oven. Being a trained chef could be a good cover for an intelligence officer. And it would make it easier to poison enemies.

"Here three electric phase, yes?" said a voice in broken English. I looked up and saw a round-faced middle aged balding man with a healthy tan looking down at me.

I answered in equally broken Russian, since my construction lexicon was still poor. "Yes, this machine needs three phases."

"I am Chernenko, Anatoly Vasilievich." I realized I was talking to the Soviet colonel in charge of construction that Uncle Lou had told me about.

"I'm Justin," I responded as we shook hands.

The hand shaking ritual is very important in Russia. I first noticed this while observing the embassy milimen. When they'd do their shift change at the little rubber shack every morning, every one of the 20 or so guards would shake hands with the others. This took time. But under communism there is a lot of free time. It was an endearing moment of asexual intimacy. The factory escorts did the same thing when they changed shifts, and when we met them. You could always tell who was getting along with whom by the manner and amount of time spent on the handshake.

Chernenko had a firm grip and a warm smile. "Please call me Vasilich," he said, relieved that we had switched to Russian. "I thought the oven connection would two phases. So now I will need to find a bigger *avtomat*."

We worked together the rest of the afternoon, pulling the extra wire from the panel to the oven and testing the connection. He patiently explained how it should be done and I learned several new terms. He was just as patient with the two young soldiers from his construction battalion under his command, when he was instructing them to move materials or dig a trench.

Uncle Lou came into the kitchen to check my work before we turned on the oven. Vasilich suddenly became quiet. He looked around with suspicion, then put his arms at his sides and waved his right hand from his hip. Lou responded from across the room with the same subtle gesture.

"In the context of something as serious as the treaty to eliminate intermediate range missiles," Vasilich said, "we are not allowed to admit we are friends. So formally we are only acquainted. Do you understand?" I put my hand next to my hip and practiced the secret wave to show my comprehension.

The pilot light came on and the oven began to whir.

"Mr. Biasotti says he will use this to make me pizza with his mother's recipe," Chernenko said. The thought of pizza excited us all. It was certainly more appetizing than fish doughnuts.

Lou turned to Chernenko. "Vasilich, I think Justin deserves a cup of your grandmother's tea, while you look in your storage room for a new *avtomat* to replace the one that burned out when we flipped the switch. What do you think?"

Chernenko warily looked left and right. Lou continued, "It's OK, we can trust him. Justin, grab your tool bag and that roll of wire and sling them over your shoulder."

The three of us traipsed out of Roosevelt towards the huts at the end of the compound, close to the factory. The cameras followed us as we walked around the back of Chernenko's hut and entered. Vasilich drew the curtains on the window. "So the blackies cannot see us," he explained. "Blackies" were bad guys who drove black cars and wore black trench coats. Russians are color confused. They call swarthy people from the Caucasus mountain area — Georgians and Armenians — "*black,*" though the white race is formally "*Caucasian.*" Yet, being "*white*" after the revolution was not a good thing, since the whites were the ones who supported the Tsar.

Lou and I sat down at a table, across from Vasilich. The shack looked like a construction foreman's office. Blueprints, tools, papers.

"How is it you don't get in trouble for this?" I asked. "I mean your side also has a rule against being alone with Americans. You don't seem at all concerned."

"It's their rule," he said, motioning over his shoulder to the headquarters of Department 162, which was in the Sixth House. "I have my own rules. I built this factory, your buildings, and lot of other buildings around here — including several generals' dachas. They can't punish me for drinking tea. What are they going to do, send me to Siberia?"

He got a nondescript bottle of red fluid from the cabinet and poured a shot for each of us. "My grandmother's tea. She's 83. Lives alone in a wooden house in the next town. Picks the cranberries herself. Keeps me supplied and sells the rest. She's a war veteran, but now she can't survive only on her pension." He put some dry crackers and a few chocolates on a plate. "Let's drink to making new friends today and eating pizza tomorrow!"

Vasilich fingered the defective circuit breaker. "Do you see this?" he said, pointing to a symbol imprinted on the charred *avtomat*. It was a circle with the letters CCCP above a sideways "K" that looked like a star.

"It's the mark of quality of Soviet manufacturing...Reminds me of a joke... Justin, please translate for Mr. Seward."

"A meeting of the United Nations Security Council had just ended. The British, French and Soviet delegates are walking down the corridor, when they come across a huge pile of freshly laid crap right in the middle of their path..." Chernenko made the shape of a mound with his hands. His eyes bulged in feigned amazement. "'Who could have done such a thing?' they ask each other. The Englishman takes his umbrella and pokes the pile a bit, then says with dignified certainty, 'It's definitely not British.'

"The others ask, 'How do you know?' He responds, 'It just doesn't *feel* British.' Then the Frenchman dips his finger into the pile, brings it to his nose and inhales deeply. He says, 'It is not French. It doesn't *smell* French'...The Soviet diplomat bends over, looks closely at the pile, rights himself and firmly says to his colleagues, 'It is not Soviet.'

"'And how do you know?' ask the other diplomats. 'Well,' answers the Soviet, 'all our crap has the mark of quality on it!' "

Our social life was controlled by the administrative escorts. They organized regular activities as well as special events and handled specific requests from the American side. This allowed for extensive interaction between us. There was nothing intimate about it, since according to the treaty the host country could and always did have an escort accompany an inspector during any off-site or inspection-related activity. The OSIA rules stated that an inspector could never be alone with a Soviet counterpart; the Russian rules were the same. Hence, in order to get a haircut, the minimum delegation consisted of five people: two American inspectors, two Soviet escorts, and a driver.

The administration escorts were mostly young ladies. They were managed by Nikolai Sapozhnikov, a non-descript middle-aged man who spoke no English. He had a hackneyed phrase that became his trademark.

"Nikolai, could we stop by the bread store on the way back to the site?" an inspector might ask.

"It doesn't seem to be on the *zayavka*," Nikolai would answer, having checked his list of approved stops, "so I'm afraid it's impossible."

"But it's on the way, and we go there all the time. Couldn't you just make a minor exception?"

"I am sorry, but that decision is not my pay level," he'd reply, with a shrug of feigned helplessness.

The escorts carried a radio when we went away from the site. It allowed them to consult with their management back at Sixth House, the headquarters of Department 162, in case of emergency. Maybe they were afraid that an inspector, having gone insane from bread deficiency, might run amok and try to scale the downtown factory wall. But Nikolai wouldn't consider the suggestion that he use the semi-functional device to ask permission to stop by the bread store. Nikolai's deputy was a retired naval officer we called the Frog, since he resembled a cartoon amphibian.

The rest of Nikloai's team spoke English. Five out of seven of them were young women.

Lyuba was a tall girl from Izhevsk with long blond hair and an earthy demeanor. When she wore her floral print dress she looked like she had just arrived on a bus from Woodstock. Larisa was another local girl. She had recently joined the Communist Party. Her impertinence bordered on obnoxiousness. Lena was a timid local with thick glasses.

The girls from out-of-town were different. They didn't take the mission as seriously as the locals. Several of them were from the same institute in Moscow. They had traveled abroad on student exchanges, and were more worldly wise.

Sarah was a Jew from Moscow with short dark hair. She had Muscovite sarcasm and always knew the latest jokes. Maria had also studied in Moscow, but was originally from Abkhazia, a province of Georgia on the Black Sea. Her demure disposition disguised a sharp wit. The diminutive form of her name was Masha. For her birthday I presented her with a package of dried mashed potatoes from the emergency supply we kept in the warehouse. She returned the gesture, presenting me with a huge brassiere, the Russian word for which loosely sounded like my last name.

Then there was Sofia, the young woman who couldn't remember my name that first day. No one was quite sure where she was from. I asked Lyuba if she knew anything about her. She giggled and replied, "She's from the underground."

Anatoly, aka Triple A, was one of only two young men on the team. He enjoyed photography and was a staunch believer in the infallibility of Lenin. "Lenin never lied," he would answer when asked why he was such a fan.

Over time, he realized the Americans didn't have tails and horns. He began to loosen up. In the beginning, though, I think he was overwhelmed — not only by the Americans and the responsibility he had been given for managing them, but also by the ladies in his group, who tended to treat him as a mascot.

Alexander was the other male escort. He graduated from Votkinsk High School with good grades in English. We called him Young Sasha.

"My birthday is in June, too," he said to me, the first time he introduced himself. I realized I had been studied. I looked askance.

"It is in your file," he continued. "You and I are both the youngest people working on the treaty." He wanted to know all about me. His curiosity seemed genuine. He liked to ask a lot of questions. I could relate to that.

Americans are not good with foreign names. To simplify things, the inspectors developed their own set of nicknames for the Russians we worked with. If a Sov had a last name of an animal or plant or object, as was frequently the case, then that person was so nicknamed — in private, of course. Mr. Losev was Mr. Moose; Mr. Lopatin and Mr. Zhukov, the two Department No. 1 representatives who worked with us on setting up the x-ray machine, became Mr. Shovel and Mr. Beetle, respectively and respectfully. Those who bore a resemblance to any celebrity were also renamed.

The Russians at least tried to address us properly, but they were sometimes doomed by the phonetics of their native tongue. The absence of the 'th' sound and the tendency to read a short 'i' as a long 'e' left us with inspector Teeador Smeets. A 'g' at the end of any word is always pronounced as a 'k,' so the famous musician could only be Stink.

The predominance of attractive young women in the escort group convinced OSIA counter-intelligence that the girls were "swallows"— female KGB agents specially selected to seduce and compromise the inspectors. In reality, the Soviets were as unprepared for on-site inspection as the Americans, and had similar problems in finding enough qualified specialists. OSIA put out a contract which Hughes won. The Ministry of Defense Industry ordered the leading foreign language institutes in the country to supply cadres. The average graduate with sufficient English skills and the flexibility to move to a small town happened to be an attractive young woman. The Soviets, in turn, believed that all American missile inspectors were trained intelligence officers.

KGB chief Shuvalov's weekly briefings began as an effort to imbue the escorts with basic counter-intelligence skills. He also wanted to probe them for their own strengths and weakness, to see how they could be useful to the Committee for State Security. Regardless of the conflict with Department No.1, the KGB was able to influence the salaries and positions of its agents, including the employees of Department 162. But Shuvalov's efforts to turn machine tool operators and college girls into spies had limited success. After a while the group meetings ceased and he began to meet with escorts individually. He tried to convince each one that he or she was his exclusive contact and that he was relying on them alone to help him in his mission. He tasked them to find out more about the interests and motivations of the inspectors.

"Ask one of them to bring you a present from his next rotation," he would say, "a winter coat, or something significant."

But he gave the same suggestion to all of his supposedly exclusive agents. When Lyuba asked Thom to bring her a winter coat from his next trip to Moscow, it became clear to the other escorts who overheard the request that their interaction with Shuvalov was not unique.

The escorts got caught-up in the power struggle between the two organizations. Shuvalov told the young ladies to stop writing *spravki* for Department No.1. The escorts stopped writing them for a while. In turn, Department No. 1 put pressure on Nikolai, the senior social escort. They told him it was his responsibility to get them to write the reports. Nikolai told the girls that if they didn't start producing *spravki* they would lose their monthly bonuses. In the end, the escorts outsmarted everyone by producing 15 to 20 *spravki* after every shift, all of which closed with the phrase, "nothing suspicious was noticed." Garbage in, garbage out.

A spy organization can't function without paperwork. The participants, who are also victims, create their own dossiers. This was the concept that Peter, the CIA officer whom I met at the FBI, had described to me. The goal is to have the victim participate voluntarily — either because they think it provides them with an exit by fulfilling the requirement of the task master, or because it massages the ego sufficiently for the participant to take pride in his role. My friend in Moscow, Valery, had told me that because the beloved bard Vladimir Vysotsky was wise enough to understand this mechanism and courageous enough to resist playing ball with the KGB, he was able to avoid being controlled by them. Others were not so fortunate.

Nikolai took his counter-intelligence role more seriously than anyone. He tried to be a "humint" mentor to others.

"My name is Jim. I am a new inspector," he said in a mock exchange with one of the escorts. "What's your name?"

An answer.

"Where were you born?"

Another answer.

"What did you do before you came here?"

Another answer.

A clever smile came across Nikolai's face. "Don't you see what mistakes you made? You answered all the questions. You should have asked me some before you gave out information. It will be the same with the Americans. They are all spies and will try to get information about the factory through you. You must be very vigilant."

We lived in this atmosphere of mutual suspicion. But we chiseled away at it through our daily interaction — building the site, inspecting missiles and participating in social events.

The spring trip to Izhevsk had been approved. We boarded the Hungarian-made Icarus bus to take us to the Orthodox cathedral and then visit the cardiology center.

The Icarus was the long bus. More important than its relative modernity was the fact that it could reach speeds of 80 kilometers per hour even when fully loaded. We would be in Izhevsk in a little over an hour. They could have given us the PAZ. That was the short bus, made in Pskov. As a PAZ passenger you were left with an inferiority complex because even the most decrepit trucks easily passed you. The PAZ couldn't do more than 40 kilometers per hour going uphill. I don't know why people from Pskov made such slow buses. Maybe it was because they had to pronounce three consonants in a row. We got the PAZ more often when the two sides weren't getting along well.

I headed down the aisle of the bus and took an empty seat. It was next to Sofia. I hadn't spent much time with her. As Mr. Moose's assistant, she didn't work the social events as often as the other escorts.

"How are you settling in, Justin?" she asked.

"Ah, you can remember my name now?" I don't know why I felt like provoking her. I guess my pride was hurt.

"I'm sorry. I'm not good with names."

"It's OK. I'm getting used to the routine, as alien as it may be."

"The saying goes, 'A forced routine replaces happiness...'"

"Who said that?"

"Pushkin. He was referring to his heroine in Onegin, who married a man she didn't love, but got used to him."

"I'm not looking to replace happiness. That sounds depressing."

"Pushkin is not depressing. Dostoyevsky can be. Why do you read him in English?" she asked, as if we had already discussed this.

"How do you know I'm reading Dostoyevsky?" Again, the creepy feeling of being under a microscope. Even what I read was on file somewhere.

"Well, we were expecting you for some time. I was escorting the rotation when your trunks came in. I did not mean to be disrespectful. Your Russian seems good enough to understand Dostoyevsky in his native tongue."

The compliment and her smile put me at ease. "Thanks," I said. "I appreciate the faith. I'll put in a *zayavka* to go to the library and get one of his books."

We pulled up to the main church in Izhevsk.

"Wow, it's an entire herd of *babushkas*," I exclaimed.

It was Orthodox Easter, one of the most sacred holidays for those citizens who were believers or those who marked the event merely out of historical inertia. A crowd of mostly older people, who had nothing to lose by publicly demonstrating their faith, was trying to get in.

Colonel Francell was sitting in front of us. Looking out the window he also cooed with admiration at the determination of the elderly women who were struggling to get past two milimen managing access at the gate of the fence that surrounded the cathedral.

As we exited the bus, we could see the stucco was falling off the walls and the gold had long since faded from the cupola. But the fence was intact. The parameters of the policemen's face control became clear. If you had a young face, you were not let in, but if you had wrinkles or an American inspector's face, they let you through. We entered the massive doors, into a sea of *babushkas*.

Their eyes were clear — blue, gray and amber, preserved like opals lying just underneath the surface in a pool of water.

Inside the church was dark and sooty, and the clothing of the old women was equally as colorless — overcoats of dark blue, flat green or gray wool, with simulated fur collars and heads covered by a shawls of drab floral print or soft wool, knitted during the countless lonely hours.

But their faces glared white and pink like whitecaps on sea, though their texture was the same as the shriveled apple of a Quaker doll, wrinkles etched by years of hardship.

"The church in my hometown was turned into a gym," Sofia said, admiring the still intact icons on the walls. "Others were turned into warehouses and museums of atheism. Many had their cupolas cut off. But Gorbachev seems to be more tolerant. A few are opening again."

Even God had difficulty finding enough living space, but at least he'd been rehabilitated.

It was wall-to-wall *babushka*, gently jostling to get closer to the front where the iconostasis was. This was a partition wall from floor to ceiling made up of panels depicting the life of the Savior, which divided the nave from the sanctuary behind it.

We floated with the current and were drawn inwards, first passing the stall on the left near the entrance, where candles were sold. Thin and yellow, they ranged in price from 20 to 50 kopecks— in general not expensive, but a sacrifice if you were living on a pension.

I produced a lighter and my candle was joined by a dozen unlit ones, clenched by wrinkled but delicate fists. The burgeoning flames began to flicker, reflected in gold-toothed smiles. The warmth in the midst of this human mass was almost suffocating. Immolation seemed imminent, as everyone bumped up against each another, candle flames held in close proximity to fuzzy woolen caps and collars. The scent of singed hair could be discerned through the sweet smell of frankincense.

Nuns dressed in black and shaped like the *babushki* acted as sergeants-at-arms. They watched for wayward candles and errant worshipers and made sure all the rules were observed: hands out of pockets; women's heads covered; no loud talking; no holding hands.

The undertow dragged us inward toward the altar. Russian Orthodoxy is busy. Every inch of wall and ceiling, every corner, was occupied by icons, paintings, gilt moldings, candle stands and brass ornamentation. On either side of the iconostasis were more icons, some in frames on the wall, others freestanding. They portrayed different saints who respond to prayers for specific needs.

"That icon is Mary the Quick Listener," Sofia said. "Place a candle on the stand in front of her in case you need something done in a hurry."

Offerings of food and other necessities, including soap, were left at the foot of another icon, to be distributed to the poor. Sofia looked apprehensively around the corner as we came closer to the front. "Candle stands in the left transept are intended

114

for prayers to the living; those on the right are for the dead," she said. "Be careful —
you might come across a corpse in an open coffin awaiting its last rites."

Standing on a raised platform before the iconostasis, the senior priest was blessing baskets of bread, eggs and other foodstuffs brought by a succession of worship-
pers. They had fasted all day and would now stand for the entire service, interrupted
only at midnight by a procession thrice around the outside of the church. At the end
of the event the blessed food would be taken home and eaten as part of the holiday
feast. There was no sermon. The Easter service traditionally consists of a liturgy, often
followed by a holiday message from the Metropolitan, head of the Russian Orthodox
church. Most of the time, the priest had his back to the worshipers. He made frequent trips through a door in the iconostasis to the apse beyond, where religious
books and accessories were kept.

Through the doorway he could be seen praying, along with his assistants. His vest-
ments of gold, silk and brightly colored velvet made the Catholic Pope's clothes seem
like casual wear. A choir, unseen on a balcony above the entry, chanted in harmony,
"*Christos Voskres! Slava Christos!*" (Christ has risen! Glory to Christ). The *babushki enthusiastically* responded, "*Voistine Voskres!*" (Truly, He has risen). Benjamin, my Mormon
bus driving coach, would have enjoyed such a lively ceremony.

The side door opened and a cloud of steamy winter mist rushed in before dissipating. The aesthetic appeal of the service was fulfilling in itself. Faith seemed secondary.

The senior priest took a break and came outside to bid us farewell. Lou asked
him a question, as Sofia translated.

"Why do you need the police to control access to the church?" Lou asked.

The clergyman thought for a moment and then said, "Not everyone has the spark
of faith in their hearts. We use them to help determine who the serious believers are."

Having a cardiology hospital as a cultural destination on the social schedule seemed
odd at first, but when I learned the history of the relationship I understood. The
doctors had cared for an inspector from Sandia National Labs who came with one of
the first groups and had a heart attack while working on site. He was treated by the
Izhevsk cardiology center, recovered and went home.

Doctors occupied a peculiar niche in Soviet society. They were paid no more than school teachers. But since they held the power of life and death in their hands, the aging, smoking, wheezing, boozing overweight Party leaders depended on them. They had great influence and respect.

For the visit to Izhevsk, Colonel Francell had brought a large coffee-table version of Gray's Illustrated Anatomy to present to Doctor Yevgeny Odiyankov, head of the center. He and his younger brother, Yury, had assembled a warm and intelligent group of medical specialists. When the surgeons weren't cutting and stitching, they were exercising other dexterous talents: writing operas and playing music; inventing apparatuses for cleaning blood; and brewing excellent moonshine. Their English was passable, and they knew a smattering of German and Latin.

"Yevgeny Germanovich," the colonel said, as we stood in Odiyankov's wood paneled office, "on behalf of the On Site Inspection Agency, allow me to present you this album of the human body. We have learned firsthand that you know how to make it work, so perhaps this will only serve as a reference for how to refer to its parts in our language. May you only have to use it sparingly and for enhancing theoretical knowledge of how to cure Americans; and may the people of Udmurtia be as thankful as we are that you are close by and ready to fulfill the Hippocratic Oath at a moment's notice."

Francell had learned how to make a quality toast during his time in the Soviet Union. This was important because both he and Yevgeny Germanovich knew that inspectors were only allowed to drink at official functions, and only when offered by the host in honor of the American guests — in order not to offend.

"Dearest colonel," responded Yevgeny, whose assistant was now passing around shot glasses filled with the hospital's own brew of cranberry vodka, "we are pleased that we have had a chance to touch the lives of the honorable American inspectors and also hope that our continued meetings will be based on choice and not need; so we can pay homage to the spirit of health and not have to spend time in battle against the angel of death."

We felt very honorable as we clinked glasses. Yury began to strum a Beatles song on his guitar.

Saturated with honor, we arrived back from Izhevsk in time to have dinner and still make the start of the night shift. No missile ever came out during the night shift. Nothing interesting ever happened on night shift. The biggest accomplishment would be publishing the next daily bulletin, to include the quote of the day and an unauthorized Farside reprint. That was as exciting as it got.

In the early days when the Americans and Soviets shared quarters in the temporary Data Collection Center at least one could wander across the hall to chat, sip tea, and share the boredom. Now, beyond the obligatory perimeter check, the night shift at best facilitated reading and talking amongst ourselves. Poker had been an option until the internal camera came on line. Now it wasn't worth the risk of a breach of discipline winding up on the ops room screen at headquarters.

The DCC reminded me of WOWO. That's not a train noise, but the call letters of the radio station in Indiana where I spent a summer during college. WOWO was a Fort Wayne, Indiana broadcasting institution whose powerful 100-kilowatt AM waves carried its message to the universe. Many people in the north half of the state regarded the station and its personalities as members of their family. When the atmospheric bounce was just right, farmers in Sweden got their grain prices courtesy of WOWO. The DCC was also loaded with buttons, dials, and panels. The polyester carpeting and double-paned glass added to the feeling of being in a radio sound booth.

There was something about America's impact on a society whose information flow was completely retarded. For several decades, under a bilateral agreement between Moscow and Washington, each government allowed the other to distribute on its territory 30,000 copies of a monthly color magazine about life back home. Amerika, with its stories of hi-tech achievements and freedom loving citizens, was popular in the U.S.S.R. Soviet Life, with its tales of achievements by ethnic minority groups and the wonders of socialist health care was not as big a hit with American readers. Still, the information flow in both directions was hardly more than a trickle.

The American portal monitoring outpost deep in the woods had a similar effect. It was like a radio antenna broadcasting to the outside world. The cultural waves radiated into the wilderness. A small island of Yankee existence beaming to the eardrum of Russia's heartland. Sometimes the signal reflected back and Russia responded.

There was an incident at the site that brought the point home. One day a Lada pulled up next to the DCC. A woman from the neighboring Bashkiria region got out. Fortunately

Jane and Darlene had been walking from the *sklad* at that moment. The woman started speaking quickly. Darlene translated for Jane. The woman said she had read in the local newspaper that there was an American doctor here and her daughter urgently needed treatment. Jane walked with the mother and daughter into the medical office in Roosevelt and started to examine the girl. I was cleaning the first floor toilet at the time.

Nikolai, accompanied by a miliman, came to the front door and demanded to see the colonel. I called the DCC and Francell came over, accompanied by Bellman, the Hughes site manager. Nikolai explained that visitors were illegal intruders and had to be removed. The colonel reminded them that the mother and daughter were now on American diplomatic territory, but said he would investigate and let them know the outcome. While Nikolai fumed on the portico, the colonel and Bellman went to Jane's office.

"From what I can tell, colonel, the girl has a damaged heart valve," Jane said.

Colonel Francell shook his head.

"We have to hand them over, Jane," Bellman said.

"Not until I've finished my examination and given the mother something to calm her down," Jane said.

It was clear from her tone that regardless of the opinion of Hughes, OSIA, the Kremlin or the White House, Jane was going to help her patients. The incident ended peacefully, and the Soviets promised to do what they could for the girl, though we knew they didn't have the technology to do a heart valve replacement. I was as touched by the Bashkirian mother's courage as I was by Jane's compassion. After Votkinsk she joined the Peace Corps, where she took care of volunteers in a number of depressed provincial Russian cities. She later moved to China to treat earthquake victims.

That night after the Izhevsk trip, Will Knight, stood in the middle of the floor with his slick dark hair and thick glasses, looking like a DJ from the 1950's. All he had to do was to turn on the microphone.

"Good evening, Votkinsk. Welcome to WVOT! The only radio station in town that brings you live, from the secret factory, the evening zoo team...Tonight we've got a great program. In addition to our usual features — news, weather, three-week mutant of the month and the trivia question — Inspector Jim Haley plans a live report from the emergency exit, where he'll be counting the bricks to make sure they are all there. Plus we'll make a surprise visit to our Sov counterparts and find out what really is in their teapot. That's right folks, the four most charming American

118

inspectors are in with ya till 8 a.m., playing all your favorites, along with a few new hits, so stay tuned…Let's start with news and weather, from Inspector Justin."

"Thank you, Will. Right now it's 8:15 p.m., -28 degrees Celsius, and dark outside. This, in English, we call 'friggin cold.' You could also say 'really friggin cold,' depending on how emphatic you want to be. Now for the news. There have been some changes to the social schedule made by the Soviets…every inspector departing the site for a visit downtown will be required to take one of the flamingoes with him. Ice fishing has been canceled since it's not possible to drill at current temperatures. Finally, the big news of the day: the Soviet side has officially decided to hand over the basements. We begin our final move in tomorrow…Over to you, Jim."

"Thanks, Justin. Now it's time for our usual call-in segment, where some of the lovely and probably just as bored young ladies of Votkinsk School Number 35 will be sharing their thoughts with us. Here's one now…" Haley pressed a button on the panel, and the speakerphone came on.

"Hello, sweetie, what's your name?"

"Lena," said the voice on the speakerphone.

"And how old are you Lena?"

"I am 17."

"And Lena, let me just ask you for the record, where did you happen to get our phone number?"

"It's not important," Lena answered coyly.

"Come on Lena, we know what's going on here. It must be Uncle Lou again handing out our calling card." (Giggles from Lena, and a few other female voices in the background.)

"OK, dear, what's your question for the inspectors tonight?"

"We are wanting to know how say in English, 'ya tebya lyublu'."

Jim smiled and said, "Translator Thom, I'll let you handle that one for us…"

Thom batted his eyes at the loudspeaker and replied, "Why sweetie, it's 'I love you,' and we sure do."

Thom was back at the microphone: "Thanks so much for calling Lena, but after all, you know the rules! Love is FOR-BID-DEN for your WVOT zoo team! But don't take it personally. We'll get back to you when we solve that one. Have a good night now!"

"We're back with Inspector Haley," Will announced, "for this week's shlagbaum destroyer award. Mr. Haley, how many shlagbaums did we lose this week?"

"Well, Will, it was a pretty tame week here at the portal. There were only two *shlagbaums* destroyed, which is two *shlagbaums* below average. And since one was destroyed by last week's winner, this week the award goes by default to a new driver, Mr. Ivan Ivanov. Ivan is 24-years-old and hails from the Bereyozovka settlement. He's been driving his truck for only eight months and says he plans to use the remains of the shattered *shlagbaum* to shore up his sagging dacha!" (canned applause).

"Thanks so much for that update, Jim. Before we move onto our next segment, let's pause for this musical selection. Tonight, we feature, once again, the latest from Guns N' Roses!"

Knight leaped on top of his small desk and played an air guitar to the blaring music coming from Mr. Haley's boombox. The desk top somehow supported his 250 pounds. The music ended, none of the windows having been shattered. Will returned to his seat…and turned to the deputy duty officer on his right.

"Right now we are talking to our three-week mutant of the month…what was your name again, Mr. Earl Smith? That's a good one, Earl. I only hope your real name is sufficiently weirder."

"Don't worry, Mr. Knight, it is," said the mutant, somewhat perturbed at the invasion of his cover.

"Now Earl, I know you are not allowed to tell us what government agency you really work for but is it true that when you join the National Security Agency you have to change your name and forget any friends, relatives, or acquaintances you've ever known who weren't born on American soil?"

"I'm sorry Mr. Knight, but I can neither confirm nor deny that."

"All right Earl, no sweat. Tell me, do you have any idea why you were selected as our three-week mutant of the month?"

"No, I can't say that I do," replied Earl, his glasses sliding down his nose towards his pocket protector.

"Well, Earl, I'd like you to take a look at the printout of you walking through the road profiler." Will passed Earl a computer printout from the infrared road profiler, showing a clear image of stickman Earl with a bulge near his waist.

"No, Mr. Knight, it's still not clear to me."

"Come on Earl, you must be joking. The only thing I can ask is, 'Is that a briefcase you were carrying, or are you just happy to be here?' "

HOW NOT TO BECOME A SPY

Earl was not that happy to be here. The bulge at his waist was the briefcase he carried with him everywhere around the site — to the dining room, the TV lounge, the DCC. Whatever he had in there must have been pretty valuable to him. I caught a glance at the contents when I passed him coming back from the toilet. Inside was a copy of Jane's Defense Weekly and a Playboy.

"Tonight's trivia question comes from inspector Confucius," Will continued. "'What if it's only one missile that comes out and then goes back in again?" Hey, that's not trivial at all. It could be costing millions of tax dollars. Now, to close the program, we turn again to the famous Irish-American bard, Mr. Thom Moore, who will read his latest poem."

"Thank you, Will. Here's a little ditty I jotted down in honor of us. It's called 'What We Do.' "

Hooray, Hooray, let's build some trust!
But don't forget to leave your lust.

Get up, brush teeth, go to job.
Come back home,
Live like a slob.

Just sit and watch the world go by,
Protecting freedom,
Lord knows why.

When I feel like eating, I take a drink.
When I feel like drinking, I take a drink,
Just to keep on my toes.
An approach that's odd,
Heaven knows.

I can't make music
And I can't make love.
Them's the rules,
Decreed from above.

Quite carefully kept
Never on the loose,
Hence hardly inept
At the self-abuse.

So we work around the clock
The only kids on the block.
Work, work, work, a baker's dozen years
Work, work, work, allaying others' fears

Please don't forget us, here among the Reds.
You say it's six o'clock? Time to be fed.

The Soviets didn't want to give the Americans control of the basements. The Washington building was less than a hundred meters from factory territory. Water and electricity were coming directly from the plant. Surely there was some device that could be installed down there which would provide vital information the flamingoes had failed to detect. Perhaps the Americans would even dig tunnels.

While the question of basement jurisdiction was still under discussion, the Soviets put up a fence around the entire building site. Two weeks later, they suddenly took down the fence and turned over the buildings in their entirety to the Americans.

Young Sasha, the escort, was heading for Shuvalov's office. He had half an hour before he needed to be on the bus to the site in order to start his shift.

"Alexander," said Gennady Petrovich, "the last time we met, I read you the list of items we observed inspector Lifflander bringing down into the basements of the Roosevelt and Lincoln buildings. Were you able to find out what he is doing there and why?"

Sasha enjoyed the attention from Shuvalov. It made him feel important and useful. He respected the Americans and the new era of cooperation the treaty brought, but that was no excuse to lose vigilance. They could not be trusted. They would be living at the factory for the next 13 years. Competent men were needed to help implement the treaty and protect the factory. Shuvalov appreciated his potential and had promised Sasha that if their cooperation was fruitful, in the fall he would write him a recommendation letter for the KGB Academy in Moscow.

"I have only been on one social event with him since then, Gennady Petrovich, and we didn't get a chance to talk about it. You did instruct me to be subtle."

"Yes, that's right. It's very important to gain their trust. I am not so worried about the Roosevelt building basement. From what we can tell, they are putting up shelves and moving canned foods there. This might make sense, since it is nearer to the kitchen than the warehouse. But we are concerned about the basement of the Lincoln building — it is closer to the factory territory. The assortment of goods he has been bringing there is baffling: shelves, wiring, furniture, carpeting, a wooden packing crate, a tarp...not just one, but two vacuum cleaners. They have so much space already. Why would they need to move those things to that basement? You need to try to spend more time with him to find out."

"There is a clue, Gennady Petrovich," Sasha said. "I made a point of walking from the Fifth House to the Sixth House and passing him as he was going into the basement. I stopped to make small talk and asked why he wants to be down there. He said he needs a place to smoke."

"But," Petrovich said, "they smoke in the Lincoln TV room, don't they?"

"Yes," said Sasha, "but that is only for cigarettes and Lifflander is a smoker of cigars."

Petrovich contemplated this. "My uncle told me he once smoked a cigar. They used to sell them in the kiosks when Castro was trading them and sugar for our weapons and trucks."

"Did he enjoy it?" Sasha asked.

"He smoked it till the end and then fell off his horse on the way home."

The basements looked to the average observer like a replica of a Turkish prison, each with a long poorly-lit corridor and three or four chambers on either side. The cement work was new and smooth. Fresh white paint graced the hallways and glossy brown paint covered the walls of the chambers. Once I got all the lights working in the Lincoln basement, it actually took on a homey look.

I had always been attracted to underground rooms. Something about being surrounded by all that earth made me feel secure. My workshop at home had been in the basement. I knew it could only be penetrated by going through the main door, on which I had mounted a digital locking system and alarm. In college I installed a similar system for our fraternity's secret meeting room, which was also subterranean. Basements represent the soft underbelly of a building — where water, electricity, gas, and most interestingly, telephone cables enter.

While pledging, I entered the basement window of our fraternity house one night, tapped into the phone line of one of the senior brothers and attached the same device I had used on the high- school PA system.

I awoke one morning in my dorm room to find my bed shaking and the enraged brother standing over me. "Pledge," he yelled, "do you have any idea why George Carlin and his seven dirty words keep interrupting telephone calls to my parents?"

Of course I had an idea. The prerecorded program I designed for this operation consisted of various obscene monologues of leading comedians interspersed with periods of silence. My self-satisfied grin gave me away.

"If I hear him again," the frat brother continued, "you'll find yourself wrapped in a carpet, stuffed in my trunk, and on your way to Hobart." A fate worse than death. I broke into the basement again that night and removed the equipment.

Access to the Votkinsk basements was from the back of the buildings through a midget-sized metal door and a re-bar grill. A cement staircase went below. It reminded me of a tomb in the Valley of the Kings. The musty smell was similar, though our basements lacked the artwork.

While the Soviets saw the basements as a point of possible infiltration, I regarded the space as underutilized real estate. Lou installed a telephone for me in the room that became my office. Next came poker tables that had been languishing unused in the *sklad*. The room across from my office became the gaming parlor. Scraps of carpet added comfort.

When I spotted a packing crate sitting unwanted on the garbage pile, I realized what needed to be done. I began to plan the hot tub room. While I lived in Moscow, I made a two-seater hot tub on my balcony. I assembled it in my living room, hopeful that the concrete floor panels would support the tub's weight. It was outfitted with underwater lamps and a side panel made from an odd piece of sheet metal which I found in a junk store. It also had an etched copper emblem of the hammer and sickle. I used spare taillights from the ambassador's old Cadillac to illuminate the step.

The Votkinsk incarnation was a four-seater, padded with packing foam and lined with a giant blue plastic tarp used to protect shipments from the elements. The drain connected to the sewage pipe of the building via a piece of conduit. It only leaked a little. The basements frequently flooded after a heavy rain, so no one would notice. The beach chairs, requisitioned along with the flamingos to give the site a suburban American appearance during the summer, looked swell on either side.

I hooked up two vacuum cleaners in reverse, to function as a source of aeration. I flipped the switch while Lou sat inside as my floating guinea pig. A glorious burst of bubbles sprang forth, but then one of the motors overheated and began to suck in water. I was able to pull the plug just before Lou got electrocuted.

"Maybe you should ask Vasilich for help," he said.

Chernenko and his chief engineer showed up under the guise of repairing light fixtures. They analyzed the situation and returned a few days later with a solution. It was a modified air compressor from a truck. They wired it to the main switch panel in the next chamber and ran a hose into my tub. The thup-thup-thup echoed loudly through the corridor but a steady stream of bubbles churned gently through my aquatic wonder-box. And you could smoke while bathing. The hot tub's christening was an occasion to celebrate.

"I'm not really sure what I was expecting," I said, as Lou and I sat in the Jacuzzi in our birthday suits. The warm water, gently agitated by the bubbles, gurgled between us and Chernenko. He was also naked but for his Australian army hat — a present from one of the OSIA officers.

"What do you mean?" Lou asked.

"Well, I invited everyone. But with 28 homophobic men and two nervous women on site, I don't know who I thought was going to join us down here."

"My grandmother is with us," said Chernenko as he poured out three shots and we clinked in honor of our creation. "Maybe you invite Darlene?"

"Are you kidding? I'm afraid to even talk to her."

"What about escorts?" Chernenko said playfully.

Lou sighed and said, "Fred Coy, one of the original inspectors, went on an unauthorized bike ride alone with Ekaterina to the emergency exit. Fred was fired and I heard they moved Katya to some job in the downtown factory. But you, Vasilich, you can sit here with us, buck naked, and you don't get in trouble. What's your secret? Is it because you're a high-ranking officer?"

"Yeah, Vasilich," I said as I held my lighter to the end of his Romeo y Julieta cigar, just above the tepid gurgling water. "What is your rank, anyway? I've never smoked with a Soviet officer before."

"Mmm," said Vasilich as he exhaled and put his nose to the fragrant brown wrapper, while beads of sweat rolled down his cheeks.

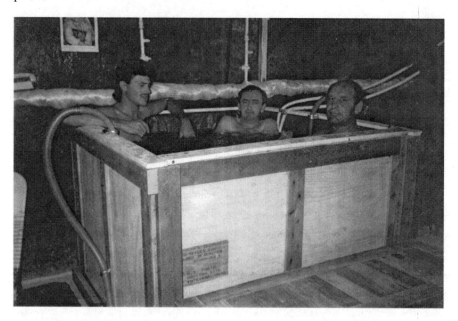

"You don't want to know my rank. You'd be shocked."

Vasilich's humor and lack of pretense always helped us forget we were living in a golden cage. But, except for such rare distractions, the social privation was beginning to get to me. I yearned for a more normal life.

Chapter Ten
Cooking Up Trouble

Once the kitchen was outfitted with all the essentials, it became the most important place at the portal monitoring facility. With no sex and limited drinking, food took on extraordinary importance. Chef Chuck was used to long stints in a confined area, making due with a limited amount of resources and pleasing a captive audience. He produced three decent meals a day and wasn't overly temperamental.

I had been helping Chuck by cleaning the kitchen and occasionally preparing breakfast. Bellman, the Hughes site manager, had offered me the second chef position but I decided not to take it for two reasons.

First, I had some doubts about his sense of reality. While we were examining the buildings before the move, he noticed the main walls were very thick — as much as three-quarters of a meter in some places. The Soviets used a combination of concrete panels and bricks. It gave strength and insulation from the cold.

"You know," he said in all seriousness when he first noticed this, "I bet they make these walls especially thick so they can move around inside 'em and keep an eye on us."

Second, kitchen work was the hardest job on site and as a full-time chef I would rarely have gotten a chance to get out. I wanted to participate in the social program.

So Hughes brought in a second chef a few months after the kitchen opened.

Tim came from the other end of the culinary spectrum. He graduated from the CIA: the Culinary Institute of America. His last job was as sous-chef at a five-star hotel in Los Angeles. He and his paring knife could turn an ordinary radish into a delicate rose in under two minutes. You could almost feel your coronary artery clogging as his homemade hollandaise sauce melted on your palate. Chuck relied on Knorr's.

Tim was a big fellow with a manic demeanor and dramatic gesticulations, having graduated from clown school before attending the CIA. Something told me he might be too wild a bird for our gilded cage.

The arrival on site of one three-week mutant with the appetite of two marked the beginning of the end for Tim. A key challenge of the chef's job, beyond being on his feet for 12 hours a day, was making the produce and other perishables last for the three-week stints between rotations, when we brought in supplies from the base in Frankfurt. This was realistic since the number of diners was always between 25 and 30. The final count was clear at the start of every three-week period and didn't vary. There was no other place to eat.

Joseph, the gluttonous three-week mutant, was a military officer. He was tall, with bushy eyebrows and a full head of curly gray hair.

Tim stood behind the hot table and noticed that Joe regularly served himself a portion at least 50 percent in excess of the standard. Tim made snide comments but Joe kept obliviously spooning away. Tim found himself having to scramble to produce extra food at the end of the meal for latecomers whose portions had been devoured by Joe. This went on for a few days, until Tim got fed up. He decided to escalate. At one point Joe entered the dining room and sat down to chat before getting his food. Tim was prepared. Having attached two large steel-wool pads to either side of his head to mock Joseph's hairdo, Tim came out of the kitchen with a full tray of macaroni and cheese and planted it in front of Joe.

"Here! Why don't we just save some time? You can eat all of it and the rest of us will go hungry for the night!" Tim said. He snatched Joe's cutlery away, slapped the oversized serving spoon down in its place and stood with folded arms as Joe calmly heaped an extensive mound of the golden yellow creation on his plate. The officer was not intimidated. The clown was even angrier. Tim was headed for full confrontation.

D-Day came when Tim surreptitiously mixed himself a pitcher of martinis and consumed it on his own just before dinner. When Bellman approached the hot table, Tim cackled in his face, grabbed three baked potatoes and proceeded to expertly juggle them. He closed the act by landing the potatoes, one by one, on Bellman' tray. Fortunately they were New Reds, not Idahos.

Bellman looked suspiciously at Tim, but only asked, "Where is the sour cream?"

Joseph was next on line. He was treated to a barrage of verbal abuse. Tim flung two meal trays across the kitchen in his direction. Joseph caught both of them and proceeded to load up. We hoped that was the end of it.

In the lounge, after dinner, I held my breath as Tim joined the discussion. Joe had gotten a cigarette out and asked if anyone had a light. "Let me get that for you," Tim said under his breath. With his BIC set on maximum, Tim torched Joe's shirt cuff and sleeve. Fortunately it was made of cotton or the burns could have been serious. We tamped out Joe as Tim walked away giggling.

Bellman and Blackstone reviewed their options. Restraining Tim for the remaining days of the rotation period was discussed. But they decided against it. Something about a lawsuit. Tim promised to sober up and calm down. He was sent out for good on the next rotation.

Hughes was now in non-fulfillment of its contractual obligation for kitchen staffing. Three chefs were necessary, since that was the minimum number to ensure two would be on site at all times. Now they were down to one. Bellman offered me a significant raise if I would take the sous-chef job. I thought about it again.

I enjoyed Chuck's company and it would be nice to have the skills. Bellman said something about sending me to cooking school in Thailand in the fall.

Chuck lobbied hard, but I held my ground. I had doubts about Hughes' ability to keep its commitments. And the social excursions away from the site were one of the few things which kept me sane. I told Bellman I'd agree to be a cook for three months until Hughes got two more chefs on site, and settled for a 5 percent pay increase. Bellman also promised to find a backup for me whenever I wanted to go to a social event.

Sofia pulled a book from her purse and handed it to me as I sat down next to her on the bus.

"It's all in Russian," I said.

"That's the point. It's Bunin. He's easy to read."

"Easy if you are a Russian."

"Bunin's plots are clearer than Turgenev's," Sofia said.

"I'll give it a try. Is it allowed for escorts to give inspectors gifts?"

"It's not a gift. I expect it back when you are done." I liked her boldness. It wasn't like Vasilich's. He was sure he was indispensable and that gave him power. Sofia acted like she had nothing to lose.

"Why did you take the job in Votkinsk?" I asked.

"It was one of the choices the state gave me after I got my degree."

"What were the others?"

"To become an English teacher at a school in a small town outside of Moscow. I would have liked to take it, but the Votkinsk job also promised apartments to those with children. Max and I finally got our own place last month."

I had seen the boy once or twice when we were still living at the hotel. Sofia had brought him to watch videos on nights when Department 162 employees were invited. He had big ears, a huge smile and brown eyes with long thick lashes like a doll.

"He's very cute," I told her. "Your husband must be handsome."

"Ex-husband...yes, he's handsome, but a bastard." She said the word 'bastard' with a British accent, though the rest of her speech sounded normal.

I wanted to know more but decided not to push.

"The prospect of working with Americans didn't bother you?" I asked.

"No, not at all. I didn't give it much thought. It was more important to get away."

"Away from what?"

She turned towards the window and continued, as if she was explaining to herself. "From everything, I suppose. Mostly from Max's father. I guess I'm just running away." Then she turned back to me. She was smiling, barely. But the smile was filled with pathos.

"I'm very good at running away," she said, "it's in my genes. I grew up in a small town in the Yaroslavl region, about 200 kilometers from Moscow. My father tends to drink too much and then gets nasty. So one day when I was about 10 my mother took my younger brother and I and ran away. We moved to Nikolaev in the Ukraine and lived with her sister Zoya and her husband Yury.

"My father caught up with us and promised to change, so we settled in Nikolaev. I eventually got married, but it only lasted a few months. My husband had the same habit as my father. I was accepted to the foreign language institute in Moscow, but couldn't complete the first year because I was pregnant. After Max was born he mostly lived with my mother while I went back to finish my studies."

"Didn't your husband want to live with you in Moscow?"

"What he really wanted to do was sit on his mother's couch and drink all day. I was able to trick him into divorcing me by telling him it would be easier to get housing in Moscow for us as a single mother. He started showing up, but my father made it clear things would be bad for him if he continued to chase me. Eventually my studies ended and I got the chance to come here, so I took it."

She seemed relieved to have told me her story. I decided that under that layer of cynicism she had a gentle strength. Raising a child on her own was very courageous.

After a pause, she asked me, "Why did you come to Votkinsk?"

I thought for a moment. I couldn't admit I wanted to advance my career in espionage. Why else had I come? I took refuge in a half truth.

"Well, I was starting to get bored in Moscow. This job provided me with a change of scenery and a chance to improve my Russian..."

Sofia smiled. "So you're running away from boredom?"

"I guess so, and I get a chance to see more of the world."

"You think this is the world?" she asked.

"It's a part of the world. Besides, when I rotate out for my vacations, I plan to travel a lot."

Shopping was another opportunity to socialize and mingle with the locals. Department No. 1 couldn't close all the stores and clear the streets when we wanted to go looking for souvenirs. Items the locals considered unnecessary or overpriced often made good gifts. A 50-ruble watch, which represented 25 percent of an average monthly salary, cost less than 10 dollars.

I wanted a couch and chair for my underground clubhouse, so Sofia led me to the furniture store. The main section had a few items on display. But they all had little signs on them that said "This item is sold."

"There is a waiting list of several months," Sofia explained. "I hope to get my furniture by the end of the summer."

"What about this stuff?" I asked, pointing to a solidly-built orange couch and two matching chairs.

"Those are made by a cooperative," Sofia said. "It's a new type of legal entity that individuals can create. They can only employ relatives and are supposed to make goods and services for consumers. But they also get to determine their own prices." When I saw the 1,200-ruble price tag, I didn't bother asking why she didn't buy this instead of waiting.

I had already mastered the three-line acquisition system. Having identified the item I desired, I confirmed the price and department number. Next, I stood in line at the cash register to pay. I then returned with my receipt to queue at the counter to pick up my purchase. I now owned a living room set for less than 200 dollars.

The furniture store had a delivery service: an old man and even older horse with a cart parked outside, ready to bring goods right to your door.

"How much for delivery?" I asked the old man. He craned his head, clearly having trouble with my accent. He picked up his ear flaps and said, "repeat, please."

"I have a couch and two chairs. How much to deliver to my home?"

"Ten rubles." It seemed low.

"You understand it's 12 kilometers from here," I told him.

"Ten rubles," the old man repeated. At that moment Triple A, who was the senior escort for this excursion, came up to me. "What are you doing?" he asked.

"Agreeing about delivery. He is asking whether it is allowed for the horse to graze in front of the DCC after they unload? The grass is beginning to sprout."

"No horse to factory!" Anatoly exclaimed, shaking his head. "I'll organize a truck." I guess the horse didn't have the right security clearance.

Waiting for a customer.

On the way back, Knight reminded Anatoly that we had requested a stop at Bread Store No. 3. Knight got on line, but as he approached the counter the sales lady told him the bread was already stale and not worth buying. Mindful that bread was needed at the site, and no other bread store was on our *zayavka*, Knight politely insisted he would take six loaves anyway. A *babushka* behind him observed this scene and took pity on the unfortunate inspector forced to purchase sub-standard foodstuffs.

"Citizens!" she shouted at the other shoppers. "They make our American guests buy stale bread." The crowd began to grumble at Anatoly about the shameful situation. He relented under collective pressure and took us to another bread store.

I bought a pneumatic pistol when we were last in Izhevsk at the gun factory store. There weren't any Kalashnikovs on display, even though it was their most famous product. My purchase went unnoticed since everyone else was focused on the hand-crafted shotguns.

The basement corridor was a perfect firing range, since there was nothing that could be damaged and the ricochets were blunted by the thick concrete walls. I had bought the latest set of Politburo member photographs from the local stationary store. There had been several major reshuffles of the governing body since Gorbachev took power, and I was trying to keep up. But now I found a more practical use for the portraits. Gorbachev and Foreign Minister Shevardnadze, who had also worked on the treaty, were excluded from target practice. If it wasn't for them, we wouldn't have been in Udmurtia anyway. But the hardcore old guard was fair game.

Gorbachev's picture also helped to keep me out of trouble. One day I was studying the effect of gun pellets on the basement corridor wall. I noticed a particularly large hole. There were lots of small holes in those walls. Though evenly painted, the cement work was rough, with a host of blemishes, bumps, and depressions. I was driven by more than just an interest in ballistics. If there hadn't been such a contretemps about control of the basements, I might have been less suspicious. When they were finally handed over to us I realized they were finished too nicely. This suspicion, combined with boredom and curiosity, sent me down a dangerous path. I was sure the place was filled with bugs, and decided to look for them.

It wasn't that I thought I could defeat them. I had learned at the FBI that it wasn't possible. A listening device can range in size from a can of peas to the head of a pin. My goal was to prove I was right.

I remembered this as I continued to excavate my newly discovered hole, located two thirds of the way up the wall, in the center of the corridor. 'If I were them,' I thought, 'I'd use a pipe microphone here.' This device consists of a metal tube the length and diameter of a ballpoint pen with a resonating chamber the size of a tuna can on the end and wires leading out. Such devices are designed to be buried deep in concrete with only the opening of the tube exposed — hardly noticeable in typical Soviet plaster work. I expanded the diameter and depth of my digging. The hole grew, but no device became visible.

The pattern in the stucco indicated work had been done after the original cement slab was laid. For efficiency's sake, I went to the *sklad* and retrieved our largest hammer drill. It made the job much easier. Above me in the lounge of Lincoln my colleagues were watching videos. I drilled. At one point they sent an emissary to inquire about the pounding that reverberated through the building.

"Just securing some extra shelving for spare toilet paper and light bulbs," I responded. Glory to the janitor!

Soon I saw something wondrous. Barney from "Mission Impossible" would have been proud. I had exposed a metal pipe about three inches in diameter in the crater. There was no technical justification for its presence in this very place. Water, sewerage, and electrical conduit were all exposed, running along the ceiling of the basement or coming down from the first floor above. We had no gas pipes coming in to any of our buildings. I trotted up the stairs, retrieved Jane's stethoscope from Roosevelt, and applied it to my discovery. No gurgling, humming, or blowing was audible. It seemed safe to attempt penetration.

A test hole through the metal neither oozed, nor wheezed, nor squirted. I was disappointed. Not even a small electric shock. I decided to proceed. Using a one-inch diameter hole-saw I made a window into the mysterious conduit. A thin bare wire was suspended in the center and ran the whole length of the pipe. I touched it. No reaction. I plucked it. Again, no reaction. I pulled it. The wire seemed to be mounted on a spring, allowing it to move back and forth. My conclusion: it was a seismic detector intended to react to vibrations from tunneling or drilling. I imagined the technician sitting on the top floor of the Fifth House, now deafened and cursing loudly, his headphones thrown to the floor.

I believed this discovery of the device was an achievement of some kind. I had to share it with someone so I invited Lieutenant Colonel Ray to review my work. We began writing furiously on my magic slate — the one item of tradecraft I had allowed myself. The magic slate has been the tool of intimate conversation for diplomats and spies in hostile environments since it was invented as a children's toy in the 1920's. Write with the plastic stylus, show your interlocutor your question or answer, pick up the plastic sheet and, with a brief *thwit,* all evidence is erased. No microphone could follow your conversation. And no paper shredder was required.

"Finally, we got evidence!" Ray wrote. Then *thwit* went the magic slate as he handed it back to me. His chest swelled with pride as he poked around in the cavity and contemplated what he perceived to be its significance.

'He probably believes he'll get a medal for this,' I thought.

Ray then took back the magic slate and gave me clear instructions: stand by for further instructions.

I was enjoying a post-prandial smoke in my basement lounge the following after-noon when the phone rang. Uncle Lou, who was on duty in the DCC, informed me that the Soviets had asked for a fire inspection of the basements. They would be down in 15 minutes. I scrambled to gather the excavation debris as I contemplated how to hide the hole. Time was short. I spotted Gorbachev's face staring at me from the portrait collection. Why not? After all, the seismic detector seemed low-tech. It couldn't have told them the precise location of the intrusion — or so I hoped. Mikhail Sergeevich got a new mission: saving my basement and my butt. The pock marked faces of the power ministers remained on the floor.

I looked down the corridor. There was something suspicious about a singular General Secretary's portrait pasted on the otherwise bare wall. President Reagan came to the rescue. I happened to have a portrait of him which we had put up during the July Fourth celebration. I placed him on the wall opposite Gorbachev. A sponta-neous gallery of peace makers.

Ray was first down the steps and looked at me with anguish. My wink put him at ease. Glancing at my impromptu gallery, he seemed satisfied with my efforts. He was followed by Mr. Moose and a fire marshal in military uniform. Behind them were two men dressed in workers smocks. But underneath they wore suits. They had dress shoes on their feet and nice watches on their wrists. They resembled the firemen who arrived in black Volga sedans to help put out the fire at the embassy in Moscow the last summer I was there. Chernenko was at the end of the delegation, looking cool as always. The Soviets moved quickly from room to room, as I offered a guided tour.

Here we play cards. *-Why?* Because cigar smoking is not permitted upstairs and it is impossible to play poker without smoking cigars. The hot tub room is here (Chernenko feigned disinterest). And here is my office, complete with a cooperative-made sofa and armchair set, demonstrating my personal support for perestroika. *-Why do you need to be down here?* It's a cozy place to think.

They concluded their inspection, having found no tunnels. They informed us this was all in violation of Soviet fire codes. Ray reminded them it was our diplomatically inviolable basement but they should feel free to bring a copy of the fire regulations to our next weekly meeting.

Alexander Vladimirovich Losev felt sympathy for Sofia. He could see how much she dreaded the meetings with Shuvalov. Today she looked especially distressed. Usually they didn't talk about it but he decided to ask. Sofia was only a few years older than Losev's daughter and had been tutoring her in English.

"So, what are they concerned about now?" Losev asked. They never used the three letter acronym in their discussion.

"They are upset about the basement situation," said Sofia. "They consider it proof that Inspector Lifflander has some kind of additional mission. They said he had been 'activated,' whatever that means."

"Well, he sure is active," Losev said.

"Shuvalov said that Lifflander's rank and position at the embassy was typical cover for an intelligence operative. What do you think?"

"I think I know how to build rockets, manage a project and not fall asleep at Party meetings. I don't know much else," Losev said.

"Shuvalov was especially upset about Lifflander's choice of targets for the shooting range," Sofia said.

"Definitely not politically correct," Losev said.

"Do all the Department 162 workers work with them?" Sofia asked.

Losev nodded. "Well, almost all. They don't bother Sarah, since she's a Jew, and they haven't trusted Jews since Trotsky."

"Shuvalov said I should try to go on more social events with Lifflander. He asked me to get 'closer' to him," Sofia said.

She was torn by the situation. She liked being with Justin. She enjoyed his enthusiasm and curiosity. His anti-establishment spirit was refreshing. They were alike in their irreverence, but for different reasons — she had no faith in, or expectation from the established order; he was just oblivious to the consequences. Or perhaps, as Shuvalov suspected, he was above the rules? At that moment, it didn't make a difference. She was disgusted by the manipulation and the threat to her free will.

"You have to agree, it's strange," Losev said. "I mean, other inspectors have had problems — Fred Coy and his one-on-one bike ride; Greg Robinson and whatever issues he had with his taxes — and they were removed. Lifflander sets up a night club and starts tearing down the building and nothing happens to him. Who is protecting him and why?"

I was thinking about Sofia as I headed back to Frankfurt after my vacation. She had been on the rotation trip to Izhevsk when I left. It seemed she was getting to participate in escort activities more frequently. She had asked me where I was going. I told her I was headed home to New York to visit family and friends. Did I have any special friends I was going to see? I told her about Richie...She seemed relieved. I sensed her interest was genuine.

I sat down at the table for the security debriefing at the OSIA office in Frankfurt. Inspectors were asked to comment on any unusual activities, events, people, or discussions they had observed during their previous tour on site. A routine procedure where there were rarely any significant revelations. But as the meeting ended and I got up to go, one of the counter-intelligence men approached me and handed me a video tape.

"Justin, would you mind taking this video back to the site? The last outbound team lent it to me from the library."

I looked at it as I tucked it under my arm. Meryl Streep stared at me from the box cover. It was "Sophie's Choice." I started to smile at the thought of her name. Then I noticed he was staring intently at me, blocking my way and trying to gauge my reaction.

"Have you seen it?" he asked, his eyes riveted on mine.

"Nope," I answered with a nearly audible gulp. "Didn't get to that one yet."

"It doesn't have a happy ending, Justin," he said, then turned and walked away.

His dispassionate countenance robbed me of the possibility to decide if the incident had been a coincidence or warning. The counter-intelligence guys always won at poker when they came to the site. A sense of dread began to build in my gut.

Then I saw Lieutenant Jake at the end of the corridor. He summoned me into the general's office. The general was not in. Colonel Francell was sitting at his desk. Also present were two civilians I didn't recognize. They had very serious expressions on their faces. Could they somehow manage to peer into my heart and learn I was developing an attraction for one of the escorts? I would be arrested and shot, my family forced to pay for the bullets. The Soviets did the same to that flake, Yurchenko — the KGB officer who defected to the West, ate several expensive meals, told a few good stories and then defected back.

"Justin," said the colonel, "we have a problem."

The butterflies in my stomach turned into bats.

"Could you please explain your recent archeology project?" he continued.

Minor relief. I told them the truth — I was a victim of boredom and bad judgment. They also seemed relieved.

The colonel continued, "Justin, you have to understand, this is very serious. If the Soviets find out and decide to make it an issue, such an incident could have repercussions for the treaty and the trust we are trying to build."

This bothered me. I believed in the treaty. After all, there aren't many good things a government can create, besides parks and peace treaties.

The men looked at each other for a few moments and then the colonel spoke again.

"As soon as you get back to the site, take down Gorbachev, seal the pipe, fill the hole, make it look like new again and discuss it with no one. This is a classified matter now."

"Yes, sir. Thank you. I am very sorry for the trouble. It won't happen again."

"Make sure it doesn't," the colonel said. As I left the room he turned to the other men and said, "he makes damn good cookies."

A lot of progress had been made in mutual understanding during the 18 months since the first group of inspectors arrived. But, demonstrating genuine Russian hospitality while overcoming diplomatic and security challenges was not easy for the Soviet side. At the Fifth House they were trying to decide who should go with the Americans to celebrate the Victory Day holiday commemorating the end of World War II.

"Nikolai Ivanovich," Sofia said to the escort leader, "there are 10 Americans who will attend the event. So how many escorts do we need?"

How many escorts? It was a good question. If you asked the teachers, students and veterans who would gather at the school auditorium to welcome their guests, they probably would have answered, "None." The Americans could find their way to the Elbe River, where their troops joined forces with the Soviets. They don't need help finding a girls' school in provincial Russia.

The Americans, on the other hand, would have said the ratio of escorts to inspectors for such an event should be 1:1 to eliminate any security concerns. Page 12 of the "Vot, Votkinsk!" manual clearly states, "*avoid placing yourself in a compromising situation. Do not become romantically involved with a Soviet Citizen. Above all use common sense and good judgment.*" Was it good judgment to invite the 30 most chaste men in Udmurtia to a social event with 200 beautiful young women aged 16 to 19?

Sofia took the initiative and decided three escorts would be enough for the event: herself, Larisa and Maria.

Spravka

9 May 1989

Report by Department 162 Administrative Escort Tarakanova, Larisa Sergeevna (Party member since February 1987):

Text: Meeting attendees included 10 inspectors from the American side, three senior members of the Votkinsk Association of Veterans of the Great Patriotic War, several staff members and students of the Musical Pedagogical School No. 2. Approximately 200 students were also in attendance.

Following the musical presentation by the students in the auditorium, which included a pleasant medley of songs from the war, intermixed with modern era songs by western composers like the Beatles, inspector Colonel Francell made a brief speech of appreciation for the kindness shown to his delegation.

Although it seemed that this part of the event has concluded, unexpectedly Lieutenant Colonel Blackstone took the microphone and stated that he was so moved by the memory of historic cooperation between the opposing camps that he must sing his own series of songs. He put on dark glasses and sang songs by a performer named Buddy Holly, with which we are not familiar. I am convinced this aspect of the American participation was unplanned. Judging by the inspectors' facial expressions, it seemed painful for them to listen to his singing. But music students were smiling politely.

It is my conclusion that Mr. Blackstone's taking to the microphone was an effort to improve his career position in the American military establishment — he then dedicated a special song to Colonel Francell, that he said he wrote himself.

Blackstone sang a song about the home state of the colonel: these words I am writing down as I heard them:"It's a blackberry pi-i-i-cking morning, it's a Min-nes-sota kind of a day!"

I am convinced that the colonel is not liking this song, since he tried to hide himself behind other inspectors; this despite his not small size.

The school principal then guided the group to a gymnasium, where the students had prepared a discotheque for the inspectors.

The senior American military personnel took up positions in the back of the hall. The esteemed veterans had discussions with Lieutenant Taylor and Captain Knight about the meaning of the medals on their chests, while comrade Elvira Bochkova, the editor of Lenin's Way newspaper, conducted an interview with Colonel Francell.

The remaining seven inspectors joined the several tens of students in the dancing activity. Lighting was dimmed. Though it is clearly against all socialist norms, the song "American boy, American boy, take me away with you," was played frequently. This clearly demonstrates the deficiency in politically correct education of the girls. Several slower songs were played, in which students took turns selecting inspectors to dance with. Inspectors seemed on the surface opposed to this degree of youthful intimacy, but I could not identify any genuine resistance.

Next, the senior student present, whom I recognized as Valentina Smirnova— daughter of a factory deputy director, declared that a contest would be held.Without providing details as to the nature of the competition, she asked inspectors to select two representatives to participate. Inspector Lifflander and inspector Haley were chosen. I could not detect any objection on their part to fulfilling this role.

Then Valentina told the two inspectors to select partners from the crowd of students, still without giving specific instructions as to the rules of competition. Many of the politically ignorant young women vocally offered themselves to these two inspectors. Haley selected a young woman of his height, but about twice as wide. Lifflander chose a taller, thinner girl.

Finally, the nature of the contest was explained. Music would be played for several seconds, while the couples each danced together on separate sheets of newspaper that were placed on the floor. Once the music stopped, the paper would be folded in half. This would be repeated until only one couple was able to dance on the paper. I am not sure at this point whether the inspectors exactly understood the rules, as it was a very loud environment, and no one was able to translate for them. Other escorts stood with the Soviet veterans and the colonel and his officers at the back of the room.

At the beginning of the contest Lifflander and Haley were smiling very much. By the fourth or fifth interlude, by which time they were compelled to cradle their dance partners in their arms in order to maintain their position on top of very small remaining pieces of newspaper, it was clear that the physical challenge was felt. Inspector Haley, despite having big muscles, made painful expressions on his face at carrying the weight of his partner.

Inspector Lifflander demonstrated no signs of displeasure, and in fact seemed to very much enjoy this process.

By the sixth musical piece, only 10 square centimeters of newsprint was left. While inspector Lifflander continued to demonstrate skill, hopping on tiptoe on this remaining space, and his partner embracing his neck, inspector Haley had several times missed the target, danced off the paper and nearly dropped his partner.

Lifflander was declared the winner and both inspectors received kisses from their partners. No other significant political or social incidents were observed.

Faithfully reported by Escort Tarakanova, Larisa Sergeevna.

Chapter Eleven
German Ancestors and a
Memorable Dinner

As I walked toward the Fifth House for the weekly Russian-American joint Spanish lesson taught by Jane I still felt an emotional high from the Victory Day dance. I remembered the warmth and the scent of that young lady in my arms, her head resting on my shoulder as we pranced to our own victory.

But Sofia's reaction left a bigger impression on me. I walked past her as I left the dance floor with my partner. She was standing at the sidelines, arms folded.

"You seemed to enjoy that," she remarked, with a clearly discernible 'humph.'

"I most certainly did," I answered, delirious with the sensation of hormones flowing through my veins. But I thought about Sofia's tone. 'Humph'— sounds like she's jealous — doesn't jealousy imply affection? The insight was intriguing.

I took off my boots in the hallway of the Fifth House and sat down next to Sofia at the table in the kitchenette.

"Donde están dos hombres calientes, horita!" Jane pronounced slowly. Sofia laughed. Maria also deciphered the meaning and smiled. Knight and I were the only other participants in Jane's informal class.

"Well, what does it mean?" Will barked in frustration.

"Give me two hot men, now!" Maria said. More laughter.

"What kind of a conversational sentence is that?" I asked. Even more laughter. We were outnumbered.

Though I liked the idea of learning another language, my real motivation was to socialize with Sofia. Her intelligence excited me as much as her tight jeans did. I had a feeling of well-being when we were together. It still hadn't occurred to me that the situation was precarious and might somehow affect my career plans. As I settled into the controlled but idyllic routine at the portal, my career ambitions began to take a back seat to more mundane matters. What can I do to make tonight's menu more interesting? Will the toilet paper last until the next rotation?

After the next entertaining phrase from Jane, I uncrossed my knees and planted my foot on the floor. I was suddenly in direct contact with Sofia's foot. Well, almost direct — my wool sock and her stocking separated us. But I could feel her and she didn't pull away. I lost my ability to concentrate on Jane's lesson. I was looking ahead and so was Sofia but I could see in my mind's eye everything going on under the table. I wiggled my toes to see if she simply didn't notice my podiatric advance. She wiggled too. She knew I was there. Before it could escalate into a treaty-threatening full-scale round of footsie, there was the sound of movement in the corridor behind us. We both withdrew. I began to wonder if anything had actually happened. And, if it had, what did it mean?

After the class, Knight headed for the DCC while Jane and I went to Roosevelt. By this time we had all developed a sixth sense. We were conscious about what we said and where we said it. If the assumption at the embassy was that the walls of your workplace and home have ears, in Votkinsk it was a fact. The walls, the floors, the ceilings, probably even the toilets. So the circular path around our yard became the closest thing we had to a cone-of-silence. From time to time the OSIA officers would "take a walk" to discuss something. One only hoped the lenses on the cameras weren't of high enough quality to facilitate lip reading. We concluded that the second floor of the Fifth House was the nerve center. We were explicitly told by the escorts when visiting the first floor, not to go near the staircase. From time to time, a man could be seen exiting with bags of what were presumably recording tape.

"You know, Justin," Jane said quietly, even though we were outside, "you two were meant for each other."

I stopped and stared at her. "What are you talking about?"

"I mean it. You and Sofia are like two little lost souls that seem to blend when you're together. I think you'd make a great couple."

With another person I would have denied it, but Jane had become an emotional authority for me — someone whose judgment I trusted about the right thing to do. She had demonstrated kindness, humor, strength and wisdom.

At that moment, my pleasant anxiety erupted into joyous panic as I realized what I was feeling and what it might mean.

"Do you realize what you're saying?" I asked, half feigning innocence and half looking for guidance.

"It could work out someday, when you both leave here."

I sensed that everything I had strived for was beginning to dissolve; that becoming an intelligence officer might not leave me with the same warm feeling I had when I was with Sofia.

"Jane, this is out of control. It's just crazy."

"Think about it."

I had. "She doesn't believe I'm serious," I said.

"That's interesting," Jane said, "she told me that's what she likes about you. She said you are a *prikolist*...said it means you are a lot of fun."

I needed to fall back and regroup. I headed to the *sklad*. Perhaps lugging a few cases of window cleaner around the site would help clear my head. Haley was sitting at his post inside the main door, writing an inventory report. Since he was responsible for the warehouse, he set himself up at a tall lectern from whose vantage point he could see the whole facility and also monitor materials and tools as they came and went.

Haley seemed to be one of the few mercenary-types that understood contentment. He was genuinely happy to be there. He was short and muscular and always sported a five-o'clock shadow. What he lacked in stature he made up for in the breadth of his smile. He was like a puppy. If he had a tail it would have wagged constantly. When he laughed, he made that noise: *hyuck-hyuck*. From anyone else it would have seemed forced but coming from him it was completely genuine.

"Why do you like working in the *sklad*, Jim?" I asked, trying to distract myself from my greater dilemma.

"It's fascinating," he said. "Lots of different things, all in their proper places. You could ask me where a half-inch stove bolt is or the two-year emergency supply of dehydrated potatoes and I could find either of them for you in 60 seconds flat...or at least tell you who had signed them out. The trick is to maintain constant control."

I envied the simple satisfaction he got from his work.

"Maybe if they get the new chef here on time," he continued, "you could fill in for me during my next rotation. You seem to be a guy who likes order."

"Yes, I do. I'd enjoy that. What are you going to do on your break?" I asked.

"I've only got one thing on my mind: to get home and play spoons with my girlfriend," Haley said.

"Spoons? What's that? Is it like spin-the-bottle? How do you play?"

"Imagine the cutlery drawer with the spoons neatly lined up, one behind the other. We just lie there like that for the first few days each time I come home."

I started to imagine me and Sofia in that position. So much for distracting myself.

The summer dragged on towards its close and the days blended together. We'd wake up, move about between our buildings for 16 hours a day like ants with a purpose, and then go back to bed. While doing inspection shifts, I found myself wishing they'd produce more missiles, just so we'd have something to do. I'd stare out the window of the DCC at the factory gate and wonder if I would I have to be satisfied ending the shift with my initials on the daily log indicating that no violations of the treaty had taken place. The most interesting thing to exit the portal in recent weeks was a brand new MAZ truck, model year 1989. What else exciting could possibly occur? A smashed *shlagbaum?* — routine, but at least something to talk about at dinner. A moose sighting while checking the emergency exit? — it happened, especially during mating season.

When weather permitted, we could chat with the technical escorts while patrolling the perimeter. Also known as portal escorts, we worked with them on all aspects of the inspection process. Shift leaders were former senior factory workers. The other technical escorts were younger, usually educated as engineers. They were an interesting crew. Barabanov was a plump character who, like Triple A, was completely brainwashed as to the glory of communism and always happy to debate its virtues. Vasnetsov was a stuttering translator who would, during informal conversation, share his firm belief that aliens were visiting our planet and Udmurtia in particular. Yerofeyev, was a very thin shift leader who smoked constantly. We called him "Tom Petty's Father" due to his resemblance to an aged version of the rock star. Kuptsov was a short, jovial, mustached escort who always wore a leather cap. Fyodorov had a sturdy frame and also worked as a shift leader; we nicknamed him "Rocky."

Over time, we got to know each other. The conversations became more personal. What do your children like to study? Where do you go on your next rotation? Had Vasnetsov really seen a UFO?

During the long hours of shift duty we found time to read the local paper, Lenin's Way. Published twice weekly, its chief editor, Elvira Bykova, was making the most of Gorbachev's *glasnost*. She was no longer compelled to fill her four pages exclusively with the wit and wisdom of the founding father, the text of resolutions from local Party meetings calling for more discipline at work and rosy renditions of the bright future.

Elvira now reported on the latest scandals, demands of the workers and the social life of the American inspectors. She objectively wrote about local politics and had features on subjects interesting to her readers. That month she was running a three-part series describing what local scientists had termed the "M" zone — a mini Bermuda Triangle in the adjacent region where strange occurrences were taking place.

It was these morsels of humanity that kept us feeling marginally connected to the local community. There were times when I appreciated the isolation, but the sense of loneliness was exacerbated on days when nothing at all happened on shift.

"Ooh, it's show time!" Lieutenant Jake exclaimed, observing two fire trucks enter the factory gate as he sat behind me in the DCC one day. That was a sign a completed rocket engine was being moved around somewhere inside. There were rumors the factory workers accidentally dropped the first SS-25 as it was being loaded onto a rail car. Whether a fire truck would be of any use if 50 tons of solid fuel ignited unexpectedly is debatable, but it was reassuring to see some precautions taken. Tom Petty's Father knocked at our door and handed Jake a declaration. In 30 minutes a six-axle rail carrying an intercontinental ballistic missile would exit the portal.

We gathered our hi-tech verification equipment. Jake got his clipboard and pen and made a test scribble to be sure the ink was flowing. I double checked the tape measure. In, out, in, out. It was ready for action. Thom pressed the button on his flash light: on, off, on, off. All set.

We left Uncle Lou in the DCC to work the lights and gates and headed outside toward the group of technical escorts who were getting in a last smoke. The diesel-electric locomotive was visible behind the rail gate. With a single toot, the portal opened and the train came out. When I first arrived at the portal the frequent toots would wake me at night. Eventually they became background noise. The sound of thunder was also unnerving if you let your imagination dwell on the possibilities. In addition to the explosive materials inside the factory, we were living at ground zero for an American nuclear attack. Sudden loud noises were unwelcome.

The same train configuration I had seen that first day began to roll through the gate. It halted across from the DCC. While Thom held the measuring tape reel at one end of the car, I trotted to the other end. We called out the length to Lieutenant Jake, who jotted it down. I then measured the width of the car and the figure was recorded. We donned our smocks. They were just like the kind we had in second grade art class. A pair of big white cotton gloves protected against static electricity discharges. I could imagine the Hercules plant in Utah, where they had clean rooms and sterile suits. But here everything was simpler. Why overcomplicate? When the space race was in its infancy the U.S. government spent six million dollars on research to invent a pen that wrote over rough surfaces and in zero gravity. Soviet cosmonauts used pencils.

Tom Petty's Father opened the small door at the end of the missile car, stepped inside, turned on the lights and then stuck his head out.

"Yes, there is a rocket in here," he said and motioned us to enter. The three of us followed single file, while Barabanov took up the rear.

We shimmied sideways along the edge of the missile's protective canister and the interior wall of the train car. Thom's Santa belly rubbed against the weapon. The dim lights illuminated A nearly complete rocket. Jake instructed me to go to the far end. I moved slowly along the rocket's length, breathing in the smells of fresh paint and propellant. I ran my hands along its length for support, carefully stepping over the struts in the floor that kept the missile in place. Perhaps for the first time since coming to Votkink I began to really think about what I was doing, and my hands trembled slightly as I held the tape measure's clip on the far edge of the canister. Thom read out the measurement and then joined me to check the diameter. The figures never differed but it was part of the verification procedure. My heart was racing as I glanced furtively at the receptacles and mounting panels along the side of the weapon. I felt like a peeping tom, looking through a window at something I shouldn't see; that no one should see; that shouldn't even exist in a sane world. Attach fins, add the warhead and nose cone, plug in a few cables and she'd be ready to soar across the ocean and turn the island of my birth into a pile of granite dust. I was in awe of the technical achievement and power of destruction.

"OK?" asked Tom Petty's Father.

"OK," responded Lieutenant Jake, and we exited the rail car.

As I watched Barabanov turn off the lights and close the door, my sentiment changed from awe to anger. It didn't make any sense. I saw the workers' faces every day when they passed by in their buses at shift change. They looked like decent people with families and pets, yet they made such horrible machines. Their government had chosen missiles over furniture, and many other basic goods people need to thrive. Colonel Francell told me that Mr. Moose had made an informal request to find a certain drug in America that the factory's chief engineer needed for his heart condition. Not enough medicine or toothpaste, but they had this nightmare weapon.

I wanted to take every member of the inspection party by the shoulders and shake them until they became conscious of what was going on. I felt like the pretty girl in the "Twilight Zone" episode that wakes up to find herself in a world of people with grotesque faces who think she is the ugly one. She finally loses her mind as they prepare her for plastic surgery to correct her "hideous" appearance. I eyed the rails in front of the locomotive and wondered if I should lie down on the tracks to prove my point and incite them to think.

Tom Petty's question shook me from my frantic reverie.

"Lieutenant Jake, do you want to open the canister for further inspection?"

It was the trump card of the treaty that ensured verification before the x-ray machine came on line. We had the right to ask them six times per year to park the rail car in the inspection building next to the *sklad* and open the ends of the canister. We could peer inside to be sure it contained a large missile. I guess this was to confirm there wasn't a huge conspiracy between the shareholders of the Hercules missile plant in the U.S. and Votkinsk factory management to bring out empty canisters. Each side would think the other was making more and more missiles, so a steady stream of orders would be guaranteed. But when you saw how the weight of the car caused the rails to sink as it passed over, you could be sure there was something very heavy inside.

"No, not this one," Jake responded as he turned towards the DCC and waved, indicating it was OK to switch the traffic light to green and allow the missile to pass.

Off she went. There was no doubt about her gender. *Raketa* is female in Russian. But she needed to be made complete. While the workers of Votkinsk were busy making the delivery vehicle, another secret factory somewhere else was making the warhead. The explosive, with a destructive power 25 times greater than the one dropped on Nagasaki, would be attached to her at an assembly facility where she would reach her final length of 29.5 meters and weight of 45 tons. A guidance system made in the Ukraine would be installed as her brain, and then she'd be carefully inserted into a launch tube on a massive seven-axel transporter-launcher truck made in the Belorussian Soviet Socialist Republic. That was how the ICBM, code named *Topol* (Poplar tree) by the Soviets, was born.

An artist's rendering of an SS-25 Launch.   US Department of Defense's **Soviet Military Power**.

Slender and fast, she had only her one giant and deadly flower, instead of many smaller innocuous ones like her namesake. Now she was ready to join her 250 sisters distributed around the country at bases in remote areas of the Urals and Siberia, like Yoshkar-Ola, Niznhy Tagil and Barnaul. Joined by a mobile command-post vehicle, the pair would sit in their garage on the base, or meander about the countryside on maneuvers, ready for a command to launch.

Her grandmother was a German. The V2 that whizzed across the English channel 40 years earlier travelled a mere 300 kilometers. Less than a third of V2s launched made it to within five kilometers of their targets. At the end of the war, the Americans and the Soviets raced across Germany to capture the technologies born out of the V2 program. This progeny was a significant improvement. Following a cold launch, in which the SS-25 is ejected from her tube by a burst of gas, her engine ignites and she travels into the upper atmosphere, then across as many as 10,000 kilometers to deliver her warhead to within a few hundred meters of her pre-programmed target.

The Topol has three separate stages of propellant. It's like a relay race, where the first runner is carrying another runner in his arms who is carrying one more runner who is carrying a suitcase. The first runner tires, and the next two carry on until the last runner pushes the suitcase to just the right place in the stratosphere so it can fall to the earth.

The rocket reaches a speed of just over seven kilometers per second — about 20 times faster than a bullet and four times faster than the advanced hypersonic weapons being developed in this millennium. The rocket's speed allows her to break the grip of earth's gravity. It's the exact speed necessary to reach sub-orbital height. If she moved any faster, she'd get stuck in orbit or head into outer space — in either case, useless for defending the fatherland. Unlike future generations, the SS-25 of 1987 had no external guidance system. Onboard equipment calculated her position and compared it to the target that was assigned just before launch.

Once she headed down the tracks away from the portal, an attack on the United States was only one of three scenarios in which she'd ever be likely to see an American again. The Soviets decided to use old SS-20 bases as launch facilities for the SS-25. So they agreed to allow American inspectors to visit from time to time in order to check the radiation emissions from the nosecone. A banned three warhead intermediate-range SS-20 gives off a different radiation signature than a single warhead SS-25. In the third scenario, Americans might get the chance to wave to her as she is driven across Red Square in a Victory Day parade.

HOW NOT TO BECOME A SPY

With the arrival of fall and the first snow, we could look forward to a change of pace and the winter social activity schedule.

Put one ski on each shoe, slide forward on alternating feet. Use poles to keep from falling down. The cross-country skiing instructions I repeated in my head implied little need for grace or coordination, so there was a chance I'd enjoy it. I was gliding through the woods on the edge of town, the moonlight illuminated the paths. It was amplified by the flakes of freshly fallen snow that covered the ground, dappled the branches of the fir trees and made everything seem sharply in focus. The silence was almost complete, except for a light crunching sound coming from under my ski tips and a brief crashing noise when Sofia fell face-down in front of me. I took a moment to regard her posterior, clad in thick but shapely polyester snow pants, before clomping my way toward her and extending my hand.

She giggled as she steadied herself on my arm and stood up. Young Sasha was right behind us.

"You are like a suitcase without a handle, Sofia," he said.

Maria was ahead of us, trying to keep up with Will. He always had to be at the front of the line.

"I'm so glad I put eating ice cream on the *zayavka*," Jane said as we all got inside the warm van. Little icicles had formed at the bottom of her earrings.

"You are turning into a real Russian, Jane," Sofia said. "I thought only we enjoy ice cream when it is so cold outside." Jane and Sofia had become good friends. They found they had a lot in common. Jane was also a single mother.

We entered the Kosmos Kafé, which seemed to be permanently closed to the general public. It was odd, since surely the general public liked ice cream, too. The White Stork cognac that the bow-tied barman kept under the counter would also have been popular.

The glass shelves behind him were nearly as empty as the stools. Still, it felt humanizing to be in a public place, even if there was no public.

We sat down to enjoy our ice cream. One flavor — vanilla. But the barman had shaved some chocolate on top and provided shots of cognac on the side.

"How was your interview this morning, Jane?" Will asked. She had met a reporter from the Washington Post who had gotten permission from the Ministry of Foreign Affairs to come to Votkinsk and interview the inspectors. But he had neglected to get

151

permission from the Ministry of Defense Industry to come to the site, so Jane had met him downtown.

"I think it went very well," she said, giggling. She was prone to giggle, but it usually meant trouble. "I told him all about the snow snakes."

"Snow snakes?" Maria asked.

"Yes, the ones that thrive at minus 20 degrees and live along the perimeter. He was surprised to hear that wasn't the only winter danger. The exploding trees are even more hazardous. I told him I had to remove a large splinter from Lieutenant Taylor's forehead last week."

"Exploding trees?"

"Of course! When the frozen sap begins to thaw ever so slightly, the birch trees tend to explode," Jane said.

"Did the reporter believe all this?" I asked.

"He said he was from Florida. How would he know otherwise?" Jane said. "But I told him there were dangers year round. The moose in heat in the spring are even scarier."

Sofia was translating this for Young Sasha, who seemed distressed by the American disinformation campaign.

"Don't worry, Sasha," Jane said to the perplexed young man. "It's the ugly side of having a free press. Let's drink a toast to our triple date. Just look at us — Will and Maria; Justin and Sofia; ...and you and me..."

Will and Maria looked at each other and grinned. I looked at Sofia carefully to see if she revealed any signs of pleasure at the idea of being on a date with me. She seemed to blush, though the color in her cheeks could have been leftover from the cold. She translated for Young Sasha, calling the "date" a "six-way meeting." We downed the White Stork. It burned momentarily in my throat before spreading its pleasant warmth throughout my body.

My adventure was just beginning. But Sadovnikov's was coming to an end. Though winter was waning, the nights remained long. For the last weekend of February 1990 we had submitted *zayavki* to do our usual activities in town — shopping, ice cream —

but the Soviets rejected them without explanation. We heard from the escorts that protests were expected. It was hard to believe that could happen in sleepy, well-controlled Votkinsk. But from our isolated vantage point it was impossible to judge. Eastern Europe was in upheaval. The final months of 1989 had seen popular protests and the demise of communism in Poland, Bulgaria, Czechoslovakia, Romania and Hungary. The Berlin Wall had been breached, and even the tiny Soviet Republic of Turkmenistan had decided to hold democratic parliamentary elections. The rest of the republics would follow suit in the next 12 months. Civil unrest had become conceivable.

Vladimir Gennadevich had been retired for almost two years. His graying hair and recent weight loss attested to how far the Parkinson's had gone. His overriding goal had been to be useful — to the Party, to the state and to the people of Votkinsk. Now he would sit at home and watch television, overcome with gloom as *glasnost* pelted him with the decline of Soviet power — the "reforms" taking place in the Warsaw Pact countries; corruption at home; the tragedy of Afghanistan; prostitution and crime. His logical part had accepted the new era. It was the will of the Party. His emotions were another story.

At first he was able to reconcile the emerging status quo by combining his faith in the Party with his sense of fatalism. But as time went on, he found that what was left of his ambition and pride were feeding a growing sense of anger and bitterness.

When that February weekend came, the idea of social unrest seemed very real to Sadovnikov. He felt that it could be directed against him in some way. He and his sons sat at home with their hunting rifles loaded, waiting.

"I will be killed first," he told his wife.

"Who needs you, for God's sake?" Elena said, in an effort to soothe him. But it didn't help. His exit from public life had left too many scars.

"There are people who would like to see the end of me," Sadovnikov said.

"You have been watching too much television, Volodya. All of that negative energy is getting to you." But Elena knew his illness was accelerating, fueled by the stress of retirement and the events unfolding around him.

Sensing her thoughts, he said, "It's as if our whole socialist world has a terminal disease, but we only just now found out about it."

"Diseases can be cured, at least most of the time," she answered. "We just have to have the will to face it, not give up, go through the treatment." She didn't know at this point if she was talking about her country or her husband.

"Organs can be operated on, but they are never quite the same afterwards," Sadovnikov countered, shaking his head. "You can even give the patient a transfusion...but the cells themselves cannot be changed."

Sunday came and went without incident. No inspectors in town and no protests.

On Monday morning Vladimir Gennadevich awoke in a good mood. Embracing his wife on the way out of their apartment, he told her he had some papers on his desk that he would like her to look at later. He shuffled slowly along the embankment in the direction of the Palace of Culture. He remembered laying the cornerstone years earlier. Reaching the top step building, he stopped in front of one of the columns that framed the entrance, took a nine-millimeter Beretta automatic pistol from his pocket and fired into his temple. He had loaded only one bullet.

In his jacket pocket there were letters addressed to family, friends and local officials, scrawled in his handwriting — now shrunken by the lack of motor coordination the disease entailed. He asked for forgiveness. He asked that no one be blamed. He was tired of fighting his illness. He said he had done this in the interest of the state.

I learned about Sadovnikov's demise when Colonel Francell and I walked over to the Sixth House. On a table in the lobby they had placed a framed photograph of him, a black ribbon stretched across one corner like a sash.

"That's our former director," Barabanov said. "He did a lot to build our town and take care of us."

"How old was he?" I asked.

"He was 62," Barabanov said. "About the average age of death of a man in our society."

That sad figure would plummet to 57 in the mid-1990s, on the chaos and stress of life after the breakup of the U.S.S.R.

"How did he die?" the colonel asked.

"He had been ill," Barabanov said, but then pointed a finger at his own temple. "He met his end standing on his feet. Just like your Hemingway. About the same age, too..."

"I remember Sadovnikov hosted a welcome meeting at the factory dacha, shortly after we arrived," the colonel said. "It wasn't long before he retired. He gave a toast. Something about how his whole life had been dedicated to building things. How he believed in creation, not destruction, and that now we all needed to believe that building peace and trust was more important than what had been built before. But I sensed he wasn't entirely at ease with what the treaty demanded."

I stopped by Vasilich's shack on the way back from the Sixth House. He was sitting alone, the curtains drawn, a bottle of his grandmother's tea on the table.

"I heard about Sadovnikov," I said. "You must have known him well."

He nodded and poured me a shot. I raised it, assuming we would toast in Sadovnikov's honor, but Vasilich pulled back.

"We don't clink glasses for our deceased," he said. "It's too joyous a sound."

Then he leaned back in his chair, looked beyond me, and said, "Every man needs a purpose. It's not possible to live any other way."

I had a purpose. In order to fulfill it I needed our social program, which was eventually reinstated. The next chance I got, I didn't hesitate to sit next to Sofia on the bus. She seemed pleased. She had been looking out the window blankly, but I saw the reflection of her smile as I moved next to her. We started rolling toward town for Tuesday night skating. The groan of the bus engine facilitated the intimacy of our conversation.

"What do you want to be in the future?" I asked.

"I don't think about the future," she said.

"What do you mean you don't think about the future? Everyone has some vision of themselves in the future."

"I just see darkness."

"Don't you think you'll leave here someday?"

"I don't know. Perhaps there is nowhere left to run to."

I was stymied. I had never met someone who had no dreams. It was so un-American.

We got out at the rink near the stadium. Knight was upset that the rental counter didn't have skates big enough for his oversized paws. He jammed his feet into a pair at least one size too small. Half the town was on the ice, moving in pairs or groups in a circle around the rink as the grating pop music played over a loudspeaker. Even some of the off-duty employees of Department 162 were present.

"Look, there's Maria," I said to Knight.

"Yeah, I know," he answered.

"It's a shame you can't skate with her, since you promised to give me a lesson."

Knight gave me a steely look. "Get out there and try making a few loops yourself," he said, "then I'll show you what little I know."

I stumbled about on the edge, leveraging the chunks of snow at the rim to help maintain my balance.

"It's just like ballet," I said to Sofia, as I caught up to her and Max, who had come straight from school to the rink. "Much harder than it looks."

Her hair was in a long braid that flopped about from under her wool cap. She was kicking a hockey puck back and forth with Max, who had a stick and was pretending to be goalie. I looked at him and realized that the current trajectory I was on would have me playing a significant role in his life. I asked myself if I had the competence to be a father figure. I concluded that whatever affection I could provide would be better than the void he had now. Besides, I thought, I had successfully worked as a babysitter for our neighbor's eight-year-old boy on several occasions. Could being a full-time dad be much more difficult?

"It's not that hard," Sofia said as she came alongside me and locked her arm in mine. I was at first surprised by the statement. Was she reading my mind?

"Let me show you," she continued. "Just point your toes in a bit, and then take turns pushing off..."

I tried not to appear nervous as I entered multi-tasking mode: I didn't want my lack of coordination to become obvious; I didn't want to break my ankle; and I was wondering how we appeared to anyone watching. I spotted Knight on the opposite side of the rotating mass. Maria was leading him. At least I was OK from our side. The goat was now the gardener. I suppressed my fear and began to enjoy Sofia's proximity.

"You're starting to get it," she said.

I continued the conversation we started on the bus. "Why do you have to run anywhere? I mean, maybe you'll meet someone..."

I felt a tugging on my other hand. Max had skated up and taken hold. "I'll help you," he said, his cheeks rosy from the cold. "You can take my stick and use it to support yourself if you start to fall..."

I felt like I was falling. I took his stick. Max slid off on a tangent to a group of boys gathered on the far side of the rink, moving the puck with his skates as he went.

Sofia shouted after him, "Fifteen more minutes, then go home and feed the cat." He acknowledged the command. She turned to me.

"Who needs us? We'd just be a burden."

"Don't be ridiculous. He's adorable. And you…you're a beautiful and fascinating woman."

"You've no idea what you're saying."

I knew exactly what I was saying. I just had no idea what I was going to do about it. But I didn't get a chance to protest.

"Handoff!" Knight shouted as he barreled towards me and grabbed my other arm. Sofia laughed and let go of me, taking the hockey stick just before my new partner began to hurtle me across the ice.

"You need to move quicker," Knight said. "Moving slowly is dangerous — it leads to instability. Anyone observing would notice that. If you move fast, fewer people notice, and you move with more stability. Let's see how fast we can move together," he said as he began to push harder. At first I was able to keep up.

"You seemed to be moving pretty slowly yourself, Will…over there with Maria," I said.

"Well, if you noticed, then I probably was moving too slowly. We both need to move faster."

He accelerated our combined mass. My skates seemed to lose contact with the ice. We were on the outskirts of the crowd, passing like two wild horses. Everything was getting blurry. He looked at me with a demonic smile.

"At some point, you just have to realize you've got what it takes and let go of your fears," he whispered as we rounded a corner.

With that he jettisoned me like a discus right there on the bend. I went straight. There was a brief moment of pleasure as I looked down at my blades cutting neat lines in the ice, a wake of frost flying off.

'Pretty cool,' I thought.

Then everything went black. Well, actually white…and cold. I had crashed into a snow bank at the edge of the rink. It felt good to stop. It must have looked more horrific from a spectator point of view. But I was thoroughly embedded. Shortly, I felt tugging on my limbs. My head popped out of the snow bank and I looked up at those blue, very concerned eyes. Sofia was the first on the scene.

"Are you hurt?"

I shook my head.

"You shouldn't go so fast until you learn to do it better."

"Sometimes," I said, "you just have to have courage and plunge right in."

Our group was the last off the ice. We said goodbye to the escorts, who were going off duty. Only Nikolai was escorting us back to the factory. As we got in the van, I noticed a man alone at the edge of the ice, observing us carefully.

The semi-annual treaty implementation review was taking place at the portal. American and Soviet diplomats and military personnel arrived from Moscow. I stood with Triple A next to Roosevelt and we watched a U.S. general carrying his own luggage as he got out of the RAFik.

"No Soviet general would ever carry his own bag," he said.

It was the little things that helped define each culture in the eyes of the other.

I infiltrated the meeting with my tray of chocolate chip cookies. I had been plotting all day how to get them into Sofia's hands. She was going to be translating for the head of the Soviet delegation. I insisted she take a second one for Max. I thought no one noticed. The officials were still making small talk amongst themselves.

My baked goods were an element of diplomacy as well. Food improves the production of mood enhancing chemicals in the brain. The entire Soviet Union was in a bad mood because it was hard to find enough good things to eat. Perhaps my cookies, now being adroitly grabbed from the tray by negotiators on both sides, would help bring about a favorable resolution to the issues at hand. The colonel used his long reach to snag a second one.

The meeting grew quiet. The general's assistant read the agenda:

1) Unsafe use of the basements by the American side.

2) Unjustified zayavki rejections by the Soviet side.

3) Delayed fulfillment by the Soviet side of the obligation for grounds maintenance.

4) Delays by the Soviet side in providing the necessary support to bring the x-ray machine on line.

Jake read out the U.S. position on the first point: "No significant alterations to the diplomatically inviolable inspector housing, including the basements, have been made by members of the American inspection team. The compressor for the hot tub was wired by a Soviet electrician. It is true that the additional lighting in the poker room and the plug for the coffeemaker in the junior chef's lounge were facilitated by disconnecting Soviet supplied light fixtures, and that the toilet is connected to Soviet water and sewage lines, but these are hardly dangerous modifications."

Uncle Lou was standing next to me at the rear of the room.

"They want to talk about safety?" he said aloud to himself. "I saw the Soviet electrician stand in a puddle of water and use a bare bulb as a test instrument on a 380-volt panel. I felt sorry for the worker who was using a jackhammer without any ear protection while tearing up a section of pavement near the Fifth House, so I brought him a pair of foam ear plugs. He thought they were American chewing gum."

I looked at the Soviets happily munching their cookies. The factory director swallowed and said, "There is some basis for the lieutenant's position."

Beard. James Beard. Baking my way out of international conflict and being publicly appreciated by both friends and enemies in the process. It was a nice feeling and one that a real intelligence officer would never experience...unless he also knew how to cook.

I could see Ray through the window. He was wearing wrap-around sunglasses as he traversed the compound, heading toward Roosevelt. It was an odd sight: a red headed, fair-skinned, black-eyed bat-like creature moving across the white snow, looking like a fashionable winter fox on a mission.

"What is this?" Ray asked, as he entered the kitchen ahead of the delegation.

"It's a cross-cultural display," I answered.

I was still miffed about the canceled *zayavki* and decided to set up a potato protest. We had a bushel of pathetic spuds that Department 162 had sold us from the factory's elite collective farm. With their small size and wrinkled texture, they paled in comparison to the Idaho champions we imported from the base in Germany. I labeled the American potato "Capitalism," the Soviet one "Communism," and displayed them on the edge of the hot table.

"Remove it, A-S-A-P," Ray said. "It's...it's not diplomatic."

I did as instructed.

For dessert I had baked a coffee cake. Fifteen minutes before the meal was to start I grabbed the pan in order to slice my creation, having forgotten it was still hot. It fell to the tiled floor in a crumbly mess.

Chuck ambled over calmly, surveyed the scene and turned to me.

"When was the last time you cleaned the floor?" he asked.

"This afternoon," I answered, not clear how that related to my decimated dessert.

"What was that supposed to be?"

I told him. He pondered for a few seconds and then put his hand on my shoulder.

"My boy, I am afraid you are mistaken. That looks distinctly like a Norwegian Spoon Cake I once made."

"I never heard of a Norwegian Spoon Cake," I said.

"That's because I just made it up...which means for sure no one else has heard of it, so they won't know that this isn't one. Shovel that mess into a big bowl, pour a little vanilla sauce on top and change the menu on the chalkboard."

Chuck told me to serve the cake in order to give the end of the dinner a more formal touch. I placed a generous portion before Sofia. She turned to me, winked, and said thank you. I floated through the rest of the meal. Both delegations expressed their satisfaction with our unique dessert. Ray said it was the best Norwegian Spoon Cake he'd ever had.

Jake stood up and proposed a final toast "to the junior chef, without whom we would not have had a reason to meet today."

"I suppose," the American general said, "if after nearly two years of working together that's the extent of the problems we have with this treaty, then we're doing pretty well."

Alexander Vladimirovich Losev read the resignation letter. Sofia came in to his office before he could summon her and sat down across from him.

"Why do you want to quit?" Losev asked. "You are doing a good job."

She looked out the window toward the lake. A sense of helplessness and shame began to overwhelm her. She felt dirty.

"They want to send me to Moscow when Lifflander will be there on the mail run," she said, her eyes welling with tears. "It's disgusting…they're telling me who I should be with, how I should use my body. I can't take it anymore." The tears fell freely and she began to sob.

Losev thought about the girl's predicament. He had his own problems navigating the intrigues between the security organizations, diplomats and Party leaders. He could imagine how defenseless Sofia felt. He wanted to help her. But he wasn't sure why. His daughter would soon be heading off to get a higher education and then start her career. He hoped she'd find herself doing meaningful work surrounded by good people who helped each other.

"Where will you go?" Losev asked.

"I don't know," Sofia responded, "I haven't thought about it yet." She realized she didn't own a suitcase. Max had managed to destroy the banana box while trying to build a spaceship. But she was sure of one thing: she would never let them control her.

"I'll talk to Shuvalov," Losev said. "You calm down. Take your time to decide what you're going to do. No point in making any sudden moves if you don't have a plan. Perhaps fate will provide another alternative."

She stood up and headed for the door.

"Sofia, do you like Lifflander?" Losev asked, almost as an afterthought.

She turned and looked at her boss with suspicion. If she told him how she really felt it could cause problems for both of them. Before she could decide how to respond, Losev began to answer his own question.

"He seems to be one of the kinder and more interesting ones of the lot," he said. Sofia nodded at Losev. She had talked with Jane about Lifflander. Jane told her he was a good man, worth caring about. Sofia felt a wave of self-confidence building inside. It was small, but enough to help her regain her composure. She thought, 'He is fun to talk to, very adventurous and smart. I feel good when I'm around him.'

"It's necessary to be very cautious," Losev said. Sofia nodded again and closed the door as she went out.

Alexander Vladimirovich wasn't sure if he meant Sofia should be careful about showing her feelings or he should be careful about trying to protect her. Rumors were spreading around Department 162 about Sofia and Lifflander. Losev knew why Sofia had come to Votkinsk and he didn't want to see her get hurt again.

Sofia walked along the embankment toward her apartment. 'My attempt to leave the factory will fail. Alexander Vladimirovich is right. Where will Max and I go? I am doomed to stay in this dreary town for the rest of my life.' Just then she remembered her mother's favorite toast:

"Don't regret what was; don't be afraid of what will be; take care of what you have."

Though Sofia was no good at planning for the future, she knew how to live in the present. That realization gave her some relief.

'And what do I have now? An apartment, my son, brief moments of being with Justin. But how can I get more?' she thought.

Then it hit her: she could play along with Shuvalov and make the situation work to her advantage.

'He wants me to interact with Justin more...so I will. I'll tell Shuvalov at our next meeting that if anything is to come out of a trip to Moscow, there need to be more chances to socialize here. The inspectors keep asking permission to go to the Ural restaurant. Shuvalov will have to tell Department No. 1 to allow it.'

The idea of spending an evening together with Justin made her feel better, even if there was no chance for them to be alone. 'What a strange way to organize a date,' she thought.

A merry group had signed up for the outing to the Ural restaurant. We waited in the RAFik for the escorts to join. I saw Sofia coming our way wearing jeans and a light gray sweater. She was followed by the Frog, who was the senior escort for the evening. Igor Vasilievich was a retired navy officer with a reputation for being inscrutable, despite his broad thick-lipped smile.

"Igor Vasilievich, will we be eating inside the restaurant this time?" Jake asked.

The last time we went to the Ural, they put us by ourselves in a garage in the backyard of the building. We left in protest after the appetizers. Department 162 later explained they were shielding us from "possible hooligan activities." None of us had ever sighted any of these phantoms, but they were used from time to time as an excuse for denying our *zayavki*.

"Yes, Lieutenant, we will eat inside the restaurant," the Frog said from the front passenger seat. I smiled at Sofia, who looked at me and raised her eyebrow mischievously.

The Ural was the only restaurant in town. It should have been a large establishment, serving hundreds of people, with a steady stream of customers coming and going. But it wasn't. It had two rooms, each seating about 35 people, and it was usually half empty. The staff of the restaurant worked very hard to keep it that way. Considering the miserly salary, patrons who didn't tip and the fact that half the food and alcohol was sold out the back door before opening time, it made sense for them to keep the curtains drawn, the lights dim and a sign saying "Closed" on the front door.

It was unlocked for us and we were escorted through the near-empty main room to our table. I wound up with Sofia and Jane on either side of me. The Frog sat across from me with Jake and Thom next to him.

There were clues to confirm it was a functional Soviet restaurant…the cutlery on the table; the triangular napkin scraps; the empty bar at the far end of the room; decorative metal panels on the walls portraying workers eating, planting, manufacturing things.

The waitress came to take our order — though this is not an accurate way to describe the process of obtaining food in a Soviet restaurant. The table was provided with one type-written menu. Of the items on the menu, only about half had a price next to them, indicating it could be possible to order such a dish. Of those, the waitress confirmed only half were available, leaving us with two or three choices. It was more of a process of reporting and agreeing than actual ordering. Vodka was offered. Following the pleading glances of the rest of the other inspectors, Jake gave his approval. Two bottles arrived. The first toast was to having a successful dinner inside the Ural restaurant. The Frog joined in. He was in a good mood.

A middle-aged couple at a table nearby observed our merriment and also tried to order vodka. The waitress told them there was none.

"What about them?" the woman complained loudly. "Where did they get it?"

"That was the last of it," the waitress responded. "We don't have any more."

"What a bunch of crap," the woman shouted at her. "We are people too, bitch. Give us some damned vodka."

"I told you we don't have any. Are you going to order anything else?"

As the woman was midway through an even louder invective-filled retort, a mili-man poked his head out from the door of the kitchen, where he had probably been stationed to keep an eye out for possible hooligan infiltration. The woman got quiet. But she turned to us and hissed, "You have everything and we have nothing!"

Jane looked at me and said, "This is like a college psychology experiment gone wrong."

"Yeah," I answered, "but it's been going on for 70 years."

The waitress went to the couple's table with her abacus and calculated the bill. They paid and left. Our merry mood returned. More toasts followed — to the women present, to the women not present, to our parents and so on down the tra-ditional list. The poorly decorated restaurant began to appear more attractive and warmer. At that moment it seemed like the nicest place in the world.

We took turns telling jokes. Even the Frog shared one: something about *Chukchi* on an airplane. It wasn't very funny but the very fact that he was telling a joke made it hilarious. The vodka helped. If *in vino veritas*, then in vodka there is enlightenment, and often courage. We all guffawed at the Frog's punch line.

Jane complimented him. "Igor Vasilievch, we didn't know you had a sense of humor."

"Here, when we open our mouths," he replied, "we either want to cry or laugh. Only one of those is socially acceptable — in public anyway."

We laughed again. Then I felt Sofia's hand on my right thigh. A wave of emotions swept over me. The first was simply the pleasure of her touch. Then awe at her brav-ery to rise up from our solitary existence and reach out. I had been fantasizing about it, but hadn't found the courage. Was it real? Until that moment we had been falling in love. When you fall, you eventually either crash or soar. She pulled the rip cord and we began to fly. I placed my hand on top of hers and pressed tightly. Then we began to explore each other's hands, legs — everything we could reach that was not in sight. Her courage was as arousing as the feeling of her skin. The loneliness disappeared... I wanted to stand up and slow dance with her to the music playing in the back-ground. At the same time I wanted to run and hide because of the impossibility of the situation. My fear passed quickly. I forced myself to revel in the moment — with no ambition or thought of consequence. Fear and love are antithetical.

We didn't dare look at each other. Had the Frog bent over to retrieve his dropped fork at that moment, it would have been all over. He didn't. It was just beginning.

Sofia and I maintained our upper body positions so as not to reveal what was going on below. My being had suddenly divided in two. One half was far away, conversing, trying to act normally, while maintaining eye contact with everyone at the table but her. But my active consciousness was centered in my hand, roaming around her wrist and gliding across her inner thigh. As my hand stroked hers I felt the softness of her skin. I felt the warmth of her fingertips as she caressed my palm. We held hands for the rest of the meal.

Even the Frog's sharp lines softened, as frequently happens when vodka is present — before the numbness sets in. The next thing I remember was the Frog pointing at his watch, albeit reluctantly. Time to go back to the cage.

Jane was in front of us, heading for the entrance. She paused at the door to the other room of the restaurant from whence the music emanated. She had the magic ability to find humanity wherever she went.

She pried the door ajar, turned to us and said with a joyous tone of curiosity that reminded me of a children's television show host, "Hey, gang, let's see what's going on in here!"

We followed her in. A wedding party was well underway. This is where the rest of the food and vodka had gone.

The newlyweds were sitting at the main table kissing deeply. We joined the crowd in chanting *"Gorko, gorko!"* to emphasize that any matrimonial bitterness can be swept away by the sweetness of a kiss.

The local accordion champion was there belting out all the favorites. Jake danced with the bride; Jane with the groom. I followed the father-of-the-bride's lead and did my best to imitate the *mazurka* in front of the bride's mother. Fortunately, I could not feel my knees anymore.

Thom had been standing in the corner, trading old sailor's stories with the Frog. The mother-of-the-bride approached and conducted Thom to a seat in a row of lovely young ladies. They had hiked up their skirts and were exposing their legs. The blindfolded groom knelt at the start of the line. He caressed the calves and knees of the first girl while she squirmed and muffled her giggles. He shook his head. The crowed egged him on. "Are you sure?" Contestant No. 2—

a similar result; then he lingered at his unseen bride. She smiled but said nothing. His next stop, at Thom's gray furry limb, was brief. "No, no, no, not for another 50 years at least!" the groom shouted, and the crowd roared. The groom then returned to his new wife, and placed his head on her lap.

More dancing, spinning round and round. As the father-of-the-bride and I locked arms, he turned to me and said, "We Soviets don't live…we just exist!" It was said not as a complaint but as an explanation. 'If this is mere existence,' I thought, 'Then I'm OK with it…'

I broke with papa and made my way to Sofia. We swayed with the music. Such joy to her movement, as her long brown hair swung back and forth. We had all passed the psych test: we might be crazy, but we were still human…even the Frog. An exaggerated sense of benevolence is another common side effect of vodka. As I looked at the happy couple, I decided we were all real. Russians and Americans had blended into one molten mass.

A glow emanated from the restaurant as we exited and followed us into the van. Sofia and I looked at each other in the safety of the darkness as our vehicle headed back to the site. I realized my career in espionage was over. For a moment I became anxious. Was I a traitor or just a human put in an inhuman situation? What about my judgment?

I finally understood I wasn't meant to be a spy. I lacked guile. I didn't want to spend my life pretending I'm something I'm not. Although I was having trouble figuring out who I really was, I had felt the passion in her touch. There was no longer any doubt about what I wanted.

Chapter Twelve
Only Blue Push-Pins are Acceptable

'What next?' I asked myself as I brought the knife down on the tomato, using my knuckles to guide the blade in an effort to keep my flesh from being sliced into the salad. This was the culinary school chopping method Tim had taught me. But the stinging sensation told me I had cut myself again. Maybe small chunks of my fingers were going into the salad. 'I hope I'm adding some flavor,' I thought. I was in a fog.

Cuts and burns from clumsy kitchen work were the outward signs of my turmoil. Inside it was worse. I was no longer one, but not yet two. My plan to become Barney Collier had unraveled. They would never let Barney fall in love with an enemy agent and still keep his bag of tricks. I wasn't too upset about my fall from spook grace. I was sure Jack would have understood. Perhaps the same thing would have happened to him if he had been here — at my age, anyway. There was a feeling of relief. I realized I would find more fulfillment in an honest and loving relationship than I would putting LSD in my enemies' cigars and trying to get people to betray their country. Secrecy and duplicity are a spy's defining attributes. I didn't have either of them.

Yet now I needed such qualities more than ever in order to conduct a relationship with Sofia. There is something inherently thrilling about a secret affair. Trying to hide the joy inside, conspiring to make a connection. The subterfuge itself was exciting. When it resulted in a knowing glance or smile from her, it brought just enough relief to keep me going.

Most of all I enjoyed the feeling of caring. It was like obsessing with a new hobby — I found myself thinking about her, when I would see her, what she was doing, was she happy, what her hair smelled like. There were moments of despair at the impossibility of it all. But

I made no effort to resist. What was the point? It's a combination of chemicals, electricity and luck. Besides, I had no concept of surrender.

But the sense of theater was still there. If we were leading normal lives, I thought, then the progression would be clear: a walk in the park on a summer afternoon; a few candlelit dates in Italian restaurants; a vacation weekend in the Bahamas and we might live happily ever after, or not — but at least we would have run the normal cycle of how people get to know each other. It wasn't going to happen this way. I needed to ask permission just to cross the road and she was a pawn in a power struggle between two security organizations. Other than that, everything was easy. What I needed was a plan. I always felt better when I had a plan.

I found Jane and Lou on a bench near the basketball court.

"See what Haley brought me from Thailand!" Jane exclaimed, showing off her left hand. Her finger was adorned by what looked like an ordinary mood ring. "It's a boob stone," she said.

"One of my ex-wives is Thai and I worked there for a while," Lou said. "I've never heard of a boob stone."

"No, really. I asked Haley to get it. If a woman wears it, her boobs grow."

Just to hear Jane refer to her "boobs" was charming enough.

"Do you really think it works?" I asked.

"Sure. You'll see."

"I want to ask you two for advice about Sofia," I said. They smiled like proud parents.

"We could fit her and Max into produce coolers and ship them out on the next rotation," Lou said. "You could unpack them in Frankfurt and walk off into the sunset."

"You know," Jane said in a hushed voice, "I know how to forge a passport."

"I have no doubt," I said. "But I need a more practical approach and I need it now."

"Don't worry," Jane said seriously. "It will all work out OK. You'll both finish your jobs here, and then I'll send Sofia and Max an invitation to visit the U.S. They'll arrive and you can live happily ever after. We'll help you." At that moment, it sounded reasonable. It was Jane's Midwestern brogue that made the fantastic sound believable, as if she was telling a bedtime story.

Regardless of how wacky their ideas were, knowing that I had Jane and Lou to help me was essential to staying sane. And I needed them to conduct my relationship. A team effort at courting was a novel approach but it was the only option. My conversations with Sofia were dragged out for weeks due to the infrequent opportunities to see each other. We passed notes back and forth, with Lou and Jane as the couriers. The relationship took on the feel of a classic romance novel, with chaperones, intermediaries, feuding families and endless pining on the part of the lovelorn. But there was no choice. We had to minimize observable interaction. We believed we were being subtle.

The day after the Ural dinner Sofia traded shifts with Maria and took the morning off. She delivered Max to the kindergarten and cried after leaving him, as she always did. Max had to stay longer than most other kids. It had always been like that. When she was a student and studied for exams Max stayed at the kindergarten all week. They never really had a home together.

'And what's next?' Sofia wondered. The question made her uneasy.

The past was a more comfortable domain. Everything was already known. Nothing to fear. She liked to remember moments she had enjoyed. Today, she would relive last night. The feeling of Justin's hands. She was drawn to his gentle, nervous hands. She wished she could hold them tightly in her own, not hiding from anyone. She could see them walking together, away from the gloomy town. But the vision in her mind refused to become more specific — what were they discussing, where were they going, what happened next? There was no clarity.

'I want to see him more,' she said to herself. 'I will go on his next *zayavka*.' But that could be to the barber. She remembered his concern while trying to instruct the barber during last month's visit.

"Here," he'd tell the female haircutter, pointing to one part of his scalp; "there," pointing to another, "and a little here." Then he'd turn to Sofia and plead, "but tell her not to touch my curls. Tell her I like my curls and I want them to stay."

Sofia liked his curls, too. She wanted to run her fingers through them, caress them. Feel his warmth — it was an alien sensation, foreign. 'He is foreign,' she thought. 'Not from here. He does not belong here and never will. But nobody can forbid me to dream about him.'

She bristled with envy when the barber moved Justin's hair around.

'No,' she thought, 'I will not go with him to the barber. No point in upsetting myself like that. I'll wait for the next *zayavka*. Besides, Igor Vasilievich might have noticed I enjoyed my work a little too much last night.'

Then she remembered Colonel Francell's favorite question. "Who cares?" he would say aloud when trying to put any difficulty in perspective. And he never expected an answer.

We tried our best to differentiate days at the portal. It was futile, but psychologically important. Sundays were days off, unless you were on shift duty or bored and felt like doing your job anyway, in which case Sunday felt like any other day. Saturdays we tried to do something appropriate — a barbecue, weather permitting; movie night when it didn't. On movie nights we continued the tradition started when we lived in the hotel downtown and invited people from Department 162 to join us. Escorts, administrators, and occasionally their family members would sit with us in the downtown hotel building in a small living room on the first floor while we watched movies. It was a cozy activity and made us feel less like social outcasts. The most popular films were "Dr. Zhivago" and "One Flew Over the Cuckoo's Nest."

Our films were not dubbed, so the English speakers in 162 got a chance to hear different accents and learn new words. For the coming Saturday's screening Colonel Francell had wanted to show his favorite movie, "The Princess Bride" — a surprisingly sentimental preference for a warrior of his caliber. But the macho faction of the inspectorate had voted him down. So we were showing "Papillon" — a story about French criminals banished to a remote colony in South America. It seemed an appropriate metaphor for our gilded cage. Department 162 confirmed that escorts would be allowed to attend.

HOW NOT TO BECOME A SPY

I waited in the lobby of Roosevelt trying not to look anxious. I had only seen Sofia once since we were at the Ural. Reports from Lou and Jane were sporadic and inconclusive. Half a dozen escorts arrived, including Sofia. Everyone went to the second floor. While the others were treated to beer, soda and a few games of pool prior to the start of the movie, Sofia and I wandered into the library next to the lounge. I left the door ajar. We sat down at the table.

I pulled out my magic slate from where I had placed it under one of the armchairs and started the dialogue.

HOW R U *(thwit)*

NERVUS, BUT HAPPY. WHAT NOW *(thwit)*

SURVIVE, THEN LEAVE *(thwit)*

WHY U WANT SUCH TROUBLE *(thwit)*

NO TROUBLE-JOY *(thwit)*

THIS IS CRAZY + HOPELES *(thwit)*

STOP BEING NEGTIVE *(thwit)*

I M AFRAID *(thwit)*

ALL BE OK. THE PLAN:

- U TEACH MAX ENGLISH

- KEEP WORKING

- ENJOY EACH'S COMPANY WHEN CAN

- FINISH JOB

- JANE INVITES YOU BOTH TO VISIT U.S.

- WE TOGETHER *(big thwit)*

She took the slate from me.

I LOVE U

My eyes savored her response before a final *thwit* made it disappear. But it was there. I saw it.

Sofia stared at me across the table, her eyes welling up. I wanted to seduce her and unravel her at the same time. She reached her hand across the table and held mine.

I thought to myself, 'the walls have ears but we have defeated them.' Suddenly I noticed the roof had eyes. Specifically, the roof of the Fifth House, not more than five meters across from the window. The camera had rotated in our direction and was peering in at us. I leapt up and dropped the blind, as if that would offer a measure of protection. Sofia gasped and then went to join the other escorts in front of the TV. I came out a few minutes later. The film had already started. Degas's unfaithful wife was standing in the crowd on the street of Marseille, waving goodbye to her husband, who was headed for Guyana.

The next day a new rule was issued by Department 162 about attending the Americans' movies: three to a couch, and no one permitted in the library. The eyes beat us.

Sofia called Shuvalov and agreed on a meeting. Gennady Petrovich was surprised. It was rare for one of the escorts to take initiative. Maybe she had learned something interesting.

"You need to stop the approvals of the *zayavki* for a while," Sofia told him. She concentrated on not displaying her agitation.

"But last time you said I should get Department No. 1 to authorize more!" Gennady Petrovich responded.

"Yes, but since the infraction at the Ural restaurant it will be suspicious if there is not some consequence," she said. "The inspectors had unauthorized socializing with our citizens. They interacted with a wedding party."

Shuvalov thought about what she said. There was some logic to her inconsistency.

"You have the right thinking for our profession, Sofia," he said. "Women are useful in this business."

"We need to make sure nothing looks too easy or obvious," she said.

"I will think about it. Thank you," Shuvalov said. "Now, tell me, have you learned anything new?"

Sofia realized she wouldn't get away without reporting something and thought about what innocuous discussion she should relate.

"Well, he is frustrated by Russian names," she said.

"What do you mean? He doesn't like Russian names?"

"No, it's not that," Sofia said. "We talked about his studies at college and how it took him a long time to figure out in our literature who was who. He calculated that someone with the first name of Alexander could be referred to in as many as seven different combinations."

Shuvalov began to count. *Smirnov, Alexander Petrovich* (last name, first name, patronymic) could be just *Smirnov* to his boss; *Alexander Petrovich* to his children; *Alexander to* acquaintances; *Petrovich* to younger friends; and *Sasha* or *Sanya* to older or closer friends and colleagues. His mother or girlfriend would call him *Shurik*.

"Well, yes, but so what? Was there nothing more?" Shuvalov asked.

"He did admit that he had a code name at one point," Sofia said.

"Ah, that's interesting. When? Was it a specific mission?"

"No, it was in Russian language class. He was called Zhorik," Sofia said.

Shuvalov was disappointed. More worthless information. He was completely frustrated, stuck between the bird-brained escorts in Votkinsk and a paranoid headquarters in Moscow. He already knew Lifflander had a degree in Soviet Studies. That was in his visa application.

But Shuvalov was sensing something in the way she described her discussion with 'Zhorik.' Her eyes seemed to brighten.

"What do you really think about Lifflander?" asked Shuvalov. "Are you developing feelings for him? You should be aware we suspect he is an enemy agent. When he worked at the embassy, he was frequently seen with the CIA chief-of-station."

Sofia calmly returned his caustic stare. "I've lost faith in men. They are all manipulative and selfish," she said.

Shuvalov was satisfied that her mind was in the right place, unaware that the last comment was directed at him and not Justin. But she was scared — scared about where their relationship was going. That was the real reason she asked Shuvalov for a time-out. It had gone too far. She felt something had to change. For now there was nothing but frustration and a near-physical pain that came when she tried to contemplate the future. Still, she fantasized about them being together.

'Now he is all I can think about…how nice it would be to have him next to me for all of my life.'

There was a lull in our social calendar. Regular activities were allowed, but Department 162 did not schedule any interesting trips to surrounding areas or meetings with locals. Those of us who cared about what was going on beyond the site felt cut off. Although we tried to focus on the entertainment available at the site, signs of stir-craziness began to appear. Inspectors were tense and easily distracted. We were accustomed to the routine, but boredom was reaching dangerous levels.

Walking out of the kitchen one day, I noticed something not quite right with the bulletin board. It was now organized. It had been a cozy hodgepodge of information: the daily bulletin; the menu for the day; photographs from social events; interesting articles from the local paper; a postcard from a former inspector or escort. Now it was neatly delineated by border tape. Every field was labeled. Only blue push-pins were in use. Normally my reaction to order would be positive. But the boredom and confinement made me eager to rebel against the clinical appearance of the bulletin board — and my own better judgment.

I was not alone. It became the topic of the day. A choice morsel of conflict that we discussed at lunch and vented our resentment about. There was no doubt as to the source of this anality. Lieutenant Colonel Raymond Blackstone had found himself elevated to the rank of temporary site commander of our remote but strategically significant outpost while Colonel Francell was on an extended trip to Moscow. Ray was mercilessly leaving his imprint. One could imagine him late at night, sitting at his desk, conducting mock inspections with toy missiles and rail cars, humming a Wagnerian tune.

And so Ray decided that all the push-pins should be one color. And the chosen color was blue. And it was very good. Too good for my liking. I proceeded to exchange the blue push-pins that had been uniformly distributed throughout the landscape of the board for the other colored ones, which had been corralled to one side.

This act of defiance was met by indignation on the part of the lieutenant colonel, and silent support from co-conspirators who had the same reaction to Ray's sense of order. Ray retaliated by reinstating the blue push-pins and removing the non-regulation colored pins from public access. This was met by a counter strike — a visit to the warehouse where 13-years-worth of multicolored push-pins were stored. A reimplementation of a non-apartheid bulletin board followed. Ray reinstated his push-pins once more and officially ordered the removal from the warehouse of what was left of the push-pin supply. He took his booty and locked it up in his office.

Left with only blue push-pins, ingenuity kicked-in. At approximately zero-three-hundred hours all blue push-pins were removed from the bulletin board to a secure location in the Lincoln basement where they were expertly spray-painted white.

At zero-seven-hundred the following morning, the gentle breeze that swept the compound carried the soft moan of a man pushed to the brink. The cliché "to snap" is not always accurate. A breakdown can produce many different types of sounds, as simple as a "gurgle" or a misfire, or the sound of a car engine's starter hitting an already rotating flywheel. A buzzing at the base of the skull can be another indication that something is fundamentally wrong. For Ray, the repainted push-pins were an affront to his person and his command.

The push-pin partisan that committed this act of sabotage added insult to injury by assaulting the few spare blue push-pins the lieutenant colonel had foolishly left in a push-pin case near the board. Ray frantically tried to replace the sabotaged white-cum-blue push-pins with genuine blue ones. But as he tempted to drive them into the board, he discovered that they had had their pins neatly clipped by a Hughes-issued wire cutter. The emasculated pins fell to the floor with a nerve-racking tinkle.

"Sir, could you please repeat that order?" Lieutenant Jake asked.

"I'll say it slowly, lieutenant," Ray hissed through gritted teeth. "I want you and Captain Knight to move my desk into the hallway so that I can have a continuous line of sight to the bulletin board at the end of the corridor. I will take the first watch, from now until 1400 hours; I'd like you to inform the captain that he will be on the second watch, which will end at 2400 hours, and then you will be on the third watch, until 0-800 hours."

"And what exactly are we watching for, sir?" Jake asked.

Ray looked at Jake like he was an idiot. "Bulletin board saboteurs, of course."

Having again re-colored the un-castrated pushpins with a regulation-blue magic marker, a seething Lieutenant Colonel Ray sat behind his desk at the end of the darkened corridor and waited for the enemy to show himself.

But in every war there is the risk of collateral damage. Uncle Lou, unaware of the current status of the conflict, wandered up to the bulletin board. As he was getting his reading glasses from his pocket, Ray snuck up like a Viet Cong in sneakers. He gave Lou a swift kick in the rear. Lou turned to defend himself. But seeing Ray's inflamed countenance and the foam forming at the edge of the officer's mouth, he thought better of it. Ray mumbled something about damage to government property and went back to his post.

Lou went off to formulate his own retaliatory strike.

Later as the lieutenant colonel sat at his desk in the hallway, he drafted a new site policy, which he published on OSIA letterhead and posted on the bulletin board:

"*MEMORANDUM for ALL U.S. INSPECTORS*

Portal Monitoring PL-23-18-90

Votkinsk, USSR 2 April 1990

Subject: Bulletin Board Policy

1. Purpose: The bulletin boards are for the purpose of providing information for on-site personnel.

2. Changes: Changes to the information on the bulletin boards will be ONLY by the express approval of the Site Commander or Site Manager.

3. Uniformity: Every effort will be made to retain uniformity on the bulletin board including one color of push-pins, proper alignment of each item to preclude a junky appearance and other steps to facilitate the efficient use of space.

4. Types of information authorized: At no time will obscene or vulgar words or pictures be placed on the bulletin boards. No one is permitted to write on any item or make a written comment about any item already posted on a bulletin board.

6. Defacing: Defacing push-pins or any item placed on the bulletin board is an irresponsible and cowardly act. As such, it must be punished through disciplinary action.

7. It is the joint and final authority of the Site Commander and Site Manger to determine the color of push-pins and the appropriateness of content on the boards, assess the proper trimming of items and to take disciplinary actions related to offensive or inappropriate behavior regarding the bulletin boards.

Signed,

Ray B. Blackstone

LTC, USA

Acting Site Commander"

Uncle Lou had decided to use art therapy to mitigate the traumatic emotions brought about by Ray's assault on his posterior. Francell returned from Moscow to find a giant blue push-pin — made out of an empty wire spool and a section of pipe — impaled in a waning snowdrift at the entrance to Roosevelt. He read the memo, which was held in place on the bulletin board by four rather shabby looking blue push-pins. Then he summoned Ray for a chat.

I went looking for Jane. The longer I went without seeing Sofia, the darker my mood became. I needed to bathe in Jane's light. It emanated from her on an invisible wavelength, but I could feel its warmth when we talked. It wasn't something I completely understood at first. But over time, while talking to her or observing how she interacted with others, I began to notice it. It came from her intense sincerity. When she listened, she was completely focused. When she spoke, you had no doubt she believed what she was saying, no matter how silly or odd her train of thought might be. She was incapable of saying anything bad about anyone. At worst, she might make an observation about something she thought wasn't right. And then only if prompted. Most of the time she'd carry you along on her wave of kindness, until you were washed of concern. At one of my lower moments, she asked me if I liked Mark Twain.

"Of course," I said.

"Didn't he say something like, '70 percent of my life is spent worrying about things that never happen'? Everything will work out, you'll see."

I thought about it, and instantly felt a little better. She was the ultimate counselor.

I needed a dose of Jane's humor and consolation and needed to know if she had heard anything from Sofia. The restricted social program was limiting the chances for interaction. Entering Roosevelt, I heard voices coming from the second floor and went up to the TV lounge.

Haley, Lou, and a few other guys were deciding which movie to watch. As I entered, the lights flickered due to a power surge at the factory.

"I guess Darlene just fired up Thunder Dong again," Haley said. Everyone laughed. Beyond the occasional comment like that, the male-female relations at the portal were polite. But that didn't change the genetically programmed fact that the human male evaluates every female he comes across as a potential mate. We develop a matrix of appropriate reactions and behavior. The few women we had — Jane, Darlene, the rare female three-week mutant — received our courtesy and respect. The matrix held.

But Jane was a wild card. Healer to all, friend to many. No one would admit to thinking of her in other than a maternal way.

What's more fun than half a dozen guys lightly buzzed on beer sitting around after watching an R-rated movie? Probably a lot of things. Jane wandered into the Roosevelt lounge, lightly made-up, dressed in a blue pantsuit and her usual funky earrings.

"What have you been watching, guys?" She asked. Her effervescence lit up the room.

We had just finished the latest James Bond movie. The secret agent was battling Soviet intelligence officers and arms dealers. I just couldn't get into it. Jane went up to the VCR to see which movie we had watched.

I sat in an armchair stroking the beer can and observing Jane. My eyes paused for a moment on her figure. Something wasn't right. I continued to stare. It might have been the warm beer or the cold night but I became convinced her breasts had grown. I compared the current image to the last one on file. No, I thought, I must be mistaken. But there it was in Technicolor. An increase of not less than two cup sizes. My matrix had crumbled. This was followed by a feeling of Freudian guilt for being interested in her body in the first place.

Jane left us to our miserable selves. We sat around in an eerie silence. I looked up to notice the same confused expression on my colleagues' faces, as if six matrices had all collapsed at once. I didn't have the courage to comment for fear of public recrimination. Fortunately others in the group were less timid. Lou broke the silence.

"Hey, did you guys notice anything different about Jane?"

"You mean her tits?" Haley asked.

"Yeah, they got bigger," I chimed in.

"I thought it was just me and my eight weeks on site!" said Lou. "Jeez, thank God I'm not going crazy! But how can it be?"

The answer could be found downstairs in Jane's office where she was laughing and tossing crumpled toilet paper in the garbage can as she handed Darlene back the borrowed brassiere.

After a few weeks, Department 162 decided to let us out of our cage. We got tickets to the cultural highlight of the year. A packed house at the Palace of Culture came to see the Udmurt championship of accordion music. Twenty-one accordionists in two hours. It was like living through two dozen consecutive Polish weddings. Contestants came from all over the republic and were mostly middle-aged and older men. Farms and factories alike were represented. The competitors chanted *chastushkhi* — Russian folk limericks — often racy, sometimes political, as they pumped the moaning box slung around their shoulders, their fingers twiddling up and down the diminutive keyboard.

After the intermission, the "Miss Advertising" contest began. Factory management had decided it had to have a modern approach to promoting its burgeoning civilian production. The consumer goods in its portfolio included folding chairs, tools, a TV-sized plastic box with a whirring motor called a *Feya* (Fairy) that was supposed to wash your clothes, and the famous Votkinsk baby carriages — which were assembled in a workshop that used to make SS-20 parts.

A dozen young beauties gathered to compete. They glided across the stage in evening gowns and bathing suits, and recited sales pitches in French, German or English ("Please buy nice foldink chairs"). Each gave a brief interview about her dreams and aspirations. The winner was to receive a scholarship to attend one of the new marketing academies in Moscow and a job in the factory's sales department.

I was sitting next to Young Sasha. Our relationship was not going well. I wanted to be friends but had begun to suspect he had another agenda. Our conversations mimicked Nikolai's "humint" lessons. Sasha would ask me questions about myself, my family and my plans, which I would freely answer. My questions were always dodged.

Once, we took a tour boat ride on the Votkinsk Lake. The captain was an amicable old man, happy to satiate my curiosity. He told me the history of the town, the lake, the Tchaikovsky estate and the dam that served as the northern border of the main factory. Sasha made a point of hovering closely, scowling as I asked the captain questions.

"Did you get all the information you need for your report?" he asked as we disembarked. I was annoyed by his suspiciousness.

"Yes, all the secrets of your 230-year-old dam are now revealed. I can draw the blueprints myself," I said.

I had been in Russia long enough to understand that the people, by nature, are open and friendly and enjoy sharing their passions and frustrations. I didn't accept provincial xenophobia as an excuse for Sasha's behavior. Maybe he was also torn between genuine affection for me and his tasking.

That day in the Palace of Culture I finally realized who I was dealing with. During a lull, Sasha turned to me and said, "Justin, where is Greg working now?"

Greg was in one of the first groups of inspectors, but had been fired. The rumor was that our counter-intelligence guys had taken him out because they discovered some ambiguities in his income tax history. Greg was later found in a Las Vegas hotel room with his cancelled diplomatic passport on the night table next to his bed. He had shot himself in the head. If Young Sasha had been chummy with Greg I suppose the inquiry would have been justified. But it was stilted — obviously an item on Sasha's list for the day.

"The least you could do is warm me up a bit, maybe offer me money," I snapped at him.

"How much?" he asked, trying to maintain composure.

Our conversation ended. A few months later he dropped out of site. Shortly thereafter Lenin's Way ran a story about an unnamed Votkinsk youth who had been sent to study at the KGB Institute in Moscow.

Using the small banya at the Votkinsk public pool was one of our regular activities. It was reserved for the inspectors on Tuesday nights. Usually half a dozen inspectors would join the outing. But with the arrival of spring there was less enthusiasm. This time only Uncle Lou and I signed up for the *zayavka*. The assigned escorts were Sofia and Anatoly, who we no longer called Triple A.

Anatoly's work with the Americans, combined with what he saw going on around him, had changed his outlook on life. We had scratched through to his humanity thanks to our luggage-toting generals, cookies and camaraderie. But he was also undergoing his own metamorphosis, like many members of that final generation of Soviet youth.

I realized how far his transformation had come when we were strolling downtown one day. He was giving me tips on how to take better photographs. Photographing the factory was forbidden, but on one side of it was a church and on the other the anchor and the Tchaikovsky estate. I stood facing the main building.

"Can you take a picture of the Lenin statue for me, with the older part of the town center in the background?" I asked.

"Why do you want him in your shot? He's clearly confused," Anatoly said.

"You seem to have reevaluated your reverence," I said.

"I was visiting my grandmother at her *dacha* recently," he answered. "She's become quite religious. She was describing what faith meant to her and as she spoke I realized she might as well have been describing the Party. Their propaganda slogans calling for more work, greater discipline, vigilance — there is only emptiness behind them. When you dig deep, there is nothing rational or specific, or even intellectual, to be found."

Anatoly said he had a cold and wasn't going to use the banya that evening. He brought along a slide projector to show some of his recent photographs of nature and architecture in and around Votkinsk. One of the local teachers joined us so he could practice his English.

Lou took the hint and kept the other two men busy with conversation. Sofia and I went into the sauna. If any intelligence service on the planet had developed a microphone that could function in the heat and moisture of a sauna, it would be the KGB. But we decided to risk it.

"We need to make a plan," I said.

She didn't respond to my statement, but instead put her hand on my knee and smiled.

"When can you quit?" I asked, struggling to concentrate.

"It's not that simple," she said, stroking my leg. My breathing got heavier. I couldn't tell if the rise in temperature was due to us or the banya. "The only way I can get out of my contract with the factory is if a family member is dying, I get pregnant, or married."

"There isn't enough room in here to manage the second of those options," I said, as I pulled her closer. "How about if I put in a *zayavka* to go to the marriage registry office and request you as the escort?"

"I suspect it would be rejected and neither of us would be seen again."

I drew close to her ear and whispered, "So tell them you have a dying relative." I kissed her neck. The eucalyptus oil in the steam mixed with her salty aroma. She tasted like an exotic tea.

"I'd need a document proving it. I might be able to convince them I have a fiancé in Moscow."

"It wouldn't be a lie," I said.

I thought about kissing her lips but I was afraid to lose myself. And I was thinking about what was going on just beyond the door.

I wanted to say in Russian, "May I kiss your lips?" But what came out was, "May I kiss your sponges?"

Sofia laughed. Thom had a similar linguistic faux-pas on International Women's Day when he went to the escorts to play them a song. He wanted to say in Russian, "I dedicate this song to all women — *with a capital W.*" But instead he said, "*with a big ass.*"

She brought her lips to mine. It was a hot and nervous kiss like the kind you get during your first game of spin the bottle. But the stakes were much higher than just our parents coming home. If the door opened and Anatoly saw us embracing he'd have to report us, despite his reformation.

We regained our composure and went out. The men were engaged in a fascinating discussion about the names of different types of trees. I couldn't focus. All I could think was, 'I want more of that.'

Chapter Thirteen
Goats, Grass, and Goodbyes

I was moving away from the factory. It was twilight, but not at all eerie. As I left the site, I noticed that the flamingoes had changed their position and were now facing south as if they were watching the spring skies for the return of their kin. I flew past the rail yard, through the last intersection, down the hill into Gavrilovka. Flowers on the windowsills inside the *izbas* were beginning to bloom. A lone fir tree stood in a field on the right, its branches waving gently in an unfelt breeze. Now moving over the creek. Ice fishermen had traded their plastic tarps for hip waders. Motorcycles with side cars had reappeared and were being washed along the bank. No one seemed to notice me. I was going to make it this time. My will pushed me forward. I was at the bottom of the hill now. I passed the Kosmos Kafe on my left and concentrated hard as I accelerated up Ulitsa Pugacheva. Then it began to fall apart. First a mist, then brightness. Before I reached the traffic light everything dissipated. I was back in my room in the Lincoln building.

My efforts to take out-of-body trips to Sofia's apartment were not succeeding. I had explained to her how it worked. All she needed to do was concentrate on my arriving in the middle of the night, while at the same time I meditated and visualized the journey from the site to her building. She'd feel my presence and I'd at least be able to see her. It had happened to me once when I was a child. I had a high fever. I floated out of my body and hovered on the other side of my room for a few moments. It was possible to induce spiritual travel. You catch the wave at just the right moment of relaxed semi-consciousness — like body surfing. But, when trying to make it to Sofia, as I got closer to the intersection and my excitement grew, my concentration would always fail.

This attempt at escape was made at the end of a hard night. The bad dream I had before attempting spiritual travel made me forget about the challenges of my love life. In the dream I was cutting the grass around the site. It was already a meter tall. The garden tractor started to move more and more slowly. Every time I turned around I could see the grass I had just mowed beginning to grow again. By the time I got more than a few meters along, it was back to the height it had been.

I got out of bed and went to the window to look at the sun rising over a purple cloud in the distance. The flamingoes had turned to face south but they were barely visible on the overgrown lawn. The thought of cutting that grass depressed me. It was a sign of defeat in battle in an otherwise victorious Cold War. I sensed that the U.S. side's resolve could weaken. We would surrender this tit for that tat, and I would find myself outside, turning the jungle into our front lawn. It would take at least a week to chop down the grass and gather it. The mower was already useless. Did we have a flame thrower in the *sklad*? I thought perhaps I might be exempted from the task by claiming my spring hay fever would make the job medically hazardous for me. I went to Jane to consult.

"You don't need an excuse," she said. "You need a goat."

"What?" I asked. I couldn't make the association between a goat and my current problem.

"A goat is a very loyal pet. It's intelligent, friendly, can be trained…and it would be happy to mow the lawn for you."

I began to imagine a small herd of goats, perhaps eight or 10, munching in formation across the yard, leaving a swath of neatly trimmed grass and several kilos of turds. It was easier to shovel turds then hack and gather grass. Her idea seemed logical.

"Do you have experience with goats?" I asked.

"Of course! I grew up on a farm in Michigan. I learned to care for a whole bunch of different animals," she said.

I had a faint recollection that the last version of the story of her childhood had her growing up in a city. But I couldn't remember for sure. Jane's exaggerated selflessness made it impossible to get any significant information about who she really was.

I had already tried my luck with pets at the portal. There was a stray dog and her two puppies who befriended me and my kitchen leftovers. Eventually, the mother disappeared mysteriously. Then the pups abandoned me. For a while I took it personally, though my colleagues assured me that they were brain damaged. They had run through the x-ray machine on several occasions when it was being tested. Now the pups taunted me from time to time, lingering near the perimeter of our site, in places I wasn't allowed to go. They would howl or yap and then disappear. No temptation of food or affection could get them to re-defect, even though I had controlled my rage when they chewed up the contents of my humidor while living in the basement during the winter.

I decided to take Jane's advice and acquire a friend and co-worker at the same time. I went to see Colonel Francell.

"May I get a goat?" I asked.

"I am rotating out in a week," he said calmly, without raising his eyes from the paperwork on his desk. I got the point. He was a man with extensive reserves of patience. It was a characteristic necessary to deal with the frustrations of trying to succeed on a mission that depended on the whims and competencies of a long chain of bureaucrats in not one but two governments. It was also a key skill for his later service as a senior United Nations weapons inspector working on the program to disarm Iraq. He was given the assignment of destroying any weapons of mass destruction that were found, even though he and most of the members of his department had already determined there were none. "I'm the Maytag man," he would say, describing the role.

I interpreted his disinterested response to my goat acquisition request as a "yes, after next week." There are no specific references to pets in the treaty or any of its protocols. Gorbachev used to say, "That which is not prohibited is allowed."

I started joining the Sunday morning *zayavka* to the local farmer's market. No one commented as I got into the RAFik several weeks in a row with a cardboard box, a small blanket, a slightly used dog collar and a leash.

Food supplies in general and goats in specific seemed to be disappearing from Votkinsk. I made my way to the livestock area of the market. A few piglets, the occasional chicken, a plethora of rabbits. But no goats. After my third visit I found three lovely kids. Fluffy, and not very malodorous. The *babushka* insisted they were already sold. I suspected a conspiracy. I could imagine a black Volga sedan pulling up to the market a half hour before we arrived, old ladies and their goats herded into the back seat and trunk, respectively, then hauled off for questioning.

Thom said he thought the goat plan was a winner.

"I can see you leading a small herd of them beasties across the yard," he said as he reclined on the couch in my basement office one morning after breakfast. "You've got a

stalk of grass between your teeth, and you're calling each one by its given name, shouting words of encouragement as they bring the lawn under control and help eliminate a
contentious point of treaty implementation. Perhaps the diplomats will create a special
commendation in honor of four-legged creatures working for world peace."

He easily conjured images in his poet's mind, which as of late had been laboring
over a new song. The song would have nightingales in the background. I knew this
because I had helped him surreptitiously record them. It was a small operation but I
was glad to have been able to put my core skills to use in his creative process.

Thom somehow got a contraband tape recorder past the customs inspection.

"I've never heard nightingales before," he told me when he summoned me to the
sklad late one night. "They are out there beyond the fence every night, singing away.
It's friggin beautiful."

I went to the "D" shelf. Haley had the smaller items arranged alphabetically. I
took a roll of duct tape and began to secure the recording device to Thom's naked
chest.

"It's an interesting sensation," he said with a grin.

"Just wait till we take it off," I said.

He suddenly looked terrified.

"Don't worry," I said. "We'll do it in the basement. No one will hear your
screams. I'll give you a shot of whiskey to dull the sensation. Besides, aren't artists
supposed to suffer?"

This seemed to reassure him. At about 3 a.m. we met in the Lincoln lobby and
made our way to the edge of our zone. We heard the gentle whirr of the cameras as
they tracked us. Once we approached the fence, Thom opened his coat, grabbed his
left breast as rehearsed, and pressed the record button. We stood there for about 10
minutes taking in the concert. The birds were rejoicing at the arrival of spring. Then
the miliman, who had been roused from his sleep by our presence, exited his shack
next to the Fifth House and began to make a nonchalant tour around the oval. He
paused when he got to us.

"They sing so beautifully," Thom said to him. "It's a sin to sleep through it." The
miliman smiled and headed back to the shack, satisfied we weren't making a run for it.

Thom finished his song a week after we made the recording. He now put the bird
tape on in the background as he sat down on my couch and prepared to press play.

"It's called 'Molenie o Lyubvi,' or 'Prayer for Love,' " Thom said as he stared at me intently. "Do you get it?"

"You mean the birds are praying for love?" I asked.

"No, I am," Thom said. "It's a play on words. Lyubov means love and Lyubov is my love…"

Whereas I had been courting Sofia, Thom had fallen head over heels for Lyuba, whose full name was Lyubov. It wasn't hard for him to find ways to spend time with her. In addition to social events, where a translator was always needed, he had his props and excuses — a spontaneous guitar lesson or concert at the escort house; an urgent need to check a translation. Whatever worked. It was amazing we found time to implement the treaty with all the romantic machinations going on. INF didn't stand for Intermediate Range Nuclear Forces, but International Nuptial Facilitator.

As Thom started to strum, the phone rang. It was Lieutenant Jake.

"Justin," Jake said, "we just spotted your former puppies chasing a herd of goats through the traffic measuring device. They're moving in the direction of the factory."

Had it been Jane calling, I would have suspected a set-up. But even if it was, what did I have to lose? I grabbed the collar and leash. Thom followed. As I ran past the DCC towards the portal I saw a herd of 20 goats moving casually across the tracks. Not so unlikely, since the secret missile factory was surrounded by woods and farmland on all sides. Clearly a farmer had let his herd loose with the expectation they would find their way back. This time he'd be minus one…if he bothered to count them.

My quest for companionship was near an end. The Soviet escorts watched with amusement from the front portico of the Sixth House. The goats trotted nervously away along the wall. My former dogs must have tipped them off as to my boundaries. The herd headed closer to the door of the factory entrance.

I shouted "*Mozhno?*" (May I?) at the escorts, but my feet were already moving. Thom and I were joined by several escorts in the ensuing goat rope. I cornered an attractive black-and-white female kid in front of the factory door. She bleated with displeasure as I held her and tried to get the collar around her squirming neck.

Looking up, I realized I was now standing in a place where no American had been before. I could have rung the doorbell. While two recently arrived milimen looked on, Rocky, the senior escort on duty, approached me. His normally jovial expression had been replaced by a "something-terrible-is-happening-in-my-life" look.

I cradled the goat in my arms and began walking back toward Lincoln. She calmed down. Clearly we were meant for each other. Rocky pointed to the curtained window on the third floor of the Sixth House, alongside which we were now standing. "They said you have to let it go."

Did I want to go down in history as the first treaty inspector to be declared persona non grata for capturing a host-country goat in a forbidden area? What if that got into the local press? I could see the headline in Lenin's Way: "Are Our American Friends Too Lonely Out There?" If only the goat had wandered into one of our diplomatically inviolable buildings, I could have offered it asylum.

"Let it go?" I asked.

Rocky nodded affirmatively. I placed her on the ground, undid the collar and watched her trot back to the herd. As I walked toward my basement I composed a classified advertisement in my head for the paper. "*Resident of Votkinsk interested in purchasing your goat. Will pay top ruble. Meet at the market on Sunday at 10:00. Purchaser will be smoking a cigar.*"

We were on the bus again. I had told myself I wouldn't sit next to her. But I couldn't resist. I just wanted to feel her leg next to mine. I imagined we could command our flesh to seep through the spaces between the fibers of our jeans and make contact. Then a moment of paranoia ensued. I glanced around to see who might be observing. Nikolai, the escort leader, was a few rows ahead, seemingly oblivious. Only the driver could see us in the mirror. The dearth of traffic didn't require him to keep his gaze fixed on the road all the time. I couldn't tell what part of us he could see. I tried to remember from my bus driver days. When I looked in the mirror it was to see if any projectiles were coming my way. And the school bus seats had lower backs.

"Welcome to Sharkan, the Switzerland of Udmurtia," said Emilia Timofeevna, as she boarded the bus. She was the Party chairman of a settlement 20 kilometers north of Votkinsk. She and the mayor, who called himself Mike, joined us at a road sign that indicated we had finally made it to a corner of the region that the escorts had been telling us was unique for its beauty.

"I hope that phrase will be added to the sign someday," Emilia said as she sat down. She was in her early 50s, with primly coiffed platinum blond hair and a long dark trench coat.

"We are very pleased you have come to visit us," she continued, after the driver handed her a microphone. "Ours is an agricultural settlement. The city center is very modest."

There were half a dozen structures, including a bread store, a general store and the town hall. In less than one minute we had driven across the heart of her metropolis.

"The population of Sharkan is 70 percent ethnic Udmurt. They mostly live on six collective farms and grow grain and potatoes. Livestock is also raised. People live simply but without want. Houses are small wooden structures without indoor plumbing. Food is plentiful, and there is enough machinery to support the work. Our first stop will be for lunch at the Kukui Collective Farm."

The barely paved road took us through vast fields, alternately fallow or colored by yellow flowers and lone haystacks. We turned onto a dirt track that led to the farm administration building.

The entire population, with freckled faces and broad smiles, had turned out to welcome us. An Udmurt band in native dress serenaded us as we disembarked. Their clothing consisted of bright green and red woven wool. The patterns looked Native American. A group of seven women in flowing skirts, colorful head scarves and traditional Udmurt breast plates made up of silver coins, chanted and jangled in time with the accompanying accordions as we made our way through the crowd into the dining hall. Farmers and their families peered over fences and through windows with intense curiosity at the strange creatures in sport coats and neckties.

Our host, a middle-aged man with auburn hair and blue eyes, stood at the head of a long table obscured by copious amounts of food and drink. "My name is Vilston Sharikov, director of the Kukui Collective Farm. I am happy to greet such honorable visitors who have come from far away to promote peace and friendship."

Captain Knight made an appropriate counter toast and we sat down. The menu was made up of local delicacies. Jellied meat, garden snails and sliced tongue appetizers were followed by fish head soup. An entire roasted suckling pig sat in the middle of the table, staring at me until his time came. The one local dish I enjoyed was the *perepechka* — a tasty cross between a miniature pizza and a quiche.

"Probably you are wondering about my name," said Vilston. "My parents were admirers of your President Vilson, who founded the League of Nations after the first war. But the radio announcer mispronounced his name, and so I am Vilston."

"But I consider myself fortunate to be named after such a man. I have friends whose parents named their children in honor of our founding fathers and their work. I know one man whose name is Vladilen, which is short for Vladimir Ilyich Lenin. And another poor soul called, Dazperma! It's an acronym for 'Long Live the First of May!' "

As we drank toasts in everyone's honor, tongues became loose. Vilston lamented the limited contact between our two countries. He was convinced all people of the world should sit at the same table, as we were now, and get to know each other. We supported his sentiments with more toasts.

"I am pleased by the direction Comrade Gorbachev is taking," Vilston continued. "I must thank him for his courage and strength in promoting reforms and changes, like those that have brought us together. There are people around him, particularly in the military, who are opposed to such progress. I have no use for such bastards. They would have us making more and more weapons. They believe we cannot live in peace."

Nikolai cringed and said, "So, what should we do instead of making rockets?"

The farm director turned to him. "How about making more tractors?"

Vilston was the fearless master of his own world. What could they do to him? Send him to work on a collective farm?

Vilston was the master of his realm.

Emilia stayed on the farm while Mike went with us to the next phase of the tour. We abandoned our bus in favor of a 'crocodile' — a large green truck with benches in a rear cabin sitting on top of six puffy tires. It easily navigated the rutted road. We drove deep into the woods. Finally, we stopped at the edge of a vast field. Hundreds of people had gathered to celebrate the end of spring planting. We had travelled back in time. They arrived on horse, by ox cart, by tractor and on foot. It was the Udmurt equivalent of the Scottish Highland games. Tug-of-war, three-legged races, log-balancing contests and other activities were in progress across the field, interspersed by families having picnics. We shed our coats and ties and began to mingle.

Will volunteered to participate in the triathlon. He and a dozen Udmurts were poised on rickety bicycles at the top of a hillock. The starter's pistol sounded. They charged down toward a small pond, where they abandoned the bikes and dove into the murky brown water. A 50-meter swim was followed by a dash around the field. As Will struggled to get his shoes on, blood streamed from his heel.

"Must have stepped on some glass in the water," he muttered as he took off. No replacement part available for that elephant-sized paw. His pale hulk, half-limping half-running, was in stark contrast to the other contestants — small, well-tanned farmers who bounded through the grass as gracefully as gazelles. Will crossed the finish line in third place. The crowd gave a loud "Oo-Rah!" He collapsed, his white sneaker stained green and red. Maria propped him up and fashioned a bandage. A wiry old man who had taken first place came and hugged Will and shook his hand.

"Are you injured?" he asked, grinning a toothless grin.

"Nothing terrible," Will answered with a wince.

A few moments later the champion returned with a vodka bottle.

"This is the best medicine we have," he said, passing it to Will. The captain downed half in three gulps before passing it back to the champion, who then finished it off.

"You Americans are more or less normal people!" remarked the champion, before going back to his family.

We helped Knight into the vehicle and set out for the last leg of the journey. The drive took us across a barren brown wasteland. Mike said it was a potato field. Then the landscape abruptly switched to a deep green. We were chugging up and down increasingly steeper slopes. We came to a stop at the base of a massive green bump — something between a large hill and a small mountain. The slope was dotted with tall fir trees. The crest appeared as a soft grassy mound in the distance. At last we understood the association with Switzerland. We had reached Kar-Gora, the first foothill of the Urals.

"The local population finds magic in this mountain," Mayor Mike said. "It has a spring whose water bubbles from within and brings health and good fortune to those who drink from it. My grandparents always told me that those who come here with open hearts and good intentions will see their wishes granted and their dreams come true."

We scrambled up the hillside and paused at the top to survey the expanse before us. No town or road was visible for as far as we could see. Just broad green fields interspersed with patches of brown earth and trees. We trudged single file through a wooded area before coming out onto a plateau. It was a field laced with small yellow flowers. A picnic had been set up for us by the manager of the potato farm. A short man with a big belly and thick glasses, Vasily Andreevich, proudly introduced us to the gathering of friends and relatives who had assembled this feast in the middle of nowhere. The last to be introduced was the Armenian shish kebab chef, who waved to us through the fragrant smoke of his improvised open-pit grill. The spring formed a small brook, which ran through the plateau. Where the brook ran closest to the picnic blanket a dozen bottles of Vodka were corralled, keeping cool.

The toasts began in earnest. The round *lavash* bread was ripped and passed along. We nibbled on fresh greens as glasses were filled.

"Well, I was right all along," Vasily said — more to the locals than to his visitors. "The Americans do not have horns and tails. And I sincerely hope they have come to the same conclusions about us..." He spoke as if the topic had been debated by the group just before we showed up.

Will reciprocated. "Indeed, as an intelligence officer, I can confirm my own discovery — we have found that there are no bears wandering the streets, despite the stereotype held by my countrymen. Instead we are embraced by humans whose hearts overflow with generosity and warmth."

His eloquence was enhanced by the 'medicine' he had received from the triathlon champion. It could have been the heat of the sun beating down or Maria's smile as she stood by his side translating, but to me at that moment Will seemed softer, smoother — no longer the angular apparition I first encountered at OSIA headquarters.

Vasily, who had been looking at Will with beagle eyes and listening intently to the toast, nodded his head. He was clearly moved.

"*Yo my yo*! (Me oh my!)" Vasily exclaimed. "That is so beautiful, Will, just beautiful. Thank you."

A cigarette and soccer break was declared between the appetizers and main course.

Sofia and I took the opportunity to stroll. We walked a few hundred meters to a nearby clearing of tall grass. We were still in earshot of the group but could view the beautiful landscape without worrying about who was watching us.

"I'm not sure how much more I can take," I said as we sat down. "I'm only 24 and I feel like I'm in prison here. These moments aren't frequent enough. I want to live like a normal person with you."

"Me, too," she said with a sigh. "It's getting more difficult. Last month they asked, 'How do you think he feels about you?'"

"What did you answer?" I asked.

"Well," she said, "I know the answer. But I said nothing. I'm afraid they want to use it against us somehow."

"I'm beginning to think our side is on to us as well." Before I could elaborate, a distressed Lieutenant Taylor appeared, nearly obscured by the tall grass. His eyes were filled with fear and his mustache was twitching like the whiskers of a mouse that just spotted a cat.

"Justin, do you know the term 'plausible deniability'? It means I have to be able to say, if asked, that you and Sofia were never alone together. So as long as I can see you, even if you are sitting by yourselves, then I can say you weren't alone. But if I can't see you then I can't say that. Do you get it? Do me a favor and move in closer to the group...please." He was pleading.

"Sorry," I said. "We'll be right over."

It had never occurred to me that I was causing problems for my OSIA friends or that Jake was actively protecting me.

We went back to the group. They had started on the main course. The flow of the brook improved as the bottles disappeared. Vasily had taken a paternal liking to Will. At the same time, the potato farm director's speech had taken the short trip through the key usages of the ever-powerful Cyrillic letter, '*yo*.' He had begun with "*yo mo yo*," moved on to "*yolki palki*" (fiddle sticks), and wound up in the inevitable "*yob tvoyu mat*" (fuck your mother). Now nearly every one of his sentences began with this phrase, used as an affectionate but earthy amplifier of his sincerity. Vasily's lexicon was a matter of habit. It came from having to prod reticent livestock and farm workers, coax faulty tractors and thank the Party for all it did for him and his people. Only slightly more touching than seeing his tan, bespectacled face reaching up for a hug from an official representative of his alleged enemy, was the tipsy but unruffled Marine reaching down to receive the embrace.

Vasily continued his stream of compliments directed at Will. They now included references to his own anatomy in addition to the comments about his mother's sex life. It was an odd contrast. After each invective, Vasily added phrases like "You are such a normal guy" and "I love your parents for making such a decent young man." Then he'd attempt another hug, to the extent his stubby arms would allow.

Vasily then beckoned the Marine to bend down as if he had a secret to share, at which point he grabbed his cheeks and planted a big kiss, "*Yob tvoyu mat, ya tak tebya lyublu!* (Fuck your mother, I love you so much!)." Finally, we managed to assemble the group on the crest of the hill for a photo, before returning to the vehicle. Vasily sat between Will and me, his sense of equilibrium now fully anesthetized. He would have rolled down the mountainside, but his momentum was checked by the accordion we placed in front of him and the Marine's right hand on his shoulder, which served to both restrain and prop him up from behind.

Will had begun to resemble what I defined as a normal, caring human being. I learned to trust him. One night I came upon him as he stood shooting basketballs at the netless rim in our yard.

"Do you know what they call you back in Washington?" Knight asked, as we stood on the court in the dark. I didn't think they called me anything back in Washington. I wasn't calling them anything here in Votkinsk, so it seemed only fair. I shook my head.

"They call you, 'The Crazy Man.' "

"Is it because of the hot tub or the goat?"

"There are people who have opinions about your relationship with Sofia."

This was not a surprise to me. Between the three-week mutants and my own lack of discretion, I didn't think I was doing a good job of hiding anything.

"Some are even saying your digging in the basement might have been a provocation organized for the other side," Will added.

It wasn't the cool night air, but the idea that I might be considered a traitor which gave me goose bumps. Me working for them? I was barely working for Hughes.

And why was Knight sharing this information with me? In my case, sentiment had outpaced ambition. But what about him? We had become friends, sharing the adventures of the social events and challenges that faced us. He was a regular poker player, though as of late he had missed several games. His excuses centered on invitations to tea at the Fifth House. Tea over poker? Such an egregious error of judgment could only be explained by insanity or love...as if there is any difference. His absences from the poker table had coincided with Maria's presence on shift. A spotlight illuminated the otherwise poorly lit stage.

I have never seen a man change so dramatically as Captain William Knight. The figure that now stood before me bore little resemblance to the hardcore Cold War warrior ready to probe his fellow men's crevices in search of communist ticks.

"They're taking bets not on *if* she will dump you after you bring her to the States, but *when*," Will continued.

It was a farce: I had wanted to become a spy more than anything else and failed; she had made every effort to avoid it, but got drawn in all the same.

"What do you think?" I asked, genuinely interested in his professional opinion.

The ball flew from his hands and danced on the rim before falling through. "I think they're probably wrong."

That was reassuring, since part of his job was to spot spies. Then again, one could argue he wasn't doing his job very well at this point. His objectivity had become limited.

"What about you?" I asked.

The dim light showed the face of a man in turmoil. My situation as a former would-be spy turned paramour of an unwilling KGB agent paled in comparison to his situation.

"I'm too close to the target. It's a problem. I think I can get it under control, but it's not easy," he said.

"Will, this is not a bombing run. This is life."

He laughed. "I don't think either of us belongs here anymore."

The doorbell to Roosevelt rang, as if visitors from down the street had come to borrow a cup of sugar. We had no neighbors except forest animals and rocket makers. Mr. Moose and Sofia arrived for the weekly meeting. Colonel Francell asked me to greet them and show them upstairs to the living room while he printed some documents. They sat on one couch and I sat opposite. Mr. Moose stared at his notepad and scribbled. I stared intently at Sofia and she stared intently back at me. We drank in the sight of each other. Several meters apart, yet nothing separated us. The more I stared, the closer we seemed to get.

Mr. Moose continued to ignore us. Sofia and I continued our staring contest. A beam of light seemed to illuminate the path between us, leaving everything else in shadow. All I could see was the outline of her face. It was all I needed.

Suddenly the beam was interrupted by the colonel. He had entered the room unnoticed and craned his large head into our goo-goo eye stream.

He looked left. Sofia's stare had lingered. He caught her gazing at me just before she turned away.

He looked right. My delay in breaking the stream was caused by momentary resentment at the interruption...then I looked away, too.

The colonel looked like a baffled brontosaurus. He straightened up and glanced at the heavens, rolling his eyes and shaking his head as if to verify that greater powers were to blame for the predicament we all found ourselves in. Finally he sat down on the couch next to me. After a scowl in my direction, he cleared his throat to attract Mr. Moose's attention. The meeting began.

But I wasn't paying attention. Will was right. I was a liability to my friends, my job and the treaty. I could probably count on Francell not to turn me in — after all, he was a fan of romantic comedies. But the spectacle of Sofia and Justin's relationship was becoming obvious to others. At the last softball lesson in the stadium, where we coached the local kids and then played a game with them, Max had come tearing around the corner while we were unloading the equipment. He jumped into my arms. One of the three-week mutants noticed the display of affection. "I guess he knows you pretty well..."

"Uh... yeah...well, all the kids here are friendly," I muttered. Tchaikovsky's slogan painted in huge letters above the bleachers of the stadium glared down at us: *The most wonderful things in the world are children, flowers and music.* It was time to move on.

Bellman tracked me down in the warehouse. I was loading canned vegetables into my wagon to lug back to Roosevelt for dinner.

"It seems we haven't managed to find another chef yet, so I guess you'll be on duty in the kitchen again when you get back from the next rotation," Bellman said.

His timing was off. The longer I went without seeing her, the worse my mood got. On top of that, I had just dropped a large can of artichoke hearts on my foot.

"No, I won't," I told him.

"What do you mean you won't?"

"We made a deal that I would be a temporary chef. For a maximum of three months. That was six months ago. I've been patient, but I'd say the Hughes personnel department needs to work harder. I'm not going to be the chef after this next rotation. I did my part. Now you share the burden with someone else."

He tried to appear calm in the face of my insubordination. But the twitching of his mustache betrayed his annoyance.

"I am giving you an assignment and you're refusing it? You know we're a team here and everyone needs to help out. I'd have to say you've got a bad attitude."

"And I'd have to say you're a bad employer if you don't keep your promises," I retorted. "It's not about team work. You're just saving money by not hiring a real chef."

"Well then," Bellman continued with a grin, as if he had me in check-mate, "I'd have to say either you come back from your next rotation as the chef or you don't come back at all."

"Are you firing me?"

"It's your decision," he said, and slithered away.

Bellman thought he had me, but he was giving me the opportunity I wanted. Sooner or later I would probably wind up being medevaced out for accidentally chopping off all my fingers. Or, more likely, I'd be removed for breaking the fraternization policy. Here was a neat, face-saving means of absquatulation. I began to feel better. After a year and a half of voluntary prison, I was being let out early for bad behavior.

Department 162 organized a picnic at Stepanovo, the riverside settlement just down the road from the portal. After eating *shashlik* we boarded a remodeled ferry boat for a ride on the Kama reservoir.

I knew it was my last opportunity to talk freely with Sofia. The environment seemed secure: no microphone could possibly function in such a breeze. I saw Colonel Francell standing next to the railing.

"Have you seen Sofia?" I asked.

He glared for a moment and then his face softened.

"I understand you are leaving us," the colonel said. "Is there no way to make peace with Bellman?"

I wanted to confide in him and tell him this wasn't just about an incompetent Hughes manager. But I sensed he knew that, and by sharing my plans I'd be taking away his plausible deniability. There was no point.

"No, colonel," I said. "Besides, he's just one factor. I think it's time for me to move on."

"We'll miss you here, Justin," he said. Then he smiled. "Sofia's a fine woman...I think you'll find her down by the stern."

I shook his hand in appreciation of his blessing. It added to my resolve and helped me to believe I was doing the right thing.

I found her sitting on the edge of the back of the boat and sat down next to her.

"We need to finalize our plans. I'm leaving on the next rotation," I said.

"I heard," she said, without looking at me. Her hair blew in my face and I enjoyed its scent for a moment. Then I gently turned her head with my hands so I could see her eyes.

"But you're leaving too, right?" I said.

"Yes. I told them I need to go to Moscow on vacation to finalize my wedding plans. I can stay with one of my friends there."

"How much time will you have?"

"Two, maybe three weeks," she said.

"Ok. I will go back to the States and organize a new visa for myself. I've got an idea of how to do it. I don't know all the details yet, but I should be back in Moscow by the start of August at the latest."

"I'll probably have to work at the factory until the end of the year so they can find someone to replace me."

"No problem," I said. "I'll get a job in Moscow, and then we can register to marry. In the meantime I'll find an apartment and a school for Max. How does that sound?"

She nodded her head and sighed. I could tell she still had doubts.

"You believe me, don't you?" I asked.

"I believe you," she answered, forcing a smile. She wrote down the phone number of her friend in Moscow on a piece of paper and placed it in my hand. Her fingers were cold.

Following the boat ride, Jane and I decided to stroll through the village before the bus departed.

"She doesn't believe in us," I said.

"It's not the *us*, it's the *her*," Jane said. "She doesn't believe in herself. But don't worry about it. I'll work on her over the coming weeks. She'll be there in Moscow. We need to toast your new beginning!"

"I think the party ended. All the bottles were empty."

"Someone around here must have something to drink," Jane said. Her eyes scanned the horizon, as if she expected to spot a tavern somewhere along the dirt road. She veered to one side and rapped on the gate of a bright blue *izba*. A young man opened the door in the fence and we stepped into the yard. A family was preparing to eat its evening meal alfresco. In her best Russian, Jane introduced us, saying we were thirsty from walking.

The owner of the house quickly passed around a few glasses and filled them with White Stork. Freshly picked strawberries from their garden plot were offered as *zakuski*.

We lost track of the time. Fortunately, Jane's loud laughter could be heard out on the road. One by one, passing inspectors who had been sent to look for us joined in. We made it back to the bus a half hour late. Strawberries shared from the basket the family gave us to take home helped assuage Nikolai's vexation. Nothing rivals Russian hospitality.

When we returned to the site, I said goodbye to the escorts who were with us. They were still struggling with the concept of a janitor being fired for not wanting to work as a chef. I shook Sofia's hand. She smiled placidly, wished me luck and turned towards the Fifth House. As I watched her walk away I realized she didn't believe she'd see me in Moscow. I was worried her cynicism would be our undoing. If you don't believe then you don't have the resolve to win. We were going to need a lot of resolve to overcome the obstacles ahead.

I went to Chernenko's hut. He tried to be cheerful as we sat at his table enjoying his grandmother's tea. The glasses left red rings on top of his blueprints. It was the first time I was completely relaxed there, not worried about who might see us or if I would get in trouble.

"Where will you go?" Vasilich asked.

"New York for a while, then...I don't know."

"Ah, New York," he said with a smile. "I haven't been to New York in 43 years."

"Well," I said, "It's about time. You'll just have to plan a trip."

"I can plan all I want," he said, "but I don't think they'll ever let me go."

Mr. Moose poked his head in the door.

"Alexander Vladimirovich," Vasilich said, "please sit down. Mister Lifflander and I are just discussing my upcoming trip to New York. We are going together to look for spare parts for the toilets."

"Well, Justin," Mr. Moose said, as he motioned Vasilich to fill one of the empty glasses, "I don't know much about New York, but you certainly seemed to enjoy your time here in Votkinsk. We liked having you. Maybe you would consider staying here and working for Department 162...if Hughes doesn't want you?"

I couldn't tell if he was kidding.

"Could you provide me with an apartment?" I asked.

"I am sure we'll find some solution. Besides, you've made many friends here. There will always be room for you." I was touched by his sentiment. He seemed sorry to see me go, despite the problems I caused.

Mr. Moose presented me with a medal honoring the treaty work. The brass coin depicted a road mobile missile with a line through it, as if it was as easily banned as smoking in public. The opposite side had the ubiquitous crossed flags and "December 1987" written on it. We clinked glasses. I said I would consider his offer.

"See you later," Bellman called out as I headed for the bus.

"No, you won't," I responded, convinced it was my farewell to Hughes and its style of management. They couldn't manage their way out of a defense-contracted paper bag — the kind that is open at both ends and costs 17 dollars apiece.

The bus was ready to depart. I hugged Jane, Thom and Lou. Chernenko stood quietly, a plaintive smile on his round face. As I boarded, he gave me his secret wave one last time. After all, officially we were only acquaintances.

My sadness at leaving was mixed with exhilaration about the adventure ahead. I savored the minutiae that I had taken for granted for the last year and half: the flight from Izhevsk to Moscow; the courtesy of the Nuclear Risk Reduction Center handlers at the airport; the sweet aroma of the Bolshevik Candy Factory at the end of Leningradsky Prospekt; the unique architecture of the Ukraina Hotel, where Will and I and the rest of the inspectors who were rotating out were spending the night.

I invited a friend who was an attaché at the U.S. Embassy to come to the hotel and have dinner with me. He was a critical player in my plan to return and be with Sofia.

"Joseph," I told him while we waited for our entrees to arrive, "what you need is a nanny. I am happy to volunteer." Embassy diplomats had the right to sponsor a nanny visa. The nanny might help take care of children, a dog, or just be a housekeeper. It was an easy route to return quickly and meet up with Sofia.

He figured out what I was up to. "Justin, even though I have no pets or children, I'd be happy to have you as my nanny. Just remember the embassy contact policy regarding locals extends to nannies, too…" I had forgotten about that. My plan was torpedoed.

Joseph left and I headed to the 14th floor bar to meet Will Knight, who had also completed his last tour in Votkinsk. He got a promotion and would now be based full time at OSIA headquarters at Buzzard Point.

"I made the standard request to go out in the city tonight," Will said. "The Nerk gave the standard refusal. They don't have the staff to escort us and are afraid we'll get in trouble before rotating out of their zone of responsibility tomorrow morning."

"This is your last time here as an inspector, right?" I asked.

"Yeah, so what?" Will responded.

"Mine too. What do we have to lose? I mean, as long as no one gets hurt."

"Right. What can they do, send us to Siberia? We just came from that direction…"

Will ordered and we drank our beers with determination. I struck up a conversation with a young American couple at the next table over. They had come to do business in Moscow. That was a strange concept for 1990.

Giancarlo, the barman, announced last call. Will and I accepted the American couple's invitation to go to their room and continue the party. The idea of "doing business" intrigued me, so I began to ask questions. I inquired as to how they got visas to come to the Soviet Union. They gave me the number of a travel agency in the U.S.

that could book a hotel room and organize a visa based on advance payment of the accommodation. I felt renewed. I felt the seven beers I had already consumed. I took down the information carefully, making sure I could read what I wrote.

My spirits were lifted by my new plan. I gazed out the window at the skyline. The street lights illuminated Kutuzovsky Prospekt as it wended its way toward the Kremlin. Finishing another beer, I noticed what appeared to be a small porch, about a meter below the window. The railing was adorned with socialist-realist gargoyles — giant concrete hammers and sickles. I felt an urge to inspect them up close.

"It's farther down than you think," I heard someone say as I headed for the window. They didn't realize who they were talking to. By that time neither did I. And I had decided this couple was out of place. Who comes to Moscow to do business in 1990? Probably they were spies too. Damned spies everywhere. So I exited the room, containing one known and two suspected spies, via the window. At precisely 2 a.m. I was dangling from the sill on the 12th floor of the Ukraina. My seersucker pants made a gentle scraping noise against the facade. What's a one meter drop at that hour and blood alcohol level? Not much. But it wasn't one meter. More like two.

Fortunately I didn't break any bones. From between the gargoyles, the White House peeked at me across the river. I gathered a few samples of the crumbling cement work with the vague notion of selling them like chunks of the Berlin Wall. I noticed a light illuminating the floor of the balcony. A small window revealed an electronics workshop located between the 11th and 12th floors. 'Bug repairs while you wait' I mused. I looked up at the window I had come through. It seemed very far away. How to get back up? Then a gorilla hand descended. Knight reeled me in.

Common sense having long since left the party, we also decided to flee. We took the American couple with us and found a taxi in front of the hotel. The miliman at the entrance looked distressed as we pulled away. The only place I knew that might be open at 3:30 a.m. was the disco at the Kosmos hotel on the north side of town. The Solaris Bar was a black hole of hard currency, frequented by Warsaw Pact businessmen, middle-eastern diplomatic brats and prostitutes. The bouncer told us they were about to close. I convinced him to allow Will inside to purchase a few take-out beers.

We were frustrated in our attempt to wreak final havoc, but fate appeared in the form of Giancarlo. He emerged from inside the Kosmos and motioned us to join him. "We go to casino," he squawked. My spy companions were suspicious.

"Where is it?" they asked.

"We go there, OK?"

"But where is it?"

"Is downtown. We go now, OK?"

We got in Giancarlo's van and soon arrived at the casino in the Leningradsdaya Hotel. At that time there were more functioning casinos in Moscow than churches.

While the spooks were busy trying to think up fake names, I put our real names in the registration book and paid the entry fee. The atmosphere was a mixture of Ian Fleming chic and Fellini Roman orgy, replete with oily foreigners and heavily made-up whores. We kept our losses to a minimum and left by 5 a.m.

The same miliman on the hotel stoop was visibly relieved to see us return. I foolishly decided to get an hour sleep prior to departure. My nightmare, in which various American and Soviet officials were attempting to restrain me while I pursued my romance, was interrupted at 7:05 a.m. by a knock on the door from Will. I made it to the bus, full of stern OSIA and Nerk faces, 10 minutes later. I dozed off as we headed to the airport, believing everything would now fall into place.

Chapter Fourteen
Co-Conspirators and
Consumed Mating

The month in America flew by. I was focused on getting back to Moscow and meeting Sofia. I wanted to have a job lined up in advance, but the pickings were slim. I connected with a few lone carpetbaggers. They were scheming about opportunities in the Soviet Union, but offered no visa or salary. I was convinced that if I could just get back there and get my personal life settled, I would find a job.

I took my savings, paid in advance for a hotel room in Moscow for 30 days, and received a tourist visa of equal length. I figured if I couldn't get things sorted out in a month, I never would. The Ukraina Hotel was a logical choice. It was a place I was familiar with and cheaper than the ones in the center. I could walk from the hotel to the embassy commercial section to check the want-ads posted there.

My preparations for the trip helped distract me from a feeling of paranoia. On the one hand, I had been told that stories were circulating about me in the treaty's counter-intelligence circles. According to Lou's reports, their counterparts in the Evil Empire had been suspiciously quiet. From the Soviet perspective I was a capitalist Zionist agent bent on infiltrating their society and recruiting its citizens. Objectively speaking, without people like me they would be unemployed. I doubt they appreciated that concept.

Meanwhile, it again turned out that my parents were less clueless than I imagined. I had regularly sent my film home to be developed. My mother commented that one young lady appeared far more often than others. Great. I had my own in-house intelligence analyst. It's amazing what parents notice. I confessed everything. No lie detector required.

"She looks like Mrs. Schier's cleaning lady...She's got a Polish girl," Barbara said.

"She is Slavic, mom. They probably all look alike to you. She's got a degree in English literature."

"What about the child?"

"He doesn't have a degree yet," I said.

"You know what I mean. Are you ready to become a father?"

I was excited about the idea. A young man would look up to me and accept my wisdom, improve on my faults and carry on my name. All this without ever having to change a diaper. It seemed like a good deal.

"I've had a great example," I said, trying to get Matt's backing.

His ears perked up along with his ever expressive eyebrows.

"All right, all right. But maybe she's after your money," he said.

"She knows I don't have any."

"Well, maybe she is a KGB agent."

"They all are. But it's not what you think. Everyone is a KGB agent there. That's how it works. You don't just call up your lawyer and ask him to sue the KGB for harassing you. All the girls have to write reports on the inspectors. It's a pointless task. They make fun of it...writing gibberish."

Matt and Barbara made peace with my plan. I guess they remembered how their own parents condemned them for entering into a mixed marriage and decided to do better by me. Or perhaps they believed I was doomed.

The first time I landed at Sheremetyevo Airport in Moscow without diplomatic status was a scary experience. In 1986, while still in college, I studied in England for a semester. When it was over, before heading back to the U.S, I joined a British group for a tour of the Soviet Union. One chap had taken Tom Clancy's "Hunt for Red October" along. Mistake. The customs officers took it away and then hand-searched the luggage of every member of our group. They made sure we familiarized ourselves with the "rulebook" for tourists before letting us leave the airport. An innocuous blue and white pamphlet, it contained far more don'ts than do's:

--*Don't take photographs of panoramic views of any city, military installations, or airports;*

--*Don't import pornographic or subversive literature;*

--*Don't engage in illicit currency exchange activities.*

Welcome to U.S.S.R.!

Departing was equally chaotic. There was no order to the line at passport control. Passengers formed a large mob. There was a white line painted on the floor across the length of the hall in front of the exit booths. A poorly translated sign hung above, instructing everyone to "Wait here until the emigration is free." If you took the sign literally in 1986, you'd have stood there for about seven years.

Returning at the end of July of 1990 to carry out the next phase of my plan to build a life with Sofia, it soon became clear that little had changed since my first arrival to that airport. As I exited the jetway, I realized I had left the West and was now completely at the mercy of the Soviet authorities. The stench of filterless cigarettes filled my nostrils. The bizarre ceiling panels made of dark copper rings provided barely enough light to find the staircase down to passport control. No place to roll your bag.

But the country had changed dramatically in the four years since I had first visited. The U.S.S.R. was now de facto minus six of its republics and democratic parliamentary elections had taken place in the Russian Soviet Federative Socialist Republic that spring. This had led to Russia declaring its sovereignty over the U.S.S.R. in the summer. Boris Yeltsin, by then an opposition politician, had just resigned from the Communist Party.

I was oblivious to the significance of these events as I bobbed along in the herd trying to make it to one of the passport booths. The crowd was made up of oilmen, baby adopters, Russians who had been visiting their emigrant relatives and a few cowboy businessmen. I wondered if there was anyone else in a situation like mine.

I handed my passport to the stern-faced border guard behind the glass. He fiddled with my documents under the counter. This seemed to take an exceptionally long time. 'Perhaps they will nab me right here at the airport,' I thought. It would save everyone a lot of effort. Maybe he was waiting for the senior officer to finish his tea and cigarette break, so he could personally supervise my arrest. The border guards are a division of the KGB. The phone in the booth rang. The guard mumbled, looked at me, mumbled again, put down the phone. More fumbling with my documents.

Perhaps they were waiting for an even higher authority to come in from the city center to take me down. That would explain the delay. The phone rang again. Another inaudible discussion between the pimply border guard and an unseen authority on the other end of the line. It seemed like 30 minutes had passed. Then, to my surprise, I heard the clump of the stamp coming down on my visa. My passport appeared. A click of the solenoid on the gate indicated I could open it and enter the country. I checked my watch. Only five minutes had elapsed since I got to the booth.

Ten dollars and two packs of Marlboro's got me to the Ukraina. I checked in, and then headed out in search of the friend whose name and address was written on the scrap of paper Sofia had handed me on the boat. Manya was a Muscovite with whom Sofia had gone to college and was now teaching English and studying acting. Sofia said she would keep Manya informed about her vacation plan and whereabouts. Fortunately I still had my CIA pocket map of Moscow, with all streets and major buildings marked and indexed in English. Every driver at the embassy had been issued one. At a glance you could find a *refusenik's* apartment or the nearest gas station. We knew it was made by the CIA since nowhere was it written on it that it was made by the CIA.

A young woman in a bathrobe opened the door of the apartment. She was expecting me. Manya — sounds like mania, I thought. Her living room looked like a movie set, with a bright lamp in the middle and darkness on the periphery. She flitted about in her robe, gesticulating with her cigarette, as she welcomed me in. Suddenly she paused, sat on the arm of a big chair, tilted her head back and took a long dramatic puff. When she finished and the smoke had dissipated I expected to hear someone shout "Cut!"

Up close she was too exaggerated to be seductive, but far away — maybe from the fifth row or further back — I could see her wowing an audience.

"Tea?" she asked in a voice made gravelly by all that dramatic smoking.

"Yes, thank you." Tea and chocolates appeared. Despite food shortages, I never met anyone who didn't have tea and at least a few chocolates. Perhaps they were only offered when an agitated foreigner showed up.

Again she dragged on her cigarette and then swooped it from her mouth with a broad stroke of her dainty fingers. The spectators in the back row certainly caught the gesture this time.

"Sofia was in Moscow for a week but had to go to Yaroslavl to visit her granny who'd taken ill. She rang me yesterday and said she'd let me know when she'd be back."

Manya's diction was perfect, and the British accent gave her a hint of condescension. I felt as if I was part idiot and part naughty student.

"Do you know if she quit her job yet?" I asked.

"I think not. She said she has to go back to Votkinsk at the end of the fortnight."

"That means two weeks, right?"

I waited for Sofia to materialize. It took me a few days to put my resume in mailboxes at the Western embassies and commercial offices. In between, I called Manya twice a day from a pay phone. I remembered the mysterious electronic workshop on floor 11½ of the Ukraina so I decided not to make it too easy for them to track me. Muscovites were generous. If you stopped someone to ask for change to make a call they'd just give you the three-kopek coin if they had it.

I scanned the bulletin board in the U.S. Commercial Office, next to the embassy. I couldn't help noticing how disorganized it was. Ray was haunting me. I spotted a neatly typed 3x5 index card with an announcement:

"The Moscow representation office of the Hewlett-Packard Company is looking for an executive assistant for its expatriate general manager. Qualifications include native English and spoken Russian, typing, administration and other secretarial skills. Please contact...."

I vaguely remembered that Hewlett-Packard made calculators and laser printers. I suspected I could get a long-term visa if I worked for a respectable firm.

I reviewed my resume: college degree, driver, mechanic, janitor, chef. Why not secretary? I fit their requirements and the job had a ring of stability to it. I called and they agreed to interview me.

The HP office was on Pokrovsky Boulevard, in one of the three buildings in Moscow where Western companies were located. All were owned and operated by UPDK, the same agency that had formerly supplied U.S. embassy personnel.

I told the German personnel manager about various administrative experiences I had. More importantly, I was already here and eager. The only thing I needed was visa support. The other benefits a foreigner might require from the company — a car, apartment, medical coverage — were my problem. He agreed to organize an interview with their general manager later in the week. It seemed like a nice place to work. The staff consisted of about 30 Russians and five foreign managers. I could smell lunch being prepared in the kitchen as I left. I had been living for a week off a cache of cheeseburgers from the newly opened McDonald's, which I stored in my hotel room refrigerator. Now I wanted a solid meal and the job at HP.

The meeting with the general manager went well. Anton was a Viennese man in his 50s, sent by the regional headquarters to bring the company's business in the Soviet Union to the next level. Everyone was optimistic thanks to Gorbachev. Anton had been with HP for 25 years. I figured it must be a good company if people stay so long. He presented the position as a chance to learn about business while working as his executive assistant — organizing meetings, handling mail and phone calls. I was to report the following week.

Manya confirmed Sofia would arrive at the Shchyolkovskoe bus station on the northeast side of Moscow on Sunday at noon. By 10:30 that morning my heart was already racing. I went to pick up a rental car. There was a stand at the hotel offering a range of Soviet models at very cheap prices. I got behind the wheel of a gray Volga, feeling nervous but determined.

With my adrenaline at full throttle, I pulled into the parking lot of the chaotic bus station. I noticed several black Volgas and police cars parked in the far corner of the lot. I tried to guess why they were there. Obviously, they had exited the underground garage on Lubyanka earlier that morning and Operation "Schmuck-In-Love" was now in full swing. I assumed the moment Sofia and I embraced we would be arrested. A uniformed miliman and a plain-clothes goon were patrolling the station together. They were clearly looking for someone in particular, but they ignored me.

I took up position near the platform where the buses pulled in. My legs were weak and I could feel myself breathing quickly in anticipation. I scanned the license plates of arriving buses to try to identify the one coming from Yaroslavl. Finally I spotted the **ЯР**. I glimpsed Sofia's head above the crowd as she stepped off, waded through the mass of people and reached her as she was picking up the payphone to call Manya. She turned and we embraced. For a few moments, as I put my arms around her, everyone else seemed to disappear. I could see only her. It was as if I had stepped into the eye of a storm. The brief sense of calm let me gather my thoughts and my doubts.

"I can go away if you want," I whispered in her ear. "It would be easier for you."

Her lips met mine. We were not about convenience.

"Where is Max?" she asked.

I hadn't seen him get off the bus with her. We began to search the area. Surely they got him and stuffed him into the trunk of one of the black Volgas. No, they hadn't gotten him; curiosity had gotten him. He decided to stay on the bus to see where it goes after it lets all the people off. Fortunately it only went to the other side of the parking lot. We found him wandering there, his little vinyl backpack drooping off his shoulders, tears in his eyes. He recognized me and ran into my arms. As we drove away, I saw the police loading a bunch of rambunctious gypsies into their vehicles.

Sofia said we needed to go to the train station to pick up her mother. She was arriving from Nikolaev, in the Ukraine, to take Max back to Votkinsk for the start of school. As we drove, I looked over and noticed that Sofia was grinning.

"You didn't believe I would be here?" I asked.

"I still don't believe it."

"That makes two of us."

We went to Kursky station and stood on the platform holding hands as the train pulled up. Tamara Alexandrovna emerged from one of the crowded third-class cars, looking fresh and relaxed. She came towards us, the afternoon sun shining behind her. She wore a bright red dress and carried a small bag. It was hard to believe she had just traveled 36 hours in a train car with no separate compartments, 60 other people and one toilet.

"Very pleased to finally meet you," she said with a slight bow and a giggle.

Once we were in the car she began to bring Sofia up to date on family news. Tamara laughed throughout her stories. It was the uncomplicated laugh of someone who easily found joy.

"Do you ever laugh like that?" I asked Sofia.

She thought for a moment. "I used to…I might again." She put her hand on mine.

There were a few hours to spare before the plane took off for Izhevsk, so we went to the newly opened Baskin Robbins at the Hotel Rossiya near Red Square. As Max slurped his milkshake, I asked Tamara to tell me more about her husband. At first she didn't respond to my question.

"You have to speak up," Sofia said in my ear. "She spent 20 years next to a mechanical loom, so she's a bit deaf." I repeated the question louder.

"He's a simple man," Tamara said. "He has his emotional outbursts, but he just needs a lot of understanding.

"Once, when Sofia was a teenager in Nikolaev someone tried to mug her on the way home from school," she continued. "When she got home she told her father. He bolted from the house in a blind fury to search for the perpetrator, but returned 30 minutes later without a suspect. 'Who were you looking for?' I asked. 'You didn't even wait to get a description!' "

Having dropped Tamara and Max off at the airport, Sofia and I decided to look for a place to stay. I still had my room at the Ukraina. But it would have been unwise for us to go there. American inspectors used the hotel and the Nerk had an office there. Besides, Soviet hotel rules did not allow for a man to have a woman in his room who was not registered as a guest. On each floor sat a *dezhurnaya* — a lady responsible for distributing room keys and guarding Soviet morality. I was too excited about being alone with Sofia for the first time to risk spoiling the moment due to a battle with an authority figure.

We went to the "Three Train Stations" square where travelers on the Leningrad, Yaroslavl and Kazan lines arrived in the capital. At the exits to the rail and bus terminals, pensioners gathered to offer rooms for rent in their apartments to Moscow migrants and visitors. We approached a middle-aged woman. She turned out to be a roving real estate agent.

"What are you interested in, one room or two? What part of town? For how long?" she rattled off the questions as she thumbed through a collection of soiled pieces of paper that constituted her portfolio. We asked for one room for a week, reasonably central.

"I have the perfect place for you. Clean, cheap. Just what you need. It does have a *babulka*, but that won't be a problem will it?"

Sofia agreed that a *babulka* was fine. I knew the word *bulochnaya* meant bread store, and *bulka* meant dinner roll. It didn't matter to me if the apartment came with bread or not. I presumed there was a Russian tradition that it's good luck to rent a place with a loaf of bread included. The agent turned to a payphone and made a call.

"Yes, I am going to send you two young people. What?...No, they're ours. Yes, they are very nice. They'll be there shortly." She put down the phone.

"Is everything OK?" Sofia asked.

"Yes," said the real estate agent. "The landlord just wanted to make sure I wasn't sending any more North Koreans. She had a bad experience once. That will be five rubles please."

For future reference, a *babulka* is not a bread product. It's a grandmother. This one was rotund and talkative. She lived alone in a two-room apartment. Her inner room was now ours. I made grilled ham and cheese sandwiches for the three of us. After some polite conversation, we bid her goodnight and went through the living room to our temporary home, closing the door behind us.

Finally we were alone together. We could hear the *babulka* snoring in the next room. No one would disturb us. We felt like children who had stolen candy and gone to our tree house to devour it. All we wanted was to devour each other. With its scant but typical decorations — Persian rugs hanging on two walls and teapots on the shelf — it seemed more like a tent than a room. We slowly undressed each other on the small bed. After more than a year of anticipation, our skin was in contact — not just our lips, but our entire bodies. The absence of inhibition seemed alien. My hands were free to caress her; my nose inhaled her scent. Our movements were gentle at first. But soon we were overwhelmed by the sensations which had been denied for so long. Her soft brown hair brushed my chest and face as she moved on top of me. Then we rolled over and she wrapped her legs around me, pulling me closer until we melted into one.

The only disadvantage of playing spoons is that you can't see your lover's face. As we lay there I thought she was laughing quietly. I wasn't opposed to such a reaction — I was happy to give her any form of pleasure. But then I felt a warm tear on my hand.

"I don't want to go back," Sofia said between sobs.

"It's only temporary," I said, as I kissed her earlobe and neck.

"Sometimes I hate myself," she added cryptically.

It was hard for me to reconcile her sorrow with my joy. We had finally consummated. Consumed mating.

"We are united against the world and can defeat any enemy," I said. "Everything we've done so far has worked. We'll be together for good soon." And I believed it.

She turned to me and I could see serenity in her face. When I told her that I loved her the words came from inside. They passed my lips, pressed close to her ear, and immediately entered her heart. They knew exactly how to go from my place of complete truth, where they could not be twisted or diminished, directly to hers.

Sofia said that as soon as she got back to Votkinsk, she would tell Mr. Moose she was going to resign. There was still a year left on her contract. He had the power to decide to release her from her obligation to the state. This was problematic, since the factory was having difficulty attracting qualified people to work for Department 162.

"Well, if he doesn't do it, I'll just have to move to Votkinsk and find a job. Alexander Vladimirovich offered me a position."

"But Udmurtia is closed to foreigners, isn't it?" she asked.

"Doctor Odiyankov told me it would be open soon. They had a vote in the local parliament. Now they are getting the agreement from Moscow."

"Still, I don't think they'd allow you to move there," she said. "Losev likes you, but they'd never let him hire you. It would be an embarrassment to the factory and the treaty…or at least some people would see it that way. I think he is scheduled to come to Moscow next week on a business trip. He usually stays at the Ukraina hotel.

Maybe if he is faced with the choice of letting me go or taking you in, he'll have to choose the first option."

It sounded like a good plan.

The reception desk of the Ukraina confirmed that Alexander Vladimirovich Losev was staying in room 731. Seventh floor. The one where they usually put inspectors and Nerk people. I walked through the lobby. I was David with my slingshot and down the hall Goliath was in residence. It wasn't him I feared, but what he represented. He had little reason to grant my request. Either way I was trouble for him, the factory and the treaty.

I knocked. A groggy voice from within responded. "Who is it?"

A good question. Who was I now? Citizen Justin? Former Spy-Wannabe Lifflander? Visiting Schmuck-in-Love?

"It's former inspector Lifflander. Would you have a few minutes to chat with me?"

A well-muscled young man answered the door. "Is this Losev's room?" I asked.

"Yes, but he is in the gym. Come back in a half hour."

'Hadn't imagined him as the work-out type,' I thought, as I took a seat on the couch near the key lady.

Two hotel detectives grilled her about the comings and goings of a particular guest. Small groups of stocky athletic-looking men came and went. There was an international wrestling tournament going on. It brought back fond memories of fairer struggles. It was the only sport I participated in during high school. I was inspired by the combination of team effort and support with the ultimately individual chance to succeed or fail — the same circumstances I now found myself in.

Nearly an hour passed and Losev did not materialize. Shortly, two OSIA officers appeared on their way to check-out. I attempted to hide behind a column, not wishing to explain myself. But they spotted me. We exchanged pleasantries. They didn't ask what I was doing there. I helped one of them carry his bag down to the lobby.

I went back to Losev's room and knocked on the door. No answer. As I turned to depart I was confronted in the corridor by the large fellow from room 731 and a squat sidekick. The large fellow pointed at his friend.

"You are Losev?" I asked incredulously.

"Yes," he answered. He seemed quite convinced.

"Alexander Vladimirovich Losev?" I queried further.

"Yes," he again replied.

"But you don't work for the Votkinsk Factory," I muttered in confused disappointment.

"No, I am a wrestler from Bulgaria. What do you want?"

"I'd like Slavs to start using a wider variety of names..." I said, and wandered away.

Sofia later told me that Losev's trip to Moscow was canceled. But she managed to convince him to let her out of her contract. She would stay until the end of the year, while he looked for a replacement. She and I agreed I'd come to Udmurtia in three months and retrieve her and Max. That gave me time to prepare.

Chapter Fifteen

"It will be bad for you."

Renting an apartment in Moscow in 1990 was not for the faint of heart. Inexperienced landlords, the absence of a legal and financial infrastructure and the variety of building types made the search feel like a game of three-card-Monte.

Fortunately, I had Valery to educate me on my options. He had grown thinner, but his sense of humor was intact.

"So, probably, you are not wanting a *kommunalka*. This is room in communal apartment made from private property taken by Bolsheviks. Too many people for each toilet. I live in *panelnoye zdaniye*, or panel building. It is prefab concrete, but walls and floors very thin. Our neighbor above has telephone conversations and I feel I am participating with her. Worst is on Eighth of March — Woman's Day holiday. This year she gets 22 phone calls congratulating her. New record. Last year was only 18.

"*Khrushyovki* are cheap, but falling down, since former General Secretary put big rush to make so many little buildings in his era. Good choice is Stalin-era building — built like Ukraina. Lots of labor and materials in those. Very solid. *Partiynoye zdaniye* is very best. They were built in recent years for the elite of the party and state apparatus. You can identify them from outside by the unique beige bricks used to construct them. Often have high ceilings and a concierge — bathtubs are bigger than those used by rest of proletariat. These apartments are more expensive, too. But you are rich American — like imported Party person. This is where you belong."

I took Valery's teasing in stride and listened carefully to his final admonishment: the quality of the landlord is more important than the quality of the walls.

I settled temporarily in a one-room apartment in a run-down building near Studentcheskaya metro while looking for a long-term solution for my new family.

The phone rang at my desk in the HP office.

"Allo."

"Dzhastin, it is Boris." My landlord, who spent more time in my apartment than I did.

"Good morning, Boris."When he called me yesterday it was also a good morning.

"Are you warm enough, Dzhastin?"

"Yes, Boris. It's quite warm there, thanks."

"Do you have enough food, Dzhastin?"

"Yes, I am fine, thank you for asking."

"Is there anything you need, Dzhastin?"

"Well, it would be nice to have a bathroom sink."

"Do you really need that?"

"Yes, Boris. I am finding it difficult to shave while standing in the shower."

"OK, I'll work on that. I haven't found the plumbing parts, yet."

"Great. While you're at it, if you could find a door for the oven, it would be useful, too."

"I have the door. But it takes two people to install. Will you be home tomorrow?"

A rhetorical question, since he came and went as he pleased, whether I was there or not.

"No, I have to work."

"Ok. I will get my wife to help."

I was well looked after but soon found a two-room place in a *partiynoye* building closer to the office. It had a playground in the backyard and a school nearby.

Time passed quickly. I enjoyed the job and making preparations for family life. The director of the school agreed to accept Max into his second grade class after the New Year holiday.

Life was not as pleasant for Sofia. The small-town rumor mill was in high gear. There were even stories that I was living surreptitiously in her Votkinsk apartment. Nelli claimed she had spotted me taking out Sofia's garbage late one night.

And the attention from the KGB had not abated.

"You know, Sofia, we have figured out what he is," Shuvalov told her.

Sofia sat silently across from him in his office, trying to keep from throwing up.

"We've confirmed it. He is a sleeper. He will wait months, years maybe…then he'll activate and fulfill whatever mission he is given. Once he has completed it, he will kill you and your son before fleeing."

Shuvalov believed such a scenario was possible. Party ideology allowed for such monsters. The Soviet State made a martyr out of 13-year-old Pavlik Morozov who, according to the communist legend, denounced his father, a farm manager with capitalist leanings, to the authorities for hoarding grain during the 1930's famine. His father retaliated by slaughtering the boy with an ax before being sent to the gulag, so the story goes. Pavlik was idealized for his willingness to sacrifice the individuality of his family bonds for the greater collective good. A park across from the U.S. Embassy in Moscow was named in honor of the boy.

"You should be very careful," Shuvalov said.

Sofia didn't respond.

It was a strange feeling to walk around Izhevsk unescorted. I wasn't walking far — from the plane to Doctor Odiyankov's car, which was waiting outside the airport fence. The cold air at the top of the gangway revived me after the stuffiness of the decrepit aircraft. But I was free. No escorts required. I was one of the first foreigners to visit since Udmurtia opened to outsiders a few weeks earlier. I registered at the hotel which belonged to the Izhmash factory. It was called the Frenchman's House because French automotive engineers stayed there in the 1970s. But they had to get special permission to come. I did not.

We left my bags and made it to the cardiology center just before the American inspectors showed up. It was the day of the Christmas concert, which included performances by the doctors and Thom Moore. He had been churning out ballads in Russian since he arrived in Votkinsk, and was now the most popular Irish-American folk singer in all of Udmurtia.

I shook hands with my former inspector and escort colleagues as they filed in. I felt welcome, as if I had only been on an extended rotation. Yet I had no status and fit into no scheme.

"Welcome, Mr. Lifflander," Losev said. "What brings you back so soon?"

I wanted to say I was here to elope with his assistant but thought better of it. "I've got a meeting with a group of factory directors tomorrow to discuss cooperation. Perhaps the Votkinsk factory could use some HP equipment?"

He smiled and said, "If you'd consider barter for our washing machines or baby carriages, we might be able to make a deal."

"I'll get the proposal to Palo Alto immediately and let you know."

Sofia was next. We exchanged a simple *privyet* and a hand shake, restraining the goo-goo eye beam before it could fully ignite. The concert began. The ensemble of heart surgeons backing-up Thom proved their hands were made for playing instruments as well as cutting flesh. The stage was decorated in a goat motif to celebrate the Chinese symbol of the coming New Year. 'This is a good omen. It's going to be a great year,' I thought.

Zhenya had set up a full day of meetings with the local industrial magnates of Izhevsk. It soon became clear there was a scarcity of hard currency. Only the paper mill director had dollars. He was going to spend them on importing consumer goods for his workers. Izhmash presented me with their catalog of export items, including sporting weapons, high-frequency chainsaws, a mechanical titanium penile erector and automobiles. The cars hadn't changed much in design or efficiency since HP founder Dave Packard visited the U.S.S.R. in the early 1960s. He said then that even his best salesman couldn't hawk one of those vehicles.

The list of items available for barter included: 880 cubic meters of galvanized waste metal, 500 tons of slag, and 4,000 tons of burned earth. Unless the U.S. Environmental Protection Agency was about to construct a museum dedicated to industrial waste, I felt it would be a real challenge to find a market for such things. There was one research institute which gave me a brochure for a device of indeterminable use. It looked very much like an iron lung. Perhaps I would be interested in barter? They offered marble, wood, and medicinal mud.

"You wouldn't happen to be going to Moscow, would you?" I asked as I sat down next to Max on the second floor of the Izhevsk airport. My new family was larger than I expected. The additional member was Koozia. He was a David Bowie cat: pure white, with one blue eye and one green eye.

"What do you mean?" asked Max, "of course — we are going with you!"

"Ooh, then I better find some tickets for you," I said. I pulled three plane tickets with our names on them from my pocket.

Sofia smiled. "Even with the tickets, I'm not sure we are going anywhere. Look at the weather..."

"Stop being so pessimistic," I said, and produced a set of train tickets with our names on them.

"And if we miss the train while we're waiting here for the plane?"

I nodded and pulled out one more set of tickets. "A less comfortable ride, but the bus goes in the right direction."

"You are clearly a spy," she said.

I leaned over and kissed her. "Retired. Just lost my security clearance, in absentia. I'll mail them back disappearing ink once we get to Moscow."

"There is no such thing as a retired spy," she replied.

The weather cleared and we went to board. At the security checkpoint Sofia showed the miliman Max's birth certificate. But instead of providing her passport, she gave him a document with a stamp on it.

"My internal passport disappeared from my apartment," she said, noticing my surprise. "The police gave me this *spravka*. I can use it as a temporary identification document. I already applied for a replacement. It should be ready in a few weeks."

We moved in to the two-room apartment I had found. It was just off Pokrovsky Boulevard, not far from my office. The smaller room was for Max. The larger one was a living room and bedroom for Sofia and me.

In our cramped but cozy home, I began to learn what it means to be the father of an eight-year-old. I lost track of the number of times I said to myself, 'Matt, now I know what you must have gone through.' I felt like issuing a blanket apology to him. Max just needed a lot of attention and a little discipline. It was a constructive outlet for my dictatorial tendencies. I made a plan for him:

--Do take out the garbage.

--Do eat all your carrots.

--Don't try to feed your carrots to the cat.

--Do wear your mittens when it is -20 outside.

--Do not lose my mittens, which I gave you since you lost yours.

--Do tell me where I can buy more mittens.

--Do change the cat's litter box.

--Don't take the cat in the bathtub with you.

--Don't forget to dry off the cat before he tears about the apartment.

If only wet fur was the biggest issue with that cat! One night I felt something strange at the bottom of the bed. By the time I was fully conscious, I understood that some deranged creature was exploding under the covers. We lifted them to find Koozia twitching and spinning rapidly. He had epilepsy. Sofia thought it might have been triggered by a fall from the ninth floor balcony while they were still in Votkinsk. I felt sorry for him. Normally dignified, he was now covered in his own urine and panting heavily. From then on he slept in a box in the kitchen. 'If these are our biggest problems,' I thought, 'then we are doing pretty well.'

The first day of school was traumatic — more for me than for Max. Upon arriving at the classroom, we waded through a turbulent sea of children. Their natural kinetic energy was further stimulated by the gaudy Soviet rock music blaring from the public address system. The director introduced us to Max's teacher, who asked me if the boy spoke Russian. Before I could explain, she added that I shouldn't worry since she spoke some English. 'Well,' I thought as I made my way toward the exit, 'she is bound to be impressed by his language skills, at least until she figures things out.'

My Russian vocabulary began to increase along with my patience. "Vinny Pookh" sounds even more comical in Russian. I was pleased with my bedtime reading skills.

Pookh never does anything complicated in any language. At one point Sofia corrected my pronunciation. Until that moment I thought I was pretty competent. Max quickly set her straight.

"You know what he's trying to say," he told her. "Besides, it's funnier when he reads like that." I thought he had been laughing at Pookh.

Max's English was also improving rapidly. He could understand most things I said as long as I spoke slowly. His comprehension was naturally better on issues concerning toys and desserts. It was weaker in the areas of homework and chores. It wasn't hard to tell when he was pleased. He learned to pronounce the phrase "It is good" with almost no accent. It was a reaction easily elicited when discussing cartoons or cookies.

Life outside our home was getting stranger. The cancer of the Soviet system that had slowly been spreading through the organism for the past several years was finally reaching the epidermis, exposing its lesions to anyone attentive enough to see them. We received food aid from Europe via the school. Finnish powdered milk and German chocolates.

Gorbachev had taken to ruling by decree in an effort to bring order to the economy and produce to the shelves. Soldiers and milimen jointly patrolled the streets. Defending against whom? Were they afraid of hordes of angered pensioners whose mattresses full of cash had become worthless thanks to the bungled policies of then Prime Minister Valentin Pavlov?

Pavlov was not a popular character. While he was on a state visit to London a joke circulated back home:

"Did you hear that Pavlov asked the British for political asylum?"

"No, I didn't hear that!"

"Neither did I, but I was hoping you had."

Ration coupons, or *talony*, were introduced for sugar, tobacco, meat and alcohol. The government was forced to spend a million dollars in hard currency importing Philip Morris cigarettes to avoid riots. The black market thrived. One advertisement glued to a lamp post read: "Willing to trade sugar *talony* for tobacco *talony* on regular basis. Please call…" The impetus for such a deal was not as healthy as it might seem: sugar was an essential ingredient of moonshine.

Food was obtainable, but not via the front door of the store. Check the basement, back door, the sidewalk, or the truck as it pulls up. Farmers markets were prospering, selling higher quality products at two to three times the state price. At one point Sofia went to the Detsky Mir department store to buy Max a winter coat. After three hours of standing in a line that didn't move, she realized it was controlled by black marketeers. They packed the line with their agents who bought the coats at 30 rubles each, then sold them for 60 rubles on the street in front of the store to buyers too frustrated to stand in line anymore.

Sofia and I were learning to live together. The rare moments of discord between us seemed insignificant compared to the greater complication of legalizing our relationship. She was still waiting for her replacement passport. I thought it odd that the document essential for any Soviet citizen to function, including to get married, had disappeared from a shelf in her one-room apartment while she was at work.

In Russian the verbs for marriage are different depending on your gender. The wife gets "behind the husband" and the husband gets "wifed." There is the implication of some kind of collision. Perhaps there are couples that can look deeply into each other's eyes and see that they are meant to spend the rest of their lives together. Ours was a "let's give it a try" approach. I remembered the newlyweds at the party in the Ural restaurant that night back in Votkinsk. It seemed they had already found a rhythm that boded well for their long-term happiness. We had a chance, but the paperwork for a foreigner was daunting. I picked up a handout at the embassy entitled "Six Steps to a Soviet Marriage."

"1. Plan Ahead: be sure to bring with you all pertinent civil documents and get translations.

2. Prepare a 'Marriage Letter' (Svidetelstvo) at the U.S. Embassy. Do not sign it until the consular officer is present.

3. Have the letter certified by the Soviet Ministry of Foreign Affairs. This will take about a week, and cost five rubles in advance.

4. Obtain an official translation of your U.S. passport at the Office of Translations on Bobrov Pereulok, 6. This will take about 10 days.

5. Take all the documents you have collected to the ZAGS (civil registry office). You will be given a marriage date approximately 90 days from the date of registration.

6. Congratulations! You are married. If your spouse wants to emigrate to the U.S., you should come to the embassy and prepare the following documents..."

I hadn't given step six any thought yet. At the ZAGS they confirmed that without the passport they could not give us a date for the ceremony. Sofia said she'd go back to Votkinsk in a few weeks to pick up the new passport. Then we could continue the process.

"My father likes to drink," Sofia said. He was about to stop by, on his way home to Nikolaev, near the Black Sea. He had been visiting his mother in Yaroslavl.

"Well, so do I...within reason."

"Well, he overdoes it sometimes...but he's a good man. Just don't take him too seriously."

"Are you implying I take things too seriously? I know how to go with the flow. If I can handle Hughes management, I can handle anyone."

"I'm sure you'll find a common language."

The doorbell rang. A tall man of about 50 stood there. Despite the cold weather, he wore no hat and his wool coat was unbuttoned. His handsome face was accented by snow-flecked wavy gray hair and bright blue eyes. I helped him off with his coat and saw that he had the broad shoulders and strong arms of a farmer. Sofia said he spent half the year working watermelon fields in Moldavia and half the year at home on his couch drinking vodka. He had a gift for growing things. One spring, he passed out on his in-laws' vegetable patch. Later, the seedlings under the soil he had been napping on emerged faster than the rest. There was a silhouette of cucumber sprouts in the form of his massive body. It took two weeks for the others to catch up.

"I brought Borya with me," Sasha said as he put down his bag. I started for the door, thinking I had inadvertently shut it in the face of another relative. He stopped me gently with his large hand and pointed toward the bag. I peered in; a bloody pig's head peered back out.

"I've got a kilo of lard and a kilo of good meat, too," he continued. Sofia told me Borya had lived with her grandmother for many years and she knew him well. As she took the bag to the kitchen, I realized I had never been personally acquainted with any food I had eaten.

Borya was tasty. I was able to forget that his face was still staring at me through the refrigerator door. After the meal, Sasha told Sofia and Max to leave so we could talk "like men."

"Will you try some Ukranian cognac?" Sasha asked.

"Oh, yes," I replied from the other end of the table. "I like cognac."

"Well, it's not exactly cognac. It's a home brew my mother and I made." He poured two shot glasses of a greenish brown fluid. We drank the first shot in honor of "getting acquainted." It burned as it went down. The flavor, which came through only once my taste buds had regained consciousness, was slightly nutty.

"Have you ever seen a walnut?" he asked.

"Yes, we have those in America."

"Then you've noticed they look a lot like a brain."

"Now that you mention it, yes. Like the human brain..."

"There is a part of the walnut," he said, moving his fingers as if he was opening a small brown cranium and removing the tiny beige brain, "between the four segments of the nut itself. It's a little wall. That's what we use to make this cognac."

He poured two more shots. I toasted to his distilling expertise.

"Almost as good as the French stuff," I lied. "So this will help me think more clearly then?"

"I don't know. It could." He leaned toward me. Without breaking eye contact he filled both glasses again, as if the neck of his reusable moonshine bottle could automatically home-in on the rim of an empty shot glass.

"What I do know is this, Justin...I am a simple country man, with few possessions. But what I do have I protect. My family is the only valuable thing I have."

"Well," I said, feeling emboldened, "we should drink to your family." His raised eyebrows showed he was pleased by my interjection. We drank.

"I don't have a fancy education or job like you," Sasha said. "All I have is my family."

His tone was a mixture of humility and aggressiveness. He stared at me for a moment, looking like he was going to hit me. Then he cocked his head to one side and said, "You seem like a good man."

We clinked glasses without further pomp and downed the contents. I was beginning to feel like a very good man — to the extent that I could still feel anything.

"…So, I need to warn you," Sasha continued, "if things become bad for my grandson and daughter…I'll take them away…and deal with you…and it will be bad for you."

The brain-joining fluid did have a wisdom-enhancing element. I realized he was not so much threatening me as describing how much he loved them, how precious they were to him. So I didn't focus on the details of how exactly things would become bad for me. I was going with the flow.

"I understand," I thought I said clearly, but I must have begun to slur my speech.

"Is your Russian good enough to follow what I am saying? Do you really understand me?" He filled our glasses again. Was he speaking Russian? I had no sense that some foreign language was involved in our interaction. Everything was perfectly clear to me. I nodded enthusiastically. Maybe I could not yet speak fluently, but I could listen fluently.

We raised glasses and he drank to his daughter's happiness with me. I think he continued speaking. Maybe about the pig or his mother or his wife. It didn't matter. His tone grew more affectionate. I guess I had satisfied him. I began to lose all sensation in the lower half of my body. This was not an unpleasant feeling but it did result in me sliding lower in my seat. I remember the revelation that Russians also put used chewing gum on the underside of their tables. Then I don't recall much of anything at all.

I crawled to the office the next morning while Sofia stayed at home with Sasha. She prepared sandwiches for him for the long train ride home. The doorbell of the apartment rang. It was the local miliman making a spot check of registration documents. Every citizen has to have a stamp in his passport indicating at what address he is permanently registered. Sofia showed her *spravka* and Sasha showed his passport. The officer thanked them and left. Milimen rarely took initiative. Was a neighbor jealous of our landlord's 300 dollars per month income and trying to cause him trouble? Or was it higher powers trying to see if Sofia had solved her passport problem without the help of the Votkinsk authorities? Such mysteries I could do without.

I talked to Sofia on Sunday night. She was in her apartment in Votkinsk. The poor quality of the phone line cheated me of the ability to judge her emotional state. She said she was going the next morning to pick up her passport and she'd be on the evening plane. We agreed I'd pick up Max from school and come to the airport to meet her.

On Monday morning Sofia entered the small office that was part of the police department. The passport bureau was responsible for issuing internal passports, recording the addresses at which citizens were registered and producing foreign travel passports — though there was little demand for them in Votkinsk.

There was no one else there. She passed her *spravka* through the little window. The woman behind the counter looked at it, read the last name, got up and went into a back room.

Shortly, Shuvalov came through one of the doors and entered the waiting room. He was carrying a passport in his hand. He motioned her to sit down on one of the benches.

"I helped expedite this," he said, handing her the little red booklet.

"Thank you," Sofia answered, knowing the conversation was not over.

"I wanted to tell you that Moscow has changed its mind. We want you to marry him. It will be much easier to track him and neutralize any threat…if that becomes necessary."

Sofia felt powerless. "But I am not sure I will marry him. And I don't know where we'll live if we do," she said.

"Don't worry. Our arms have a very long reach. You'll be asked to help, of course. But we can find you anywhere, and we can protect you. You won't be alone."

Sofia looked straight ahead without reacting.

"Have a pleasant trip back to Moscow," Shuvalov said as he stood up and departed.

Anton, my boss at HP, looked up from his keyboard and nodded affirmatively in response to my request to leave early. I walked along the boulevard. The falling snowflakes were illuminated by the lights suspended on wires above the street. In the third floor classroom where the after-school group met, two children were drawing quietly. Neither of them was mine.

"Where is Max?" I asked the teacher.

She looked at me with confusion. "He didn't come after school today. I think he left early."

'Great', I thought, 'I've been a father for barely a month and I've already misplaced my kid.' I went to the director's office. He was having a staff meeting.

"I'm sorry to interrupt, but I'm trying to find my son. He seems to have left."

"Yes," said one of the secretaries. "His mother picked him up a few hours ago."

"Are you sure it was his mother?" I asked, now completely baffled.

"Well, yes. Why? Is everything OK?"

"I'm not sure."

I walked quickly toward our home. A queasy feeling began in my stomach. I wanted to think that they were waiting for me in the apartment. Sofia must have arrived on an earlier flight and wanted to surprise me. But why take Max early? It felt wrong. A slight buzzing noise started inside my head at the base of my skull. Very subtle at first. Like I had been hit with a blunt object.

I opened the door to the apartment. No wife, no son…not even a cat. Their few belongings were gone from the still open drawers and cabinets.

I looked at the shelf near the door. A note read:

We have to leave. It simply will
not work. There are too many
complications and differences.
This is (my) decision. Please
forget about us and go on with
your life. S

Not "Love, S," or "Hate, S." Just "S." My heart was pounding. The humming inside my head reached full volume. It was like getting an insufficient dose of a general anesthetic. A creeping dullness — then you expect to pass out. But you don't lose consciousness. You know pain is coming. Panic sets in as you anticipate it. You want to ask for more anesthetic but there is no one to ask.

At the same time a defense reflex kicked in. Something akin to the one that compels you to turn the wheel at the last moment to avoid a head-on collision. I began to formulate a plan. Where could they go? If they stayed in Moscow they would probably go to Manya's, though she would hardly have room for them along with her parents

229

and grandmother. If they were leaving town, then the only places they might go are Nikolaev or Votkinsk. I thought about the trains and planes that might take them away from me: train No. 50 at 18:15 from Kazansky station to Votkinsk; another at 19:00 from Kursky station to Nikolaev. A plane departing Bykovo at 20:00 to Izhevsk.

I called Manya. She denied any knowledge of Sofia's actions. I didn't trust her, but she sounded concerned. Then again, she was an actress.

I jumped in the car and headed for Kazansky train station. The Italmas express to Izhevsk hadn't left yet. I ran to the passenger waiting room and asked the guard if I could go in to look around even though I didn't have a ticket. He refused. I felt the veneer of kindness and adventure wearing off. The reality was foul and damp, like the film of mud on the marble floor of the station. Rage welled up inside me at this sense of helplessness. I was about to shove the guard out of my way, but noticed a miliman standing nearby and got a hold of myself. Peering through the filthy window into the dimly lit room I scanned each face. They weren't there.

I drove to Kursky station a few kilometers away. It was just as filthy, but friendlier. The female attendant at the waiting room for mothers and children took pity on me and let me inside. But I didn't find them. I headed towards the platform where people would be gathering to board the train.

A human mass was moving through the station, carrying bags, boxes, carpets and television sets. It gave the impression that war had just been declared and an exodus was underway. The dank passageways crammed with passengers — coming, going, waiting — left me feeling soiled. When a man several meters away coughed, I held my breath instinctively, as if his infectiousness was magnified in the cramped environment. Even the snowflakes falling on the platform felt dirty, like dust from a crumbling structure. Among all that filth there was no sign of my family.

I raced along Volgogradskoe Shosse towards Bykovo airport. Despite the snowfall, the airfield showed signs of life. The board displayed half a dozen flights. Izhevsk was on time. I walked resolutely through the first and second floor waiting areas, scanning the face of every passenger. Sofia and Max were not there.

I drove mindlessly back towards Moscow, my tires not feeling the potholes that had recently filled with snow and me not feeling anything at all.

CHAPTER SIXTEEN
I DON'T UNDERSTAND

I learned perseverance at an early age. A pit bull lived at the landscaping nursery near where I grew up. He was beige and his name was Vick. He had a game he liked to play. Vick wandered the aisles with a plastic flower pot in his powerful jaw. Approaching a customer, Vick would make it clear he wanted someone to try to remove the pot from his mouth. I observed this many times. I felt sure that Vick was not conscious of his guaranteed success. He wanted to test himself and garner attention. I never saw anyone defeat him. He grinned back at his challengers, snarling and drooling, never letting go.

Once, while Matt was engrossed in shrubbery acquisition, I decided to out-muscle Vick. We struggled for about 20 minutes, neither of us willing to concede defeat. We battled among the neat rows of bushes and plants. With my strength waning, I gave a final heave and landed in a bonsai tree with three fourths of a plastic flower pot my only prize. Vick trotted off with the other quarter still wedged in his happy, frothing mouth.

Now, my part of the plastic flower pot consisted of a few articles of their clothing, some photographs and white, furry dust bunnies skirting the baseboards of my apartment. I tried to analyze what went wrong. Was I to blame, or had there been someone else all the time? I couldn't find enough evidence to support the vague explanation she put in the note. Maybe I didn't want to. I had framed a photograph of Sofia sitting at the Kosmos Kafe. I remember how happy she was that day. I placed five or six bowls of ice cream in front of her and took the picture. She looked at me now from behind those bowls, content with life's simple pleasures.

Maybe she figured out living with me was not a simple pleasure. Were we together long enough for her to make such a judgment? She seemed satisfied with my parenting skills. Max was happy. The cat definitely had no grounds for complaint.

I tried to remember any arguments in the midst of our bliss. I couldn't think of any. But my mind always blocks out negative memories. One day while we were making a salad she told me that a woman is like a tomato, all soft inside and in need of gentle handling.

Then she said, "Men love with their eyes, but women love with their ears." I couldn't remember ever speaking harshly to her. Once, I expressed my dissatisfaction with the cutlery drawer. I had bought one of those dividers and always put the forks, knives and spoons in their respective slots. After washing the dishes she would put the cutlery back all mixed up. I don't think I raised my voice. But I remember she made some comment at that moment about being accustomed to living alone. The significance of the statement didn't sink in.

Then there was the orange juice incident. Food was supplied with great irregularity even in the state hard currency stores and not at all in the ruble shops. I ordered the juice from a Danish catalog company and received a monthly shipment to my office. Having been a chef in Votkinsk, I learned what it meant to stretch supplies between rotations. Moreover, I was the one lugging the stuff home. So I would only order what I thought was reasonable for a family of three to consume in a month. As far as juice was concerned, that meant one glass a day per person, which equaled two cartons a week or eight cartons per order. The math was clear.

To my chagrin, I discovered Sofia was consuming a whole carton every day by herself. I lectured her on my belief that self-denial was good for the soul. But they had had 70 years of self-denial. I just didn't get it.

The day after their disappearance I called Tamara. Even if they hadn't gone to Nikolaev, maybe her mother would have some insight for me. I also knew that Tamara's 50th birthday and retirement celebration was scheduled for the beginning of April. This was a big event in the life of a worker. Perhaps Sofia would attend.

"No, I haven't heard from her," said Tamara cheerfully. "I hope she'll attend, but I'm not sure."

"I'd like to come too, but your city is closed."

"Closed for my birthday?"

"No, I mean closed to foreigners. Can you send me an invitation by fax or something?"

"What is a fax?"

"It's like a telex…How about a telex? Can you go to the post office and send me a telex invitation to visit you in Nikolaev?" I was having a conversation with a nearly deaf person over a bad phone line. It was like screaming at myself.

She said she understood. I eventually got the telex. The protocol department of the Ministry of Foreign Economic Relations, which was responsible for the accreditation of HP in Russia and its foreign employees, said Nikolaev was still closed to foreigners and I was forbidden to go.

I waited a few more days and dialed the number of Sofia's apartment in Votkinsk. She picked up the phone.

"Can you please tell me what happened?" I asked. "Why did you leave?"

"There is nothing more to say," she answered. "It's all there in the note."

"I still don't understand," I said, but she was silent. So I did what any sensitive male would do. I threatened her.

"I must know the truth. If you won't tell me on the phone, you'll just have to deal with me in person." She was still silent and the conversation ended. It was painful, but my determination lingered.

On the floor of the lobby at CIA headquarters in Langley it is written: "Know the truth, and the truth will make you free."

I went to see Manya. I found her at home, again in her bathrobe and slippers, smoking a cigarette.

"After all, you are a foreigner…there were bound to be cultural differences," she said.

"What culture? I don't have any culture," I protested.

"You don't know all of her past. It's complicated. Perhaps she wasn't meant to be part of your happiness."

The Russian sense of fate irritated me. In earlier times they enjoyed dueling and invented Russian roulette. These people played chicken for keeps.

"Why are you Russians ready to give up on happiness so easily?" I protested.

"Well," Manya said, as if it was a minor revelation, "we never expect it anyway, so I guess it's not so hard to part with. You'll get over her in time. You should take comfort in the old saying, 'Out of sight, out of heart'..."

"Out of *heart*? We say out of *mind*. There's a cultural difference for you. My mind has nothing to do with this."

Manya continued to expound on her view of the situation. Sofia couldn't find a job (which was not true — she had several leads in the short time she was with me); Max wasn't happy (I had seen no signs of this).

"Your explanation seems a bit rehearsed," I said.

Her face flushed ever so slightly. "There are greater forces here at work than you can handle," she said.

It was enough of a hint to lead me to believe that Sofia was not acting out of free will — that circle around the word "my" in her note was another scrap of evidence.

"Did you ever do any Shakespeare, Manya?" I asked, grinning with satisfaction.

"No, we do contemporary pieces," she answered. "Why do you ask?"

"How do you say in Russian, 'The lady doth protest too much'?"

I convinced myself I had a chance. Perhaps some of those 'greater forces' would have a heart, as well as a mind. But I needed a new plan.

I had learned from Anton that in Russia know-*who* is more important than know-*how*. He spent a lot of time tracking *who's who* at the relevant ministries, meeting officials and looking for creative ways to "cooperate" — which in Russian business parlance means anything from sponsoring a conference to purchasing millions of dollars' worth of equipment. Corporation or Communist bureaucracy, it makes no difference: the key to business success is manipulating relationships.

I was taking notes at a meeting with Anton and the other senior managers. They were preparing an agenda for the upcoming visit of an HP vice-president for Europe. I applied my wisdom to my personal crisis and came up with the following theory: if I could arrange a meeting between the Minister of Defense Industry and the visiting HP vice-president, I would impress the management of the missile factory — which is a subsidiary of the ministry — and maybe even the local KGB branch, by my high-level connections. Perhaps they would then reconsider their treatment of my fiancée. It seemed to make sense and it was the only idea I had at the time.

Yevgeny Odiyankov, the cardiac surgeon from Izhevsk, had told me that he was an old friend of Defense Industry Minister Belousov. Yevgeny and I had stayed in touch after my departure from Votkinsk. As a respected leader in Izhevsk he was easily elected to the new national assembly, called the Congress of People's Deputies, which had been created by Gorbachev in an effort to breathe some representative life into the stagnant system inherited from his predecessors. Yevgeny traveled regularly to Moscow to attend sessions of congress, where he sat on the health committee. We saw each other frequently. Our friendship grew. I began to call him Zhenya.

Doctor Yevgeny Odiyankov

He was proud of my joining such a reputable firm as HP, which at the time was more famous for making first-class medical equipment than niche products like computer printers. Zhenya told me that if my company ever wanted to cooperate with any of the defense industry factories in their conversion projects, he could facilitate a meeting with the minister. "Conversion" of defense industry manufacturing to production of more consumer goods was one of the key elements of Gorbynomics. HP wanted to be a supplier for that process. I proposed a meeting between our VP and the minister to Anton. He liked the idea. Yevgeny gave me the contact at the ministry.

Vadim Grekhov was responsible for international relations at the Ministry of Defense Industry, which made him chief arms trader for the nation. Fluent in English, he also spoke Farsi, French and German. Vadim traveled the world from Havana to Hanoi peddling weapons to the socialist camp.

He was also the front man for the ministry's interaction with foreign companies. I dialed his number. It was busy. The busy signal was one of the hallmarks of doing business in the Soviet Union. There were no multi-line telephones or PBXs. The power of a bureaucrat was measured by how many phones he had on his desk. Sometimes when you got a ringing signal and thought you were about to be connected you'd get blasted by an electromechanical raspberry sound for a moment before being segued back to the busy tone. Even if you did get through there was only a slim chance that the person you were looking for was near his desk. At best you'd be told to call back. Soviet phone culture dictated that it is the responsibility of the caller to pursue the called — to keep redialing until your fingers bleed or you get the person on the phone. Message taking was an anomaly. I would stun customers who called our office merely by saying, "He's not in right now, but maybe I could help you, or take a message?"

The 11th attempt got through.

"Hello, I am looking for Mr. Grekhov," I said in Russian.

"It is me," he answered.

"My name is Justin. I am with the American company Hewlett-Packard. I was given your coordinates by Doctor Odiyankov who said you could help us to organize a meeting between our visiting vice-president and the minister."

"Yes, I am aware of this. We can speak English, if you prefer."

We switched to English and agreed that he would come to our office for a preliminary discussion.

It was easy to recognize Vadim in our waiting room. Our typical visitors were mid-level functionaries at the few ministries who had hard currency and were allowed by Cocom — the Western trade agreement that limited technology sales to the East — to buy our equipment. The buyers were neatly dressed but their garb was almost exclusively of Soviet manufacture. Occasionally a foreign businessman would come to secure equipment for his company or joint venture. As of late, a new type of creature had begun to appear: the proto-entrepreneur. These were typically young men who worked for or had recently left a state engineering institute or technology firm. They were trying to take advantage of the minor liberalizations in the economy to set up their own companies to do systems-integration or technology distribution. They almost always carried a Samsonite knock-off black plastic briefcase with aluminum trim.

Vadim didn't resemble any of these characters. He was a well-groomed man in his late 40s. He bore the usual signs of someone with access to foreign goods. His suit had a warm color and sharp cut. His eyeglass frames were not the thick brown plastic ones with fat glass lenses. They were made of metal and thin plastic. He wore attractive calf skin shoes — not clunky *galoshy* or the cheaply made summer shoes that looked fine on the boardwalk in Odessa but smacked of East European kitsch in contrast to the rich carpeting of the HP office.

We chatted briefly before Anton stopped by to discuss the objectives for the upcoming meeting. Vadim had a rapid yet formal way of speaking English. He eyed Anton and me carefully while we spoke. We agreed on the agenda and Anton bid him farewell.

Vadim's own agenda was more selfish. It was revealed as I drove him back to the ministry after the meeting. My Volga required the level of attention most Soviet cars needed to get from point A to point B without stalling, flooding, overheating or losing a wheel, so I drove slowly. Once we had set out, his manner became less formal but the conversation seemed planned. It was as if he knew he needed to express a lot of information in a short period of time.

"I was the last Soviet official out of Baghdad before your people started bombing the hell out of the place…man, the crazy stories I could tell you."

He had the annoying habit of overemphasizing slang to demonstrate his language proficiency.

"I'm fed up with this bullshit Communist bureaucracy," he continued. "Makes me drink too much!" "Do you enjoy chasing the ladies in Moscow as much as I do?" "Are you well paid? My salary sucks."

He told me to stop the car a block from his office. Shaking my hand, he repeated his insistence that we get together again after the high-level meeting. I was left with the feeling that he wanted something more from me but couldn't understand what. 'Most unusual,' I thought, 'that a person in his position would excuse his driver for the afternoon and ask me for a lift.'

As I pulled up to our office building it finally hit me. The word jumped out at me from a memory of a training manual I had read at the FBI: Grekhov was plagued by **MICE**. Money, Ideology, Compromise, Ego — the four main reasons why people betray their country. Vadim thought I was an intelligence officer. He was making it clear he had something to offer. Me, the 25-year-old love-sick former driver-mechanic-janitor-chef, now skilled at making coffee and typing memos. He had no idea that all I was competent to offer him in return was a lift to his office, a few of Chuck's best recipes and refills for a stapler.

HP vice-president Franco Mariotti, Anton and I attended the meeting with the minister, along with Zhenya and Grekhov. Franco was pleased because he got to meet a high-level Soviet official. Anton was pleased because Franco was pleased. The minister was pleased because he got to use the word "conversion" several times while describing his industrial empire and efforts to make more consumer goods and promote joint-venture possibilities. I was pleased because I did some good for HP and, hopefully, myself. Zhenya was pleased because everyone else was pleased.

On the way out the minister proudly showed off some samples of items made by his factories. They were displayed in glass cabinets around the conference room. They included everything from model missiles to folding chairs.

"What about baby carriages?" I asked the minister. I knew the answer, but by asking I speciously felt I was strengthening my position.

"Yes, we even make baby carriages," he replied.

A few days later I met Vadim again and we exchanged protocols from the meeting, which listed the action items for both sides. As we stood up to depart, he opened his briefcase and handed me a document.

"Here is a copy of an internal report about the problems we've been having at the ministry with accelerating conversion at our factories. I'm sure you'll find it useful." I glanced at the cover page. It had about 20 signatures, including the minister's.

I read through it. It wasn't classified, but it was a blunt assessment clearly not meant for external consumption. I remembered that Knight was in New York working on a master's degree in Soviet economics in the evenings while organizing the UN's hunt for Saddam's SCUDs by day. I was sure he could use such original material for his thesis so I sent him a copy of the report. He asked where I had obtained it.

Feeling empowered by my recent machinations, I bought a round-trip ticket to Izhevsk for the weekend. Anton gave me Friday off so I could catch the morning flight. Zhenya contributed his driver, who met me at the airport and took me to Votkinsk.

The sun had already set by the time we rolled down the hill towards the lake. "Rocket Man" by Elton John was playing on the tape deck. *"Mars ain't the kind of place to raise your kids. In fact it's cold as hell..."* Phonoverism: when the music inadvertently corresponds to your immediate reality. I had already been infected by the ability to recognize and appreciate the important role symbols play in Russian life. I took the song as a good omen. As we pulled into the courtyard of Sofia's building, the driver asked me if he should wait. I decided that would be an admission of defeat and sent him on his way.

I knew her building and apartment number from her passport *spravka*. I rode the elevator up and rang the bell. An old man who looked very much like my deceased grand-uncle from Brooklyn answered the door.

"Is Sofia Alexandrovna at home?" I asked, still not able to imagine what Uncle Al was doing in her apartment.

"No such person here," he responded. "You probably want block number one — this is block number two."

Damned socialist housing. All the buildings look alike. I went into the next block and again knocked at apartment 153. No answer. I rang the bell a couple of hundred times but there was no life within. I waited about a half hour. I considered knocking on the neighbor's door. But I already felt exposed and night was falling. Trying to make it out to the portal monitoring facility to sleep was out of the question — the soldiers at the post near the switching yard probably wouldn't take kindly to a former inspector creeping around in the dark, and my ambitions would become even more public. The only other native Votyak whose phone number I had was Anatoly Vasilievich Chernenko, the construction colonel. But I feared I might get him in trouble if I asked him to harbor me.

It was getting later and colder. I walked down to the embankment and across the dam to the anchor and started to hitch. A car with a young couple stopped. With no questions about my accent or intentions, they took me to Izhevsk. I spent the night on Yevgeny's couch. I dreamed that Vick came up to me and let me take the whole flower pot from him. He winked at me before trotting off.

I returned to Moscow and called Sofia again on Monday.

"I guessed you were coming," she said. "Max and I spent the weekend with some friends."

I thought I heard a man's voice in the background.

"Who is that?" I asked.

"A friend of mine," she answered.

'Fine,' I thought, 'I can play games too.'

"Well, OK. I won't be bothering you anymore," I said, and hung up.

The next day I bought another round-trip ticket to Izhevsk for the following weekend.

As I found myself again entering her building I was sure this time the element of surprise would be on my side. I knocked. Sounds came from inside. My pulse quickened as the door opened. A man of about my age stood there, with no shirt and more hair on his chest than I would ever have.

"Is Sofia home?" I asked, as if my presence on her doorstep at 8 p.m. on a Friday night was a routine occurrence.

"No," he said brusquely, "she isn't."

"And who are you?" I asked.

"I'm her fiancé," he answered.

While I tried to process his statement, Koozia came to the door, ambled indifferently past the hairy interloper, and began to rub against my leg.

"Well," I said, "that's interesting, since I am also her fiancé."

"You are *not* her fiancé," he said, pointing a finger at me, "and if I were you I would leave and never return...or else it might become bad for you."

Again, this mysterious "badness" was lurking in my future. I was caught off guard and entirely unskilled at making threats, so I remained silent. He grabbed the cat and slammed the door.

I retreated to the stairwell to contemplate my situation. The sounds of children returning home after playing outside in the snow echoed through the building. After about 15 minutes the alleged fiancé departed via the elevator. I pouted in the darkness, unobserved and feeling vulnerable.

But that vulnerability gave me strength I hadn't expected: it forced me to think how to defend myself, both immediately and in the long term; to open my mind to all possible scenarios and solutions.

I must have sat there for another hour ruminating. Either she had been spirited away and they had put this fuzzy thug there to frighten me...or he was legitimate...which would mean I had a competitor all the time. Sofia had decided after a month with me that he was the better man. Yes, he had more hair on his chest. But I had redeeming qualities, too. As I thought about this second variant more and more, it seemed like it just might be true. Maybe I wasn't worthy. But what about Koozia? He acted like he had never seen that guy before. Could I trust the cat? What is the world coming to when you *have to* trust a cat? If she only had a dog. Even a small dog.

I needed clarity so I rang the neighbor's doorbell. I wasn't really sure what I was going to ask them. *"Excuse me, but would you happen to know if that hairy bastard is really her fiancé?"* It didn't seem an appropriate conversation starter. But the thin walls and collective conscience of Soviet apartment life assured me that they would have some information. A plump woman in her mid-30s opened the door. A small boy hid behind her knee.

"Sorry to disturb you, but I was just wondering if you knew when Sofia might get home. My name is Justin and I've come from Moscow to visit her. I was expecting to find her here."

The woman smiled knowingly and said, "I'm Vera. Sofia had to go on a business trip suddenly. I think she will be back next week."

I thanked her for the information and wished her a good evening. My emotional and practical privation must have been written on my face.

"Where are you going?" she asked, alarmed.

"Well, I'll go back to Izhevsk tonight."

"That's not possible. The last bus has already departed and it's minus 30 outside. Why don't you stay here?"

I could have been a stray dog foaming at the mouth with fleas leaping off in all directions and a Russian stranger would have offered me shelter. I was worse than a stray dog. If I was an American spy — as Sofia had told me the local security organs believed — and these folks harbored me, things might become "bad" for them.

"You're very kind," I said, "but I couldn't bother you. Besides, I 'm sure I'll get a ride."

I stood at the anchor for about an hour. It was past midnight. I couldn't feel my toes or fingers anymore. I envisioned myself the next morning, frozen solid like Jack Nicholson at the end of "The Shining," a grimace on my face and one hand leaning on the anchor for support — a monument to obstinance greeting everyone arriving by the main road. Maybe this is what fuzzy tits meant when he said it would be bad for me. I felt pretty bad.

A cold death or room-temperature surrender? I trudged back to the neighbor's apartment.

"It seems there is no more transportation going to Izhevsk tonight," I said to the man who opened the door and introduced himself as Vera's husband Kolya.

"There is nothing surprising about that," he said and ushered me in.

"I really don't want to cause you any trouble," I said.

"It's the least we can do to show you some hospitality," Kolya said. "After all, I pass by where you used to live in front of the factory every day. I sometimes wondered what it would be like to take one of you inspectors home and have you meet my family...and now you just show up!"

The warmth inside their home was metaphysical. Vera and Kolya seemed to know who I was and what I was on about. Sofia was friendly with them. Their boy, Sasha, was Max's playmate. They claimed they had no details about Sofia's love life.

They had a teenage daughter named Yulia. She was at that precious stage in life where the obliviousness of adolescence had worn off but the discretion of adulthood had not yet stifled her. Yulia peppered me with questions about life in Moscow and America as we sat at their table and enjoyed a meal. Vera finally sent her off to bed. I fell asleep on the couch, the weight of my defeat alleviated by their uplifting generosity and 100 grams of Kolya's White Stork. I slept soundly and took the bus back to Izhevsk the next day.

Vadim Grekhov's unexpected appearance on my TV screen several months later lifted me out of the funk that had plagued me since my last foiled attempt to see Sofia.

I had been watching the state news program, which wasn't usually entertaining. Bureaucrats explaining new concepts and economic mechanisms of Gorbachev's perestroika. Factories increasing production of consumer goods. Social problems exposed for public discussion. It was like a car engine designed to run on gasoline had suddenly been fed diesel. The mechanics were trying to make adjustments and even swap components while it was still running. But it was sputtering and about to stall.

The program that followed was a documentary about how he had betrayed his country. Vadim had just been arrested for espionage. The KGB interrogated him at their headquarters on Lubyanka Square. They labeled him "an enemy of the people." I couldn't believe they still used that term. Vadim had spent a month at the highest point in Moscow, confessing how he had spied for the British intelligence service. They say from a windowless basement cell on Lubyanka you can always see Siberia.

Grekhov was no longer a well-groomed, smooth-talking respected member of the establishment. Colonel Francell would have said that the accused spy looked like "a soup sandwich." I had always wondered what he meant by that. Seeing Vadim's pathetic figure — gaunt, disheveled — I finally understood. It's the stale sandwich you get for free with a bowl of soup. His voice broke as he told the primetime audience his story. Vadim said he had been blackmailed, recruited, equipped and abandoned by his MI6 case officer after providing useful information. The narrator's solemn voice told us that traitors are always betrayed by their handlers.

I wasn't surprised by Vadim's arrest. He admitted to the interviewer he had done it for the money, although there had also been compromising material to coerce him. Vadim was even easier to recruit as a spy than my coupon man Kuzmich had been for his task of distributing alcohol coupons.

The TV report made the story seem so exciting. The KGB had code-named him "the Sheik." The spy equipment the Brits gave him was clever, but of course inferior.

A notebook computer with hidden data storage; a camera with dual emulsion film — the visible negative with a child's portrait, the invisible one containing secret plans of Soviet weapons.

The feeling of an unwelcome bond with Vadim gnawed at me. We were both abandoned, in trouble, and ultimately responsible for our situation. He got what he deserved, with some help from me.

Knight sent me a thank-you note for forwarding him Grekhov's memo about military conversion. In it Will said that he had shared it with a fellow student who was a British diplomat. I had inadvertently aided the arms dealer in betraying his country. Recalling the conversation I had with him in my car, the British could have used all four of Vadim's MICE to persuade him to work for them. I don't know which one was his primary driver. Maybe he saw the writing on the wall about the end of the U.S.S.R, as others Soviet bureaucrats had. But they were either planning to learn how to make a profit, hunker down and muddle through the tribulations that mother Russia would face, or emigrate. Becoming a willing traitor was not an obligatory path. On the other hand, maybe he had just gone mad. A lack of socks and smokes could drive any man to the brink. But I had no sympathy for him. Traitors always get caught. Do handlers feel remorse or disgust when one of their agents is captured? I guess it depends on which mouse is in play.

Grekhov finally got *what* he wanted, just not from *whom* he wanted. I think they call it "re-gifting:" when one intelligence agency decides not to recruit a potential agent but passes him to a friendly spy organization.

According to the TV documentary, the Brits got Vadim and Vadim got 10 years of hard labor, forfeiture of all his possessions, and no right of correspondence. His mission was over. Maybe he felt relieved. He would simply disappear. I tried to imagine how he would look in 10 years. If he was a soup sandwich now, he'd be a moldy crust by then. The final comment in the broadcast was from Vadim's defense lawyer. He praised the court's professionalism and said how satisfied he was with the proceedings. I guess he wasn't working on a contingency basis.

The similarity of our predicaments was irritating. Then I remembered the narrator's final comment. He reminded the audience that Grekhov was an example of what happens when you lose your commitment to your country.

The difference between us was suddenly clear. My despair began to dissipate. Thoughts of redemption seeped through. I was still committed to her…and to us.

I unplugged the television and lay down on the couch. Vadim's story inspired me to make a new plan.

As spring approached, I attempted to reestablish communications with the little apartment in Votkinsk. I believed that by demonstrating dedication and determination I might get closure and at least a semblance of truth. The intercity telephone connections to Udmurtia were particularly bad. I could dial 50 times and get through only once. The conversation would be cut off after just a few minutes. There was a joke about the phone call being disconnected so the KGB could change the recording tape, but the poor network infrastructure was just as likely the cause.

I did manage to get Sofia on the telephone a few times. She seemed glad to hear my voice, but would then become morose. She said she was having a hard time and that everyone knew about us. She didn't want to elaborate on the telephone. I don't know what I was expecting to accomplish by those phone calls. I just wanted Sofia and Max to come back.

I eventually found a better way to communicate. It was called Uncle Lou's express diplomatic mail service. He was still on site. I was able to pass letters to him via the embassy mail system. The Votkinsk inspectors had a mailbox at the embassy entrance. Lou passed my notes to Sofia when no one was looking. The easiest method was to slip them into her coat pocket while she was on the second floor of Roosevelt, translating at one of the weekly meetings. My messages were consistent. I was sympathetic, but still in search of an explanation. I got no written responses from her, but Lou reported to me on the situation in general and her comments in specific. She told him she was again trying to quit her job but the local 'authorities' were giving her a hard time.

At the end of May I sent her my final plea:

"Please see me one last time so you can explain what happened. You owe me that. I will come to Votkinsk at the end of June; I think we can make it work together and defeat any enemy, within or without. If you don't agree, you can offer me a cup of tea and send me on my way. I still love you."

CHAPTER SEVENTEEN
TRUST YOUR DOCTOR

Max answered the phone.

"How are things there?" I asked in Russian.

"Excellent!" he answered brightly. "It's starting to get warm. I found three frogs down at the pond. But I didn't bring them home because I thought mama might not like it."

"A very smart decision, though I am sure Koozia would have enjoyed playing with them. Where is your mother?"

"She is still at work with the Americans."

The distance between Moscow and Votkinsk disappeared. I saw the small boy alone for the evening, in the small apartment, in the small town far away. I didn't want to drag out the conversation. No need to give away extra information. Besides, they might run out of recording tape. My goal was to get her reaction to my last note, but I realized Max probably wouldn't know.

"When she gets home be sure to tell her I called. What else is new there?"

"You know," he said, "I really liked it in Moscow. But I left my chess game there. Couldn't you bring it to us?"

"I don't know," I said, "maybe I can find someone who will bring it."

Suddenly his voice dropped to a low but audible whisper, his hand clearly wrapped around the receiver's end to augment the confidentiality of our conversation.

"We know you will come," he said in passable English. "We are ready. It is good." His excitement, and the answer that I hoped for, soothed me for a moment. I held my breath and felt the blood pounding in my chest and wrists. But the phone line had no mercy. I tried to cover up.

"Uh, yeah, well that's nice," I said loudly, in an effort to drown out any other details he might have cared to add. "Listen, I have to go now, but take care of yourself and say 'hi' to your mama for me, OK?"

I put the receiver down. 'At least he's not discreet enough to ever become a spy,' I thought.

The next phase of my plan involved the collusion of a number of witting and unwitting co-conspirators. On the unwitting side there was the Hewlett-Packard Company. As the executive assistant to the general manager I had become acquainted with the products and managers of all five sales units. I had introduced Zhenya, head of the cardiology center of a reasonably-sized population center, to the medical equipment sales department as a potential customer for their products: cardiographs, ultrasound equipment, defibrillators. When Zhenya told me he was planning to host a conference in Izhevsk for health care professionals of the Ural region at the end of June, I proposed that HP participate with a small demonstration stand. The demo equipment would have to make it there somehow. I could drive it. That would get me as far as Izhevsk with a legitimate excuse.

Anton liked the idea. He agreed to spare me for a few days so I could dabble in sales.

Thanks to the burgeoning liberal atmosphere, many areas of the country formerly closed to foreigners were declared open. But non-Russians still needed to inform the Soviet authorities if they wanted to go outside the city of their residence, even if it was to an officially "open" area. And some parts of the country — municipalities and various roads — remained closed. I had what I thought was the latest map issued by the Ministry of Foreign Affairs. It looked like the route from Moscow to Udmurtia was open. An official notification had to be sent from the company to the accrediting ministry's protocol department — for us it was the Ministry of Foreign Economic Relations — naming the travelers, dates, means of transportation and itinerary. This was then processed through various security bodies. The trip was considered automatically approved if you didn't hear back from the ministry within 24 hours of departure.

I arranged to use an HP Volvo station wagon to transport the demo equipment, so I included the number of that bright yellow license plate on the ministry notification. The route was more problematic. Moscow-Izhevsk-Moscow was clear. But a question remained: should I risk including Izhevsk-Votkinsk-Izhevsk on the request?

Declaring this lonely stretch of road would blatantly expose my plans. Not declaring and driving it anyway would create an excuse for an official reprimand or expulsion. In normal circumstances the latter result would be unlikely. But in my case, where I believed there were those who would like nothing better than to banish me permanently from Soviet soil, it seemed to be a real possibility.

I decided to throw up a smoke screen. I included on the itinerary the three additional cities in Udmurtia a tourist might possibly consider visiting. After all, Zhenya told me the conference agenda would include side trips to Udmurtia's historical sites. Izhevsk-Glazov, the ancient city that was the republic's original capital; Izhevsk-Sarapul, where a famous brewery founded a century earlier still stands, not far from the chemical weapons storage tanks; Izhevsk-Votkinsk, where the Tchaikovsky estate awaits any visitor who can get to it.

Zhenya agreed to travel with me by car from Moscow to Izhevsk. He thought it would be fun to make a road trip he hadn't done since his student days. Having the doctor at my side gave me a sense of comfort. His aplomb and wisdom would improve our chance of success. And he would be good company for the 1,200 kilometer drive. Zhenya had an elfin twinkle in his eye. An intense man, he often contemplated the suffering of his countrymen. But he subtly exuded the hope and optimism he had for his nation as he witnessed the beginning of real change.

I began to get ready for the long trip along desolate two lane roads, populated by pot-holes and frequent GAI check points. The rare gas station occasionally had gas, but other services —repair or rest stops for weary, hungry, or bladder-challenged travelers — were non-existent. I checked the car from radiator to exhaust pipe and prepared the necessary supplies: oil, brake fluid, water, sandwich meat and bread for two days, five full gas canisters and a funnel. I assembled these materials and the demo equipment in a corner at the office. Zhenya recommended a departure of 5 a.m. That would get us through Gorky before rush hour, when the roads would become congested with trucks.

One of the other secretaries noticed my pile. "Do you really think they are going to let you go?" she asked. I realized the female contingent of our office had figured out what I was up to. It's very hard to deceive a woman who doesn't want to be deceived.

On the eve of departure I came back to my desk to find a note that our contact from our sponsoring ministry's protocol department had called. It could only mean one thing.

Nikolai Petrovich was not a nice person. I had dealt with him concerning various issues for Anton. In theory, he was there to serve us. But in reality, the concept of customer care had not been adopted by any Soviet bureaucrat. Usually, when we needed something from Nikolai Petrovich, it took no less than 10 calls to find him and have him tell you that he'd get back to you. If it weren't for the fact that our office manager lived in the same building as he did and they walked their dogs together, Hewlett-Packard might have disappeared forever into the mass of documents that endlessly circulated in and out of the ministry.

"Nikolai Petrovich, this is Justin from HP returning your call."

"Yes, Justin," he said with enough joy in his voice to indicate that something unpleasant was about to happen to me. "It seems that the authorities have rejected your request to travel."

"Which authorities?"

"Well, there are many authorities. We could say it is the GAI."

"Why?"

"You plan to travel through a restricted zone."

"But I checked the map. There are no restricted zones between here and Izhevsk."

"No, you are not correct. There is still one closed area on the way. I think it's a 10-kilometer section beyond Gorky. When I was stationed in America, your authorities wouldn't allow me to travel from Washington to New York by car."

"Nikolai Petrovich, I am very sorry that our authorities did that to you, but I don't see what that has to do with the situation here."

"I am just telling you that it happens there, too. So I have done my job and informed you. There is nothing more I can do."

There was no point in arguing with him. The decision wasn't taken at his pay level. I checked the Ministry of Foreign Affairs map again and realized I had overlooked a small patch of road that lay on the east side of Gorky. I hadn't noticed it because, as part of an overall movement to restore the historical names of streets and cities, Gorky region had been given back its original name: Nizhegorodskaya region, and I got confused. I called Zhenya at his hotel to let him know he'd need to find another way to get home.

"It's strange," Zhenya said. "I talked to the head of the Udmurt Ministry of Internal Affairs and he said he had been informed of the trip." It felt oddly comforting that the local police were expecting us.

"You know," the doctor continued, "there is a law that a People's Deputy can commandeer an automobile to fulfill his duties. I would say that since you are driving me, and I am returning from the Congress, we are within the letter of this law. I think we go anyway."

I weighed the situation. I risked negative fallout on myself and HP. But I would have a well-connected lawmaker by my side.

I loaded the car and retrieved Zhenya from his hotel. By 6 a.m. we made it to the outer ring road of Moscow and started eastward. Travel, movement forward, the sense of direction, gave me a feeling of purpose. The morning light began to stream through the birch trees on either side of the road that led us through the Vladimir region. The sun rose over the horizon ahead. I began to relax.

In between major towns and cities there was desolation. It was too early for the GAI, but as we completed our 400th kilometer and the heavy traffic indicated we were getting close to the city of Gorky, I grew nervous about being stopped.

A few hundred meters before we got to the main GAI post on the Moscow side of Gorky, a tremendous storm suddenly gathered in the clear blue sky. The road was drenched by sheets of rain. Even the heartiest GAI retreats to the dryness of his booth in such circumstances. We cruised past unmolested. We wanted to stop and visit Nobel Prize winner Andrei Sakharov's apartment, which had become a shrine to *perestroika*, but the rain and risk of being detained made us reconsider. Zhenya and I drove on in silence through the soaked city. We finally crossed a massive bridge over the Volga River, before heading out of town.

The downpour continued and the GAI continued to stay dry. We traveled through the few remaining kilometers of the "closed zone." As we entered the Tatar Republic, the clouds cleared and the sun shone brilliantly on the highway ahead. We celebrated by pulling over for ham and cheese sandwiches.

Approaching Kazan, we slowed to join the long line of trucks waiting for the ferry to cross the river and enter the city. The main artery across Russia was congested by a wait of a day or more to use the ferry. Zhenya thought we might be able to get preferential treatment due to his status or my yellow license plates. We pulled to the head of the line and had a brief discussion with the GAI controlling the embarkation point. They checked our documents, found them in order and put us on the next boat. We were now more than half way to Izhevsk. While the craft chugged across the bay, Zhenya and I stood at the rail.

"I've never travelled in such a fine automobile," he said. "I can finally forgive them for Narva."

As was often the case, his smile and the twinkle in his eye told me it was OK that I had no idea what he was talking about.

"What is Narva and who is to blame?" I asked.

"The Swedish army defeated Russia there in 1700. But think nothing of it. We eventually won in Poltava, and put the Swedes and the Ukrainians in their place. But to be honest, neither Russia nor the Ukraine could make a car like a Volvo. I've dreamed since childhood of riding in a foreign-built automobile. Ours don't compare."

My naiveté and youthful sense of righteousness frequently combined to produce a curious indignation at what I saw going on around me. It was not that I didn't understand. I just did not accept. I knew that Zhenya was a man who enjoyed a good philosophical conversation.

"I honestly don't understand why people here put up with so much," I said. "You put the first man in space, but the cars are crap, you stand in long lines just to get across a river, there are pointless traffic police on every corner; shortages; sadistic bureaucrats — I mean, people complain, agree on the absurdity, but they do nothing...why?"

Zhenya thought for a moment, and then said, "It's because of the swaddling."

"Swaddling?"

"Yes. We are wrapped tight in linen cocoons, like mummies, or bugs, from the moment we are born for the first several months of our lives. Every one of us. We can't move our hands or legs. Completely helpless. And that feeling becomes ingrained and stays with us until we die. On the other hand, the swaddling does have one nice side effect: it gives us very expressive eyes. How else can we let mama know we are hungry or need to be changed?"

I nodded. I had noticed the eyes.

Zhenya continued. "It's really all about control. Take, for example, the entrance to any public building. It has four, five, maybe six pairs of doors. But all of them are locked except one, so people have to struggle to get in and out. But if they need to urgently close the facility, they only have to lock one set of doors; or if they are looking for someone, they only have to monitor one place. Why do people put up with it? I think they are just tired. Tired of being guinea pigs in the 70-year experiment to build communism.

251

"But it's not a purely modern phenomenon," he continued. "Read our literature from the last century: Bunin, Leskov. Nothing new. It manifests itself in unyielding fatalism. We wind up resigned to accept whatever happens, with no expectations. So we are easily manipulated and pitted against one another. It's a sick combination. It will take several generations to cure. Maybe that's why I became a doctor. I'm fascinated by the healing process."

At midnight we turned off the main highway at Yelabuga, onto the road that would take us the last 200 kilometers to Izhevsk. This stretch was in far worse condition, heavily pitted and cracked. I continuously swerved between craters. The swarms of insects slapping into the windshield were unfazed by my maneuvers.

Shortly, a pit across the entire width of the road caught both rear wheels. The air rushed out of the tires via the dented rims. Zhenya was calm as we pulled to the side and inspected the damage. Despite the absence of moonlight, the vast flat landscape was illuminated by a multitude of stars. Soon our eyes adjusted. I could see the treeless expanse, the road stretching out on either side of us. No other vehicles were visible.

"We only have one spare," I told him dejectedly.

"No problem," he said. "The left one seems worse. We'll replace it, hammer back the right rim, then pump it up."

A tire pump and sledge hammer were standard equipment for his Soviet trunk, but not for my Western mind. I had neither.

"Zhenya, I have to tell you this fine *importnaya avtomashina* you have been complimenting since we left Moscow, unlike its domestically-made cousins, doesn't come with an air pump as standard equipment."

He was incredulous. "I can't understand this," he said.

"I suppose it would be understandable if you ever saw the roads in Sweden."

Zhenya nodded. There was nothing left to do but smoke. After his third cigarette, headlights appeared on the horizon from the direction of Izhevsk. Now the trick was to hail the vehicle without getting run over. I flashed the headlights while Zhenya waved from the shoulder. A Kamaz dump truck ground to a halt. The driver not only had a pump and a hammer, but his uncle had once been Zhenya's patient. We were on our way in 20 minutes. But there were no more compliments for my car.

By 2:30 a.m. the lights of Izhevsk appeared on the horizon and the *izbas* became visible, indicating we had reached the edge of the city. Zhenya was concerned about the possibility of my car being stolen. I considered this unlikely. It made for a unique sight, there being no other such vehicle within a 500-kilometer radius. Plus, automobile theft was still in its infancy in Russia. We parked under the window of his first floor apartment. He told me later the only reason he stopped worrying was because he spotted a KGB Volga parked not far away, keeping an eye on my Volvo. They even followed his younger brother, Yury, around the city the next day while he searched for a place to repair my rims.

The next two days were a blur. I met the HP medical equipment sales manager at the Izhevsk airport. We set up our demo stand and literature at the cardiology center, outside the conference hall. The event was a success. We met many new potential customers and spread the word about the company.

I dropped my colleagues at the airport, politely refusing their offer to accompany me and the equipment back to Moscow. Then I headed to Zhenya's and the comfort of his couch. That night I did not dream.

I set out very early in the morning for the drive to Votkinsk. My pulse quickened at the idea of seeing Sofia and Max. I suppressed the paranoia that something would prevent me from reaching them and I hoped that my ongoing persistence had convinced her I was part of her fate.

The one GAI post on the outskirts of Votkinsk was deserted.

'Well, here I am', I thought, 'for the third time coming to Votkinsk, to liberate my once and future family, and I don't even know for sure that they want me.'

I rolled down the hill, past an *izba,* towards the lake. It dawned on me, as I passed the anchor, that if my Volvo was an oddity in Izhevsk it was a UFO in Votkinsk. I had to find an inconspicuous place to park. I decided that the best landing site would be at the back of the Palace of Culture. The hill leading to the stadium behind would shield it from prying eyes. Locking the doors, I felt the cool morning air and a hint of warmth from the sun. I thought of Sadovnikov ending his life on the front steps. Here I was, still trying to begin mine.

Walking the few hundred meters along the stadium, in the shadow of the slogans, I felt like a cross between Neil Armstrong and a wanted criminal. I took a deep breath as I pulled on the door to the corridor leading to the wing where Sofia's apartment was. It was locked. What to do? Pound and risk waking the whole floor? I blew my cover and went to the building where the inspectors used to live. It had turned back into a hotel for visitors to the factory. The sleepy administrator let me use the phone. I dialed Sofia's number and she answered.

"Can you open the corridor door please?"

"Yes," she said, with no surprise in her voice.

I opened the door of her apartment and stepped inside. Finally, on my third try I was there. She stood brushing her hair in front of the mirror. Max was asleep on a cot in the corner, separated from the rest of the room by a bookshelf. I watched her as she preened, not even looking at me. Women are amazing. You can wait for months, travel thousands of kilometers, and build up ineffable desire. They just brush their hair.

I was still wrestling with my own disbelief. I could actually see her. She was just a few meters away. And there was a chance she would come back to me. I didn't have the bandwidth to get upset at her apparent obliviousness.

On the other hand, maybe she was as nervous as I was and just needed something to do with her hands. My guts were as twisted as the rubber band on a balsawood airplane. Finally she finished and walked over to me. We embraced. I felt a slight release of tension, but it seemed to me she was trembling. She took my arm and we went outside.

We walked down the hill towards the embankment as a cool morning breeze came off the lake. The town was nearly empty. We walked along in silence before stopping at a bench that overlooked the water.

"You don't give up easily," she said.

"No, I guess I'm kind of stubborn," I said.

"Why did you come back?"

"I needed to hear two things from you," I said. "The first is the truth about why you left."

"Because I've always been influenced by fairy tales," Sofia responded. "A prince I could never have dreamed of entered my life. And I began to believe. But then I came back to pick up my passport and they were waiting for me. They said we should get married, and that they would always be able to find us.

"At that moment I remembered another fairy tale, about a Tsar who gets captured by a demon in a well. The demon agrees to spare his life in exchange for taking the Tsar's newborn son by the time he comes of age. I could see that demon's bony finger poking out of the well, wagging in the direction of the palace, screeching 'Remember your debt!'

"That Tsar had everything, but he couldn't enjoy life because he constantly dreaded the moment when the demon would appear and claim his due. I decided you were better off without me. I didn't want us to live in fear. And I didn't want to give them the satisfaction of thinking they controlled me. So, I did the opposite of what they wanted."

"And now?" I asked. "I mean, fairy tales are nice, but I'm real. Haven't I proved that?"

Sofia's eyes widened, as if she was still swaddled but needed to say something.

"Yes," she answered. "I've decided to believe more in the first fairy tale. But that was just part of it. I also need time to adjust to not living alone anymore."

"I get the point," I said. "You don't like being controlled. Honestly, I don't really care where the knives and forks go."

I wondered if I had evidence to back up my claim. I hoped that by running the gauntlet of her rejection and not giving up, I proved I was flexible and could adapt to any challenge.

"I want so much for you to give us another chance," I said, "so we can get back to the task of learning to live together."

"I think you're worth the effort," Sofia said, "...as long as you really aren't a spy."

"No, that mission is over. I failed...thank god."

"So why didn't you get removed because of the basement digging? They took that as proof that you were an intelligence officer."

"The whole thing demonstrated a distinct lack of intelligence. I nearly did get booted, but I guess my cookies and my charm saved me. It's the truth."

Up until then she had been making eye contact with me, but now she turned her head towards the lake. As if talking to herself, she continued.

"There is no way I could get used to the idea of them controlling me. I want to love you on my terms, not theirs."

"And you couldn't believe me when I told you that we could handle whatever they threw at us?" I asked.

"I still don't. And it will take me a long time to believe that. The only thing I do know is that I miss you very much and that I'm tired of running away — from them and from you. I had decided not to go with you but when I held you just now and felt your strength, I realized where I belong."

"Well, that answers my second question. But what about your disappearances when I came looking for you?"

She looked pained. "The first time, they told me you were coming and offered to let us stay at the *dacha* for the weekend. The second time I just guessed."

"Who the hell was the guy with the hairy chest?"

"That was Nelli's cousin. I asked him to help me get rid of you." She laughed. "I'm glad it didn't work."

We kissed and the town of Votkinsk began to stir.

She went back to her apartment to pack and I went to get the car from its hiding place. I could tell from the hand prints all over the windows that my camouflage effort had not fooled a herd of passing school children.

I loaded Sofia and Max's few possessions into the car. He said goodbye to his fellow yard urchins who had gathered near the vehicle. Koozia was tossed into the back in a cloud of fur, where he promptly found himself a comfortable spot between the cardiograph and the defibrillator. At least if he had an epilepsy attack on the way to Moscow I could revive him.

The trip back was uneventful, except when I got stopped for speeding in the one place I was forbidden to be. The GAI waved me down. I pulled over.

"Do you think he'll fine you?" Sofia asked as the traffic inspector approached the car.

"Perhaps there is a rule that says you can't fine a foreigner when he is speeding through a zone closed to foreigners," I said.

I rolled down the window. A clump of white fur wafted into the inspector's face. He looked at my documents and asked how I got to be in this particular place where I didn't belong. I began a long and poorly pronounced explanation about the People's Deputy, the medical conference, the flat tire, the sick cat and so forth.

Overwhelmed, the cop handed me my documents and waved us on. What could he do? Order me to return back to where I had come from? In an earlier time he would have done a lot worse. But the regime was faltering and its mechanics were preoccupied. We drove on toward Moscow.

"Do you want a sandwich?" Sofia asked, motioning to the bag that Zhenya's wife had prepared for the trip.

I shook my head. I was completely full.

Epilogue

A Museum Quality Result

Sofia, Max and I were curled up on the bed in a Washington hotel room watching the TV as events unfolded in Moscow in August 1991. Gorbachev had "fallen ill" at his *dacha* in the Crimea and eight hardline Communist leaders had begun preparations to storm the parliament building across the river from the Ukraina Hotel — the very White House where Zhenya and other democratically elected representatives were trying to make new laws to bring Russia, kicking and screaming, into the modern world. The plotters had code named their plan "Operation Thunder," perhaps in honor of Darlene's oversized, dark and artificially twitching device, which was bound to run out of steam once the batteries died.

In typical Soviet fashion, the leaders of the coup had taken various bureaucratic steps to ensure their success, while completely ignoring the significance of the individual. The KGB doubled the salaries of its personnel. Its famed Lefortovo prison, former home to Raoul Wallenberg and Alexander Solzhenitsyn, was emptied of existing prisoners to make room for new ones. Pskov, in addition to making slow buses, saw an order of 250,000 pairs of handcuffs placed at its metallurgical factory, while a printing enterprise in Moscow was given the task of producing 300,000 extra arrest forms. What would happen to the 50,000 people they expected to arrest but not handcuff remains a mystery.

Hordes of *babushkas* had joined the civilian defenders of the White House. In between serving tea, singing songs and dancing, they helped set up defensive barriers.

After only a few days, the coup attempt would fizzle out like a cigarette in a moist shot glass, but we didn't know it then. Sofia said we should check on Manya, who was house-sitting for our explosive cat back in Moscow. I bit the bullet and placed a call from the hotel.

"Is the cat OK?" I asked.

"Koozia is fine," Manya said tersely, "he's gone down to the barricades. And I'm fine too, thank you."

I suppose I should have expressed more interest in her, the well-being of her theater, or the state of the nation as a whole. But I was entirely focused on making sure my new family got the most out of its first visit to the United States.

We went out for a walk on the mall, which was baking as usual in the summer heat.

The grass had the same dog-eared appearance that I remembered. Too much sun, too many feet. But its tactical disorder was compensated by its strategic symmetry. All the architectural lines of America's capital went in the right directions.

Max lunged for a lethargic squirrel. Despite the 30 degree temperature, the rodent was able to summon a burst of energy and make it safely to a nearby tree branch.

"Do they have ice cream in America?" Max asked.

"Yes, many different flavors," I answered.

"How many?" Max was suspicious.

"At least 31," I said.

"Oh, just like in Moscow. When can we see whose is better?"

"Let's stop in to this museum. Then we can go for ice cream."

Sofia and I took his hands as we crossed the street and walked up the steps of the Smithsonian Air and Space Museum.

"We are going to look at some interesting machines," I told him.

A replica of Sputnik floated in the air above our heads.

"Max, that's the first machine to ever go into space, put there by Russians." He was enthralled enough to forget the ice cream issue. "...And on the right is the American Apollo capsule. It's the first spaceship that took humans to the moon and back."

In between these two fantastic vehicles, up against the eastern wall, there was a recent addition to the collection that I wanted my wife and son to see.

Two missiles — one Soviet and one American, stood side by side. They had been put on permanent public display in honor of the INF treaty.

"There are good rockets and bad rockets," I told Max. "These are the last two intermediate range missiles. They used to be bad. Once, each country had many of them pointed at the other, ready to fire. But now they are at peace. If you listen carefully, you can hear them whispering to each other about how happy they are to be here. Their countries made a decision to get along and destroy almost all of the bad rockets."

Max perked up his ears for a moment to see if he could hear anything above the din of the tourists.

"So there are no more?" he asked.

"Right. No more."

"Is that why you and mama got married, because America and Russia decided to get along?"

"Well, yes, you could put it that way."

"That is very good," he said in English, with no trace of an accent.

ACKNOWLEDGMENTS

I started writing this story a month after I first arrived in Moscow in the fall of 1987. I believed, as do all young people who leave home seeking adventure, that something special was happening to me and I needed to capture it. I continued my narrative in the form of letters to my parents over the years.

I am thankful to my late mother Barbara for saving those letters. I have long since forgiven her for surreptitiously sending them off to various major publications insisting they put her son's genius in print. I only uncovered her machinations when I started to receive rejection letters, though I had never submitted anything. Barbara also forced me to take typing lessons one summer long ago, since she knew I'd never be able to express myself via my Lifflander handwriting. At least I got a chance to thank her for that while she was still alive.

My father, Matthew, was always just as supportive, giving me editorial advice, asking his faithful assistant Helen Guelpa to chime in with her suggestions, and leveraging all his connections in the publishing industry to get my manuscript reviewed by some of its biggest players. My early attempts may not have been ready for publication, but I received useful constructive criticism.

This edition also garnered a hefty number of rejections. I was told that a story about how America and Russia had an intimate and productive relationship long ago is a tough sell these days. But since I believe the Russian and American people will once again ignite that relationship, and that maybe my insights will help accelerate that healing process, I finally decided to self-publish. I am sorry Matt didn't live to see my book make the light of day — but he knew it would, and his faith was something that kept me going.

I'm grateful to the slew of friends who provided feedback and tried to help me get published over the years: Solomon Karmel, Jamie Schoenfeld, Vanessa Tiongson, Thom Moore, Kevin Cuffe, Glenn Altschuler, Nick Lane, Michele Berdy, Tim Perell and Mary Ann Naples, and Paul Luftig.

My Russian friends were just as supportive and encouraging: Boris and Maya Chirkov, Yuri and Olga Yelashkin, Gulnara Khasyanova and Andrei Vitter, Rita Nyago, the Trifonovs, the Degtaryevs, and, of course, Valery Lemzikov and the Odiyankov brothers. I hope when the Russian translation comes out later this year, they won't be disappointed. I also want to say thank you to the people of Department 162 who have welcomed me into their homes and shared their stories over the years.

Though I hardly deserved such attention 30 years later based on the B's I earned in his class, my Russian professor from Cornell — now department head — Slava Paperno gave me a thorough edit and huge encouragement. And I'm especially appreciative of the final edit done by my friend and colleague in journalism, Lena Smirnova. She found the patience and sensitivity to properly manage her former editor and help him make his work a much more enjoyable read.

There were so many who helped to fill in the gaps, including Elena Sadovnikova, who befriended my future wife and opened her home and her heart to me when I finally got a chance to meet her. Ambassador Carey Cavanaugh and Dr. Igor Khripunov, of the University of Georgia, shared their memories of Vladimir Gennadevich Sadovnikov's visit to the United States. Ambassador Jack Matlock sat with me for several hours last year and shared his reminiscences of the period. The Moscow Times not only helped me to reach a professional level of writing and editing, but also jogged my memory on details of some of the events, as did Sergei Roy's articles in Moscow News, Anatoly Golovkov's article in Ogonyok, and articles from The Washington Post and Wikipedia.

To all the individuals who worked on the Intermediate Range Nuclear Forces Treaty on both sides — at the U.S. On Site Inspection Agency, Hughes Technical Services Company, the Soviet's Nuclear Risk Reduction Center and the workers at the Votkinsk Machine Building Factory and the Morton-Thiokol plant in Magna Utah: I hope I have done justice to the spirit of the mission and reminded you of the importance of your work. You have much to be proud of and are all part of my story, literally or figuratively.

Specifically I'd like to thank the U.S. military officers who were there and have remained my friends over the years: Douglas Englund, George Connell, John Sartorius, Barrett Haver, Scott Ritter and Stuart O'Neil. Their humility and faith in the treaty were an inspiration.

Finally and most importantly, I thank my wife for finding the courage to believe in us.

Justin Lifflander
justin.lifflander@rambler.ru

About the Author

A graduate of Cornell University, Justin Lifflander arrived in Russia in 1987 as a driver-mechanic for the US embassy in Moscow. A year later, he moved to Votkinsk in the foothills of the Ural Mountains, where he inspected missiles at a production plant as part of the Intermediate Nuclear Forces Treaty (INF) between the U.S. and U.S.S.R. There he met a young woman assigned to keep an eye on him for the local KGB.

After his stint as a weapons inspector, Lifflander moved to Moscow and got married. It was the first of several marriages between inspectors and escorts.

He worked as an executive for Hewlett-Packard Russia for twenty years. He then served as the business editor for the Moscow Times daily newspaper from 2010 to 2014 and authored several articles about Russian-American relations, the tragicomedy of life in Russia, and cigars. He now holds American and Russian citizenships and resides in Moscow with his wife, son, and mother-in-law.

A monument to the INF treaty stands in the yard in front of the Votkinsk Machine Building Factory, near the U.S. inspectors' housing.

The plaque next to the warhead reads:

"Votkinsk Factory Production Association, Udmurtia, Russia

In accordance with the treaty between Russia and the USA on the liquidation of their intermediate range missiles (INF), for the first time in history during the period from 1 July 1998 to 31 May 2001, a treaty to destroy strategic nuclear weapons was implemented. Here, next to the Votkinsk Machine Building Factory, a residential complex was constructed for thirty American inspectors who continuously verified the fulfillment by Russia of its commitment to no longer manufacture missiles covered by the INF Treaty. (The same work was carried out by Russian inspectors in the state of Utah in the USA.)"

Photo courtesy of the Votkinsk Machine Building Factory, Department 162.

CPSIA information can be obtained at www.ICGtesting.com
Printed in the USA
LVOW10s1317090115

422170LV00021B/250/P